QUICK REVIEW

Sum & Substance

EVIDENCE

3RD EDITION

◆

Professor
Steven J. Goode

A West Publishing Affiliate

Editor	Roberta Simon, Esq.
Production Coordinator	Seth Barondess
Cover Design	Johnson Gray Advertising

Special thanks to Alvina Norman, Loyola University School of Law, and Anh-Thu Mai, Pepperdine University School of Law.

ISBN   1-57793-006-1

Sum & Substance Quick Review of Evidence is a publication of
Sum & Substance, a division of West Professional Training Programs, Inc.

This product was printed and published in the United States of America.

TABLE OF CONTENTS

CASEBOOK TABLE

	Mueller and Kirkpatrick 3d ed	Carlson, Imwinkelreid and Kionka	Strong, Broun and Mosteller 5th ed	Sutton and Wellborn 8th ed	Waltz and Park 8th ed	Weinstein, Mansfield, Abrams and Berger 8th ed	Green and Nesson 2d ed
Chap IV General Provisions							
A. Limited Admissibility	86-88	63	43-50	379-81; 393-95	41		187-99
B. Limiting Instructions	88	63	43-50	393-95	41		188
C. Preserving Error for Appeal	48-57	92-96	36-43	377-85	43-45	76-82	
D. Preliminary Fact Questions for the Court	91-93	96-101	13-24	54-61; 213-22; 392-93	135-39		52-60
Chapter V. Relevancy							
A. Basic Principles of Relevancy	59-77; 94-95	133-44	212-14	1-10	64-77	1-18	25-60; 69-95
B. Excluding Relevant Evidence	78-86; 88-90	237-38	214-29	1-10	77-81	18-82	60-61
C. Discretionary Exclusion: General Principles	78-86; 88-90	238-42	214-39	1-10	77-81	18-82	61-68
D. Discretionary Exclusion: Similar Happenings Evidence		355-66	237-58	24-31; 35-38	414-20	1056-62	242-57
E. Discretionary Exclusion: Other Common Examples	82-84; 96-114	242-52	253-55; 340-43; 402-05	31-35; 626-35	351-65; 836-43	18-24; 45-73; 133-46	61-64; 95-132
F. Specific Relevance Rules: General	505-24	371-77; 667-97	230-35; 43-57	108-37	421-39	1070-92	133-74
G. Character Evidence	463-86	339-50	258-67; 275-88	41-54; 84-100	366-81; 405-11; 439-47	1019-56	175-89; 231-57; 310-57
H. Habit and Routine Practice Evidence	499-505	351-66	268-75	100-08	411-14	1062-70	257-65

	Mueller and Kirkpatrick 3d ed	Carlson, Imwinkelreid and Klonka	Strong, Broun and Mosteller 5th ed	Sutton and Wellborn 8th ed	Waltz and Park 8th ed	Weinstein, Mansfield, Abrams and Berger 8th ed	Green and Nesson 2d ed
I. Other Crimes, Wrongs, or Acts Evidence Admissible for Non-Character Purposes	487-99	366-70	288-308	54-84	383-411	953-1018	184-231
Ch. VI: Hearsay							
A-D. Hearsay Defined	115-78	419-36	642-78	138-55	82-131	596-638	404-25
E. Hearsay Exemptions	145-53; 180-211	328-35	678-700	155-86	115-16; 236-41; 508-14	643-80	465-72
F. Other Hearsay Problems			906				
G. Limited Admissibility			647-50				
H. Silence			653-55	155	110-12	633-37	
Ch. VII. Hearsay Exceptions							
B. Admission by Party Opponent	211-63	440-49	700-32	195-227	162-88	680-724	425-65
C.1 Spontaneous Statements	263-76	451-61	757-67	258-69	139-62	765-76	482-85
C.2 State of Mind	276-306	461-76	767-97	269-309	209-36	776-813	485-92
C.3 Business Records	313-26	476-85	807-32	315-30	253-76	813-55	494-500
C.4 Public Records	326-44	485-92	832-46	330-48	276-91	856-69	500-09
C.5 Learned Treatises	344-45	492-94	905	349-52	293-94	915-16	
C.6 Past Recollection Recorded	306-13	524-28	797-807	309-14	241-52	337-44; 352-59	492-94
C.7 Catch-all Exception	399-414	539-40	889-904	356-76	302-12	924-39	510-49
D.1 Unavailability Defined	346-57	503-05	846-56				466-67
D.2 Dying Declarations	368-72	520-24	871-75	253-57	131-39	899-907	478-82

	Mueller and Kirkpatrick 3d ed	Carlson, Imwinkelreid and Kionka	Strong, Broun and Mosteller 5th ed	Sutton and Wellborn 8th ed	Waltz and Park 8th ed	Weinstein, Mansfield, Abrams and Berger 8th ed	Green and Nesson 2d ed
D.3 Declaration against Interest	372-93	511-19	875-89	227-52	199-209	725-65	475-78
D.4 Former Testimony	357-68	506-10	856-71	186-95	188-99	870-98	472-75
D.5 Statements of Personal or Family History	393-95	517-20			294-95	907-11	
E. Prior Statements of Witness	145-53; 180-211		678-700	155-86	115-16; 236-41; 508-14	643-80	465-72
F. Miscellaneous Exceptions	395-99	494-500	905-06	352-56	291-96	911-14; 916-24	
G. Confrontation Clause	418-62		733-56	178-86; 210-13; 356-76	312-50	638-40; 670-80; 705-24; 746-65	567-688
Ch. VIII: Witnesses					627-55		
A. Competency	525-56		468-74; 478-90; 501-14	404-30; 432-45		258-318	366-98
B. Oath or Affirmation	530-32		474-78	419-25		289-92	368
C. Personal Knowledge	556-67	145-47	514-19	430-32		296-99	367
D. Exclusion of Witnesses	577-81		490-94	561-70	456-57		
E. Examination of Witnesses	559-77		494-501	501-46	12-16; 241-46; 448-61	330-52; 469-86	361-666; 398-404
F. Impeachment	583-685		567-640	445-500	448-56; 461-520	486-595	265-310
Ch. IX: Opinions and Expert Testimony	687-759		308-43; 520-67	571-647	725-35	359-469	817-937
Ch. X: Authentication	965-91	148-215	415-42	648-73	620-26; 836-43	182-211	939-978
Ch. XI: Best Evidence Rule	993-1017	405-18	442-67	674-90	612-20	211-40	978-1015
Ch. XII: Privileges							
A. Privileges in General	865-67	547-59	908-10		522-24	1348-49	689-696

	Mueller and Kirkpatrick 3d ed	Carlson, Imwinkelreid and Kionka	Strong, Broun and Mosteller 5th ed	Sutton and Wellborn 8th ed	Waltz and Park 8th ed	Weinstein, Mansfield, Abrams and Berger 8th ed	Green and Nesson 2d ed
C. Attorney-Client Privilege	868-919	575-99	925-69	700-46	522-46	1435-1526	705-797
D. Physician-Patient		601-17	977-92	746-50	546-62	1551-71	
E. Psychotherapist-Patient	920-26	601-17	977-92	746-50	546-62	1551-71	704-05
F. Clergyman			992		569-70	1571-72	705-05
G. Accountant			993		570-71	1572-73	
H. Marital Communication	937-43	561-72	910-25	691-95	562-68	1541-51	806-807
I. Parent-Child		572-73			572	1582-83	808-15
J. Miscellaneous	943-63	619-59	993-1057	750-832	572-611	1349-1434; 1573-84	696-704
K. Spousal Testimonial	925-37	561-72	910-25	695-700	562-68	1526-41	797-806
Ch. XIII: Judicial Notice	837-63	743-54	360-84	886-906	662-87	1266-1347	
Ch. XIV: Burdens of Proof and Presumptions	761-836	701-41	97-189	833-85	688-724	1099-1265	1017-96

CAPSULE OUTLINE

I. INTRODUCTION

II. 10-5-2 HOUR STUDY GUIDE FOR EVIDENCE

III. ANALYTICAL AND EXAM APPROACH

A. EVIDENCE AS AN OBSTACLE COURSE. [§1.0]

Numerous grounds upon which a court may exclude a particular piece of evidence, each an independent obstacle (objection). Each must be hurdled before the evidence is deemed admissible.

B. APPROACHING EVIDENCE PROBLEMS: HEAR PA BROWN. [§1.1]

The various grounds for objection: **HEAR**say **P**rivileges **A**uthentication **B**est evidence rule **R**elevance **O**pinion testimony **W**itnesses **N**otice (judicial notice)

> **NOTE: Answering An Exam Question. [§1.11]**
>
> Run through HEAR PA BROWN in your mind. Be sure to discuss all plausible issues.

C. THE FEDERAL RULES AND THE COMMON LAW. [§1.2]

Federal Rules of Evidence (FRE) enacted 1975. 34 states (plus Puerto Rico and the military) have codes of evidence based on FRE. Most other states follow common law rules.

IV. GENERAL PROVISIONS

A. LIMITED ADMISSIBILITY. [§2.0]

Evidence may be admissible for one purpose but not another, or admissible against one party but not another. May be admitted under doctrine of limited admissibility.

B. LIMITING INSTRUCTIONS. [§2.3]

When evidence is admissible only for a limited purpose, judge must, upon request, instruct jury to consider the evidence only for its admissible purpose.

C. PRESERVING ERROR FOR APPEAL. [§3.0]

Must take all required steps to preserve for appeal erroneous rulings by trial judge regarding admission or exclusion of evidence.

1. GENERAL PRINCIPLE. [§3.1]

Whichever party now complains on appeal that the judge erred must have done everything necessary to inform the judge of the evidence rule in question and its application to the evidence in question.

2. ERRONEOUS ADMISSION OF EVIDENCE. [§3.11]

Party complaining on appeal that trial judge erroneously admitted evidence must show that (a) it specifically objected to the evidence; (b) it did so in timely fashion; (c) evidence was inadmissible on stated grounds; and (d) admission of evidence affected substantial right of the appellant.

a. Specific Objection. [§3.111]
Objection must be stated with sufficient specificity.

b. Timely Fashion. [§3.112]
Objection must be made at first reasonable opportunity.

(1) Motions in Limine. [§3.1121]
Motion **in limine** — motion made prior to trial seeking ruling on some evidentiary issue likely to arise.

c. Affirm Unless Inadmissible on Stated Grounds. [§3.112]
If objection failed to state proper legal basis for excluding evidence, judge's decision to admit will be upheld even if evidence should have been excluded for some other reason.

3. ERRONEOUS EXCLUSION OF EVIDENCE. [§3.12]

Party complaining on appeal that judge erroneously excluded evidence must show (a) it made offer of proof at trial; (b) evidence could not have been excluded on any ground; and (c) exclusion of evidence affected substantial right of appellant.

a. Affirm If Inadmissible on Any Ground. [§3.122]
Even if evidence excluded in response to objection raising invalid ground for exclusion, ruling will be affirmed if there exists any valid reason for excluding the evidence.

D. PRELIMINARY FACT QUESTIONS FOR THE COURT. [§4.0]

Admissibility or inadmissibility of evidence sometimes turns on existence or non-existence of some preliminary fact. Sometimes, court decides whether the preliminary fact exists before ruling on admissibility; other times, jury decides.

1. GENERAL RULE: COURT DECIDES WHETHER PRELIMINARY FACT PROVED. [§4.1]

Court decides any factual issues related to questions such as whether (a) a witness is qualified as an expert, (b) a statement is hearsay, (c) a hearsay statement falls within an exception, or (d) a statement is privileged. Judge uses preponderance of the evidence standard; is not bound by rules of evidence (except privilege rules).

2. JURY GETS TO DECIDE A FEW: "BARK". [§4.2]

Four preliminary fact issues left to the jury. **B**est Evidence Rule; **A**uthenticity; **R**elevance; **K**nowledge.

V.   RELEVANCY

A. BASIC PRINCIPLES OF RELEVANCY. [§5.0]

Evidence must be relevant to be admissible, but not all relevant evidence is admissible.

1. DEFINITION OF RELEVANCY. [§5.1]

A piece of evidence is relevant if it has any tendency to make the existence of any fact of consequence to the case more or less probable than it would be without that piece of evidence.

2. TWO ASPECTS OF RELEVANCY. [§5.2]

(1) The evidence must logically tend to prove what it is offered to prove; (2) it must be offered to prove something relates to an issue that the substantive law deems of consequence to the outcome of the case.

3. RELEVANCY vs. SUFFICIENCY. [§5.3]

Evidence may be relevant even though it is not by itself adequate to sustain a verdict.

4. DIRECT vs. CIRCUMSTANTIAL EVIDENCE. [§5.4]

a. Direct Evidence. [§5.41]
Proves a consequential fact directly. No inference need be drawn from the evidence.

b. Circumstantial Evidence. [§5.42]
Requires factfinder to draw inferences from the evidence in order to conclude that some consequential fact exists.

5. CONDITIONAL RELEVANCY. [§5.5]

Evidence is conditionally relevant when its relevancy depends on existence of another fact that has not yet been proved. Court should admit such evidence either (a) upon introduction of evidence sufficient to support a finding of the existence of the other fact or (b) subject to introduction of such evidence.

B. REASONS FOR EXCLUDING RELEVANT EVIDENCE. [§6.0]

Two basic reasons: (1) extrinsic social policies; (2) although relevant, admission would lead to less accurate factfinding.

1. EXTRINSIC SOCIAL POLICIES. [§6.1]

Subordinate accurate factfinding to goal of promoting some other social concern.

2. ACCURACY IN FACTFINDING. [§6.2]

Probative value outweighed by danger that it will confuse or prejudice jury, or is not worth time required for presentation.

3. DISCRETIONARY EXCLUSION. [§6.21]

FRE 403 requires court to exclude relevant evidence when its probative value is substantially outweighed by countervailing concerns such as danger of unfair prejudice, confusion of issues, or misleading the jury, or by considerations of judicial efficiency (e.g., undue delay or presentation of cumulative evidence).

4. SPECIFIC EVIDENCE RULES. [§6.22]

Some rules deal with specific categories of evidence, setting forth when such evidence is admissible and when it is not. E.g., character and habit evidence, evidence of liability insurance, and proof of prior sexual conduct.

C. DISCRETIONARY EXCLUSION: GENERAL PRINCIPLES. [§7.0]

1. FACTORS IN EXERCISING DISCRETION. [§7.1]

a. Nature of Case. [§7.11]
Most likely to exercise discretion to exclude evidence when offered against a criminal defendant.

b. Importance of Issue. [§7.12]
Less likely to exclude when evidence goes to issues central to the case.

c. Efficacy of Limiting Instruction. [§7.13]
Court will generally exclude evidence only when cautionary limiting instruction will not provide sufficient protection.

D. DISCRETIONARY EXCLUSION: SIMILAR HAPPENINGS EVIDENCE ("SHE"). [§8.0]

Courts exercise power of discretionary exclusion on case-by-case basis; generally, courts tend to approach certain types of issues in same way.

1. "SHE": IN GENERAL. [§8.1]

Issue arises when party wishes to use evidence of other events or transactions between parties now involved in litigation, or involving other party or parties similarly situated, as proof of occurrence in question. Generally, courts reluctant to admit such evidence; probative value is outweighed by countervailing concerns. But likely to admit similar happenings evidence in certain instances.

2. "SHE": PRIOR OR SUBSEQUENT ACCIDENTS. [§8.2]

Evidence of other accidents or injuries offered to prove negligence of party or dangerousness of condition is admissible if proponent shows the other accidents or injuries occurred under substantially similar circumstances. But court may still determine that probative value is substantially outweighed by danger of confusion or waste of time and therefore exclude evidence.

3. "SHE": OTHER CONTRACTS OR DEALINGS TO PROVE TERMS. [§8.3]

Where dispute exists as to terms of contract between parties, evidence of other similar contracts between parties generally admissible.

Sum & Substance QUICK REVIEW of Evidence

4. "SHE": OTHER CONTRACTS OR DEALINGS TO PROVE AGENCY. [§8.4]

When authority of agent to make a contract is disputed, evidence of similar contracts entered into by purported agent ordinarily admissible even if parties are different.

5. "SHE": NON-OBSERVATIONS AND NON-OCCURRENCES. [§8.5]

Using evidence that event or condition was not observed, or that other injuries did not occur, to prove non-existence of the event, condition, or injury.

a. Non-Observation to Prove Non-Occurrence in General. [§8.51]
Ordinarily, such evidence inadmissible unless proponent shows that event or condition probably would have been observed had it occurred.

b. Absence of Business Record to Prove Non-Occurrence. [§8.52]
May prove that event or transaction did not occur by evidence that there is no business record of such an event or transaction upon showing that it is practice of business to regularly record all such events or transactions.

c. Absence of Similar Accidents. [§8.53]
Evidence that place, particular product, or similar product has been used over period of time without any accident occurring similar to one in issue is admissible if proponent establishes (1) place or product involved was used significant number of times under substantially similar conditions or circumstances and (2) witness would have heard of any previous accidents.

6. SHE: SALES OF SIMILAR PROPERTY TO PROVE VALUE. [§8.6]

Evidence of selling price of particular piece of property may be used to prove value of similar property. Proponent must satisfy court of substantial similarity in nature of properties and market conditions.

7. SHE: PREVIOUS CLAIMS OR LAWSUITS TO IMPEACH PRESENT CLAIM. [§8.7]

Defendant may seek to offer evidence of prior similar charges made by plaintiff or complainant.

a. Chronic Litigant. [§8.71]
Evidence that tends to show only that plaintiff or complainant is chronic litigant is inadmissible.

b. Prior Fraudulent Claims. [§8.72]
If plaintiff or complainant has previously made similar fraudulent claims, such evidence is admissible to prove falsity of present claim.

8. SHE: CAUSATION. [§8.8]

Evidence of what happened to other persons similarly situated is admissible to establish causation if causation is complex issue.

9. SHE: BUSINESS CUSTOM TO PROVE CONDUCT. [§8.9]

Evidence of established business practice is admissible to show practice was followed on particular occasion.

E. DISCRETIONARY EXCLUSION: OTHER COMMON EXAMPLES. [§9.0]

1. REENACTMENTS, DEMONSTRATIONS, AND EXPERIMENTS. [§9.1]

When a party seeks to prove fact by reenactment, demonstration, or experiment, the evidence is admissible only if proponent shows substantial similarity of material conditions.

2. INDUSTRY STANDARD TO PROVE OR DISPROVE NEGLIGENCE. [§9.2]

Party may offer evidence of industry standard as relevant evidence of reasonable conduct.

3. STATISTICAL EVIDENCE. [§9.3]

Statistical evidence, if improperly used, presents danger of unfair prejudice and is sometimes excluded, especially if proponent is unable to prove the accuracy of the data underlying the statistical calculations. Where proponent is able to do this, however, statistical evidence will be admitted.

4. PHOTOGRAPHS AND REPULSIVE OBJECTS. [§9.4]

Gruesome photographs and repulsive objects often objected to on ground that prejudicial impact substantially outweighs probative value. Requires case-by-case determination. Most often, objection overruled.

5. JURY VIEWS. [§9.5]

Court has very broad discretion with respect to allowing in-court exhibitions and out-of-court jury views of matters and places in controversy.

a. View of Scene. [§9.52]
Permitted only under strict safeguards and only where counsel and parties are present.

F. SPECIFIC RELEVANCE RULES: GENERAL. [§10.0]

While preceding sections discuss court's general power under FRE 403 to exclude relevant evidence, FRE (codifying common-law practice) also contain specific rules governing admissibility of certain classes of relevant evidence.

1. SUBSEQUENT REMEDIAL MEASURES ("SRM"). [§10.1]

Evidence that a party took remedial measures following the occurrence of an accident or injury is inadmissible to prove the party's negligence or culpable conduct.

a. Elements. [§10.11]
Exclusionary rule applies only if (1) a party (2) engaged in some remedial measure (3) after the accident or injury that is subject of suit.

b. Remedial Measure Defined. [§10.12]
Any measure that would have made the accident or injury less likely to occur, e.g., repair or improvement, design changes, change in procedure, policy change.

c. Reason for Exclusion. [§10.13]
To promote extrinsic social policy of encouraging parties to take safety measures. Based on belief that parties are less likely to take safety measures if they fear this will be used as evidence against them in subsequent litigation.

d. Inadmissible if Proving Negligence. [§10.14]
Excludes evidence of an SRM only when offered to prove party's negligence or culpable conduct.

e. Proper Uses of Subsequent Remedial Measures. [§10.15]
SRM evidence offered to prove something other than the party's negligence or culpable conduct is admissible.

(1) Ownership or Control. [§10.151]
To prove ownership or control.

(2) Feasibility of Precautionary Measures. [§10.152]
If party claims that product, policy, site, etc. could not have been manufactured or operated in safer way, evidence of SRM admissible to show change was feasible.

(3) Impeachment. [§10.153]
To impeach party's testimony.

f. Strict Product Liability Case. [§10.16]
Jurisdictions differ as to admissibility of SRM evidence in product liability cases brought on strict liability theory. Arguments for admissibility: (a) neither negligence nor culpable conduct is an issue in such a case; and (b) economic forces compel manufacturers to make their products safer. Most federal courts reject these arguments and exclude SRM evidence in strict product liability cases. Many states accept these arguments and admit SRM evidence in such cases.

2. COMPROMISES AND OFFERS TO COMPROMISE. [§10.2]

Fact that a party offered to settle claim or actually settled claim inadmissible to prove validity or invalidity of claim or value of claim.

a. Reason for Exclusion. [§10.24]
Based on extrinsic social policy of encouraging out-of-court settlements. At common law, also some feeling that such evidence was irrelevant because offer to compromise might result from desire to avoid lawsuit, as much as belief that one was not liable.

b. Express Admissions During Negotiations. [§10.25]
Evidence of conduct or statements made during compromise negotiations also inadmissible. This includes express admissions made during negotiations.

c. Dispute Requirement. [§10.26]
Rule protects settlement evidence only if offer, settlement, or statement is related to a claim that was disputed either as to liability or amount of damages.

d. Proper Uses of Compromise Evidence. [§10.27]
Compromise evidence inadmissible only when offered to prove validity or invalidity of a claim or amount of damages. May be admissible when offered for another purpose.

(1) Bias or Prejudice. [§10.271]
To prove bias or prejudice of a witness.

(2) Undue Delay. [§10.272]
To rebut a contention of undue delay.

(3) Suit on the Compromise Agreement. [§10.273]
When plaintiff brings action to enforce terms of settlement agreement, evidence of agreement is admissible.

3. OFFERS TO PAY MEDICAL OR SIMILAR EXPENSES. [§10.3]

FRE 409 excludes offers to pay or actual payment of medical, hospital, or similar expenses occasioned by an injury. Sometimes referred to as "Good Samaritan" rule. But rule does not ban other statements made in connection with offer, e.g., statements of fault. The common law does not have such a rule.

4. OFFERS TO PLEAD. [§10.4]

To facilitate the plea bargaining process, certain pleas are inadmissible in either a civil or criminal proceeding against defendant who made the plea. Neither a withdrawn guilty plea nor a nolo contendere (no contest) plea, regardless of whether it is withdrawn, may be used against defendant. But evidence of guilty plea that is not withdrawn is not protected.

a. Statements Made During the Plea Process. [§10.42]
FRE 410 also protects statements made during plea discussions and the actual plea proceeding.

5. LIABILITY INSURANCE. [§10.5]

Evidence that person was or was not insured against liability is not admissible to prove that person acted negligently or wrongfully. Such evidence is admissible, however, to prove other things, such as agency, ownership, control, or the bias or prejudice of a witness.

a. Reason for Exclusion. [§10.51]

To promote accuracy in factfinding. If offered to prove negligence, it has little or no probative value but may be quite prejudicial. May have substantial probative value when offered to prove something other than negligence.

G. CHARACTER EVIDENCE. [§11.0]

One of the trickiest areas of the law of evidence concerns the admissibility of evidence of a person's character or of a person's character trait.

1. THREE STEP PROCESS. [§11.1]

Always analyze character evidence problems by asking the three following questions (What-May-How?):

1. What is the evidence being offered to prove?

2. May character evidence be used to prove this? If so, ask the third question.

3. How may character be proved?

2. POSSIBLE USES OF CHARACTER EVIDENCE. [§11.2]

Crucial to distinguish among the several purposes for which character evidence might be offered.

a. Character as an Element of a Claim or Defense. [§11.21]

A person's character might itself be an element of a crime, claim or defense. In such a case, evidence of the person's character will be direct evidence of a fact critical to the case. When character is itself an element of a claim or defense, evidence of character is admissible.

(1) Negligent Entrustment or Hiring. [§11.211]

Where Plaintiff claims that Defendant negligently entrusted his car to Driver, Driver's character as an unreliable driver is something that Plaintiff must prove to make out his claim.

(2) Defamation — Truth as a Defense. [§11.212]

When defendant in a libel or slander case asserts truth as a defense, the character of the plaintiff becomes an element of defendant's defense.

(3) Entrapment. [§11.213]

Some versions of the entrapment defense to a criminal charge focus on defendant's predisposition to commit the crime, making defendant's character an element of some entrapment defenses.

(4) Custody Action. [§11.214]

Courts may consider a party's character in deciding who should have custody of a child.

(5) Mental Condition or Competency. [§11.215]

In cases raising issues such as the sanity of defendant, competency of testator to make will, or mental condition of respondent to civil commitment proceeding, character is an element of the claim or defense.

(6) Proving Character When It is an Element of a Claim or Defense. [§11.216]

May be proved through reputation or opinion testimony or specific instances of conduct.

b. Character Evidence Used to Prove Conduct. [§11.22]

A party might want to introduce evidence of someone's conduct in order to prove how that person acted on a particular occasion; i.e., as circumstantial evidence from which jury is to infer that the person acted in conformity with his character on occasion in question.

(1) General Rule: Inadmissible to Prove Conduct. [§11.221]

Character evidence not admissible as circumstantial evidence that a person acted in conformity with his character on a particular occasion.

(2) Rationale. [§11.222]

Probative value outweighed by danger of unfair prejudice.

c. Non-Character Evidence. [§11.23]

Sometimes evidence looks and sounds a lot like character evidence, but is really not.

(1) Self Defense — Pre-Emptive Strike. [§11.231]

If theory of self defense is that defendant reasonably feared victim was about to inflict severe bodily harm on him and so struck the first blow, victim's character is not the issue; what defendant reasonably believed about the victim is.

(2) Injury to Reputation. [§11.232]

In defamation cases, damages are measured according to injury to the plaintiff's reputation, not his character.

3. METHODS OF PROVING CHARACTER. [§11.3]

In theory at least, three ways that might be used to prove a person's character: (a) reputation; (b) opinion; and (c) specific instances of conduct. Which of these three types can be used under the rules depends on what the evidence is being offered to prove.

a. Reputation. [§11.31]

Evidence of a person's reputation in the community.

(1) Foundation Required for Reputation Testimony. [§11.311]

Reputation witness must have knowledge of the person's reputation, although witness need not actually know the person.

(2) Relevant Community. [§11.312]

Traditionally, reputation in community in which person lived. Courts now accept reputation in other significant "communities," such as place of work.

(3) Substance of Reputation Testimony. [§11.313]

Witness allowed to state only that the person's reputation in the community for relevant trait is "good," "bad," "excellent," "terrible," etc., and may not give reasons why that reputation exists.

b. Opinion. [§11.32]

Witness may testify to opinion of another person's character. Not permitted at common law, but now allowed under FRE and in many states.

(1) Substance of Opinion Testimony. [§11.321]

Witness may state only opinion of person's character and may not give reasons why she holds that opinion.

c. Specific Instances of Conduct. [§11.33]

Evidence that a person has engaged in specific acts might tend to establish the person's character. This method presents greatest danger of unfair prejudice and so use is limited. Specific instances may be used when character is itself an element of a claim or defense, but may not be used when character is offered to prove conduct.

4. CHARACTER TO PROVE CONDUCT: EXCEPTIONS TO GENERAL RULE. [§11.4]

General rule: evidence of a person's character is not admissible to prove conduct (i.e., as proof that the person acted in conformity with that character on a particular occasion). General rule applies both in criminal and civil cases. But three important exceptions:

a. Character of an Accused: Putting Character in Issue. [§11.41]

Criminal defendant may offer evidence of pertinent trait of his character to prove his innocence. Often referred to as "putting character **in** issue." Do not confuse this with cases in which character is **an** issue (that is, when character is an element of a claim or defense).

(1) Must Be Pertinent Character Trait. [§11.411]

(2) Method of Proof. [§11.412]

Only by reputation and opinion testimony.

(3) Prosecutor May Rebut. [§11.413]

If defendant offers evidence of his good character, he is said to put "character in issue" and prosecution may rebut.

(a) Reputation and Opinion. [§11.4131]

Prosecution can call own reputation and opinion witnesses to testify to defendant's bad character.

(4) Cross-Examination of Defendant's Witnesses. [§11.4132]

Prosecution may ask defendant's reputation witness whether witness "had heard" about specific acts of defendant that would reflect badly on defendant's reputation. May ask defendant's opinion witness "do you know" about specific acts of defendant that might bear on opinion.

(a) Form of Question. [§11.41321]

At common law, precise form of question put to reputation witness on cross-examination was very important; but now that opinion witnesses permitted under FRE and in many states, distinction is of diminished importance and has probably been abandoned in federal courts.

(b) Pertinent Trait Only. [§11.41322]

Specific acts referred to in prosecution's "have you heard" and "did you know" questions must relate to character trait that witness testified about on direct examination.

(c) Prosecution Bound by Answer. [§11.41323]

Although prosecution may ask "have you heard" and "did you know" questions, it may not introduce evidence to prove that the specific acts actually occurred, even if witness answers in the negative.

(d) Limiting Instruction. [§11.41324]

Defendant is entitled to a limiting instruction telling jury that the question is being asked only to test witness's familiarity with defendant's reputation and is not evidence that defendant committed the specific act.

(e) Good Faith Requirement. [§11.41325]

"Have you heard" and "Did you know" questions limited to instances of conduct that prosecution believes in good faith actually occurred.

b. Character of Victim. [§11.42]

Criminal defendant may offer evidence of the character of his victim in order to prove the victim's conduct and his own innocence.

(1) Self Defense: Victim as First Aggressor. [§11.421]

In this theory of self-defense, defendant argues that victim struck the first blow. Evidence of victim's violent character is offered as evidence that victim acted in conformity with his violent nature on this occasion; that is, to prove that victim started the fight.

(2) Method of Proof. [§11.422]

Defendant can use only reputation and opinion testimony to prove victim's character. In a few jurisdictions, defendant may introduce specific acts by the victim.

(3) Prosecution May Rebut. [§11.423]

Prosecution may rebut by cross-examining defendant's witnesses or by calling its own reputation and opinion witnesses to testify to victim's good character. In addition, in a homicide case, if defendant offers any kind of evidence that deceased victim was the first aggressor, prosecution may call reputation and opinion witnesses to testify to victim's peaceable character.

c. Character to Attack or Support Credibility. [§11.44]

Third exception to the general rule: allows evidence of a witness's character to be used to attack or support his credibility. Special set of rules governs when and how evidence of character may be used to attack or support credibility and is discussed below. (See §53.0 et seq.)

5. EVIDENCE OF PAST SEXUAL BEHAVIOR. [§11.5]

Every jurisdiction has passed some form of "rape shield" law that strictly limits admissibility of evidence of victim's past sexual conduct.

a. Criminal Cases—General rule. [§11.51]

FRE 412 severely limits, in any criminal proceeding involving alleged sexual misconduct, the admissibility of evidence of an alleged victim's other sexual behavior or predisposition.

(1) Other sexual behavior. [§11.511]

Evidence that any alleged victim engaged in other sexual behavior (actual physical sexual contact, activities that imply sexual contact) is generally inadmissible, as is reputation and opinion evidence.

(2) Sexual predisposition. [§11.512]

Evidence offered to prove an alleged victim's sexual predisposition is inadmissible.

b. Criminal cases—Exceptions. [§11.52]

FRE 412(b) enumerates three exceptions under which sexual misconduct or predisposition evidence may be admissible.

(1) Source of semen or injury. [§11.521]

Accused may offer evidence of specific instances of an alleged victim's sexual behavior to prove that someone other than the accused was the source of semen, injury, or other physical evidence.

(2) Sexual behavior involving alleged victim and accused. [§11.522]

Accused may offer evidence of specific instances of sexual behavior between the accused and the alleged victim to prove consent. Prosecution may offer evidence of specific instances of sexual behavior between the alleged victim and the accused to the extent such evidence is admissible as other bad acts evidence.

(3) When constitutionally required. [§11.523]

Evidence of other sexual behavior or predisposition is admissible when exclusion would violate the accused's constitutional right to confrontation or due process.

c. Civil Cases—Generally [§11.524]

General rule of inadmissibility in criminal cases also applies in civil cases involving alleged sexual misconduct. [FRE 412(a)]

d. Civil Cases—Exceptions [§11.525]

FRE 412(b) allows such evidence to be admitted if otherwise admissible under the rules and probative value of the evidence substantially outweighs the danger of unfair prejudice to any party and the danger of harm to any victim. Evidence of an alleged victim's reputation is admissible only if it has been placed in controversy by the alleged victim.

e. Procedures. [§11.526]

A party that wishes to offer such evidence must file a written motion at least fourteen days prior to trial, unless the court for good cause relaxes the time limit, which specifically describes the proffered evidence and the purpose for which it is being offered. The court may not admit such evidence without first conducting an in camera hearing.

6. THIRD EXCEPTION TO CHARACTER EVIDENCE RULE IN SEXUAL ASSAULT AND CHILD MOLESTATION CASES. [11.6]

Federal Rules 413-415 allow character evidence to be offered in certain criminal and civil cases.

a. Criminal Cases. [11.61]

In criminal cases in which the defendant is charged with sexual assault or child molestation, the prosecution may offer evidence that the defendant has committed other acts of sexual assault or child molestation for its bearing on any relevant matter, including as evidence of the defendant's character.

b. Civil Cases. [11.62]

In civil cases in which a damage claim is predicated on the commission of a sexual assault or act of child molestation, evidence may be offered that a party committed other acts of sexual assault or child molestation for its bearing on any relevant matter, including as evidence of the party's character.

c. Notice Requirement. [11.63]

A party intending to offer evidence under this exception must provide notice to its opponent at least fifteen days prior to trial.

H. HABIT AND ROUTINE PRACTICE EVIDENCE. [§12.0]

FRE 406 specifies that evidence of a person's habit is admissible to prove that the person acted in accordance with that habit on a particular occasion.

1. HABIT AND CHARACTER EVIDENCE DISTINGUISHED. [§12.1]

Habit: typically regarded as a regular response to a repeated, specific situation. Character: relates to a generalized description of a disposition or trait.

2. CORROBORATION AND NECESSITY LIMITATIONS ABANDONED. [§12.2]

FRE and many states have abandoned common-law limitations restricted habit evidence to situations where there was indeper corroboration of the conduct, or where such evidence was necessitate absence of eyewitnesses.

3. ROUTINE PRACTICE. [§12.3]

Organization's custom or routine practice admissible to prove that organization acted in conformity with its routine practice on occasion in question.

I. OTHER CRIMES, WRONGS, OR ACTS EVIDENCE ADMISSIBLE FOR NON-CHARACTER PURPOSES. [§13.0]

Evidence of a person's character ordinarily is inadmissible if offered to prove that the person acted in conformity with that character on a particular occasion. But such evidence may be admissible if offered to prove something **other than character** from which conduct on a particular occasion is to be inferred.

1. RATIONALE. [§13.1]

When evidence of other acts is offered to prove something other than character, balancing of probative and prejudicial value tilts towards exclusion, but danger still exists, and such evidence must still be treated with care.

2. "MIAMI COP." [§13.2]

Purposes for which other crimes, wrongs, or acts evidence (sometimes referred to as "extrinsic offense" evidence) may be offered: **M**otive; **I**dentity; **A**bsence of **M**istake or accident; **I**ntent; **C**ommon plan or scheme; **O**pportunity; **P**reparation.

a. Motive. [§13.21]
Evidence that defendant had motive/to commit the crime.

b. Identity. [§13.22]
Evidence that defendant committed other similar crimes using the same distinctive modus operandi as that used by the perpetrator of the charged crime.

c. Absence of Mistake or Accident. [§13.23]
Evidence of other crimes, wrongs, or acts may tend to prove that person possessed knowledge of what he was doing or of consequences of his act.

d. Intent. [§13.24]
Prosecution must prove that defendant had the requisite criminal intent. In many criminal cases, courts restrict "other crimes" evidence to those cases in which defendant contends that he did not have the requisite intent.

e. Common Plan or Scheme. [§13.25]
Evidence that defendant committed another crime, wrong, or act as part of a plan or scheme to commit the charged act.

f. Opportunity. [§13.26]

Evidence of other crimes, wrongs, or acts to prove defendant had access to the scene of the crime or knowledge or capacity to commit the charged crime.

g. Preparation. [§13.27]

Evidence of other crimes, wrongs, or acts to show defendant's preparation for the charged crime.

3. "EXCEPTIONS". [§13.3]

These uses of "other crimes" evidence do not violate the character rule because the evidence is not being introduced as evidence of character from which conduct is to be inferred. It is being offered as proof of guilt that does not require an inference to be made about defendant's character.

4. PROCEDURAL CONSIDERATIONS. [§13.4]

a. Quantum of Proof Required. [§13.41]

Other crimes, wrongs, or acts evidence is not restricted to acts for which defendant has previously been arrested or convicted. Jurisdictions vary as to strength of proof necessary to establish that defendant committed the other crime, wrong or act.

(1) Federal Standard. [§13.411]

Supreme Court has held that prosecution is required to introduce only enough evidence so that a reasonable juror could find that defendant committed the other crime.

b. Discretionary Exclusion. [§13.42]

Courts may exclude other crimes evidence on the ground that the danger of unfair prejudice substantially outweighs its probative value.

c. Notice. [§13.43]

FRE 404(b) requires prosecution, upon request by the accused, to provide reasonable notice of the general nature of any other crimes evidence it intends to introduce at trial for any purpose.

d. Acquittal. [§13.44]

Evidence of another crime may be offered by the prosecution even if defendant has already been tried and acquitted for that crime. This does not offend the Double Jeopardy Clause.

VI.   HEARSAY

A. HEARSAY. [§14.0]

(Basic hearsay and more sophisticated hearsay).

1. HEARSAY DEFINED. [§14.1]

A statement, other than one made by the declarant while testifying at the trial or hearing, offered in evidence for the truth of the matter asserted.

2. THE HEARSAY PROBLEM. [§14.2]

Problem arises when a witness testifies to an out-of-court statement and the probative value of the statement depends on the credibility — sincerity, communicative ability, perception and memory — of the person who made the out-of-court statement.

3. BASIC HEARSAY. THREE-STEP ANALYSIS. [§14.3]

(1) Is there an out-of-court statement? If so, (2) What is it being offered to prove? (3) Does its probative value depend on credibility of declarant?

a. Is There an Out-of-Court Statement? [§14.31]
Statement may be (a) oral,(b) written, (c) conduct intended as a substitute for words.

b. Does the Probate Value of the Statement Depend on the Declarant's Crediblity? [§14.33]
If all we care about is whether the statement was made by declarant (i.e., we don't care whether declarant was lying or mistaken), it is not hearsay. If we care about declarant's credibility (i.e., probative value of the statement depends on whether declarant was lying or mistaken), it is hearsay — subject to the qualifications concerning More Sophisticated Hearsay.

B. NOT ALL OUT-OF-COURT STATEMENTS ARE HEARSAY. [§14.331]

Several common situations in which an out-of-court statement is relevant simply because it was made and is not hearsay.

1. EFFECT OF STATEMENT ON LISTENER. [§14.3311]

Where importance of statement derives from effect it had on person who heard it, it is not hearsay.

2. STATE OF MIND OF DECLARANT. [§14.3312]

If state of mind of a declarant is relevant, statement made by him may be circumstantial evidence of state of mind, regardless of its truth.

3. LEGALLY OPERATIVE FACTS. [§14.3313]

The substantive law imbues some statements with legal significance; e.g., words of contract, statements of donative intent, statements indicating open or hostile possession, words of libel or slander. Also referred to as "verbal acts" or words of "independent legal significance."

4. IMPEACHMENT AND REHABILITATION. [§14.3314]

Prior statements of witness offered to impeach or to rehabilitate him are not offered for their truth and are not hearsay. However, there are special rules dealing with the use of such prior statements.

C. SOME DEFINITIONS. [§14.4]

1. "OUT OF COURT". [§14.41]

Any statement other than one made by a witness while testifying at the present hearing is "out of court," even if it was made at a previous court hearing.

2. "DECLARANT". [§14.42]

Person who made the out-of-court statement. A witness and declarant may be the same person.

3. DECLARANT MUST BE A PERSON. [§14.43]

Hearsay rule reaches only statements made by persons, not machines or animals.

D. MORE SOPHISTICATED HEARSAY PROBLEMS. [§14.5]

The three-step analysis will always identify statements that clearly are not hearsay. If probative value does not depend on declarant's credibility, statement is not hearsay. But we cannot always say that a statement is hearsay simply because its probative value depends on declarant's credibility. Whether or not such a statement is considered hearsay depends upon the precise way in which hearsay is defined. Common law definition is broad; FRE is narrower. In each of the five categories below, probative value of declarant's out-of-court statement or conduct depends on declarant's credibility. To determine whether such an out-of-court statement is hearsay, figure out into which category it falls. Under FRE, only first two are hearsay; under common law, all five are hearsay.

1. EXPLICIT VERBAL ASSERTIONS. [§14.51]

Verbal statements (oral or written) that assert directly what they are introduced to prove.

2. NON-VERBAL CONDUCT INTENDED AS AN ASSERTION. [§14.52]

An act or gesture intended to convey a message offered as proof of that message.

3. NON-VERBAL CONDUCT NOT INTENDED AS AN ASSERTION. [§14.53]

An act or gesture not intended to convey a message, but that is offered as evidence that the actor believed something and that the belief was accurate.

4. NON-ASSERTIVE VERBAL CONDUCT. [§14.54]

Declarant uses words but does not intend to make an assertion. Nevertheless, his statement is offered as evidence of something implicit in the statement.

5. VERBAL ASSERTIONS USED INFERENTIALLY. [§14.55]

Although declarant makes a verbal assertion, his statement is offered to prove something implicit in the statement rather than the truth of the statement itself.

a. Common Law View. [§14.56]

Based on the famous English case, Wright v. Tatham, common law view is that all five categories are hearsay.

b. Federal Rules. [§14.57]

Non-verbal conduct not intended as an assertion is not a "statement" and thus is not hearsay. Thus, Category 3 is not hearsay. Moreover, since FRE 801 defines hearsay as a "statement . . . offered for the truth of the matter asserted," if there is no assertion (Category 4) or a statement is being offered to prove something other than what was asserted (Category 5), it is not hearsay.

E. NON-HEARSAY BY EXEMPTION. [§14.6]

Although a witness's own out-of-court statements are ordinarily hearsay if offered for the truth of the matter asserted, FRE and most modern codes also declare that certain types of prior statements by a witness are not hearsay. In addition, admissions by party opponents are defined as non-hearsay.

1. PRIOR STATEMENTS OF WITNESSES. [§14.61]

Out-of-court statement of trial witness is not hearsay if witness is subject to cross-examination about the particular statement and it falls into one of three categories:

a. Prior inconsistent statements. [§14.611]

Out-of-court statement is inconsistent with witness's trial testimony and statement was (a) given under oath, (b) subject to penalty of perjury, (c) at some other trial, hearing, proceeding, or deposition.

b. Prior consistent statements. [§14.612]

Out-of-court statement is consistent with witness's trial testimony and is offered to rebut charge of recent fabrication or improper motivation or influence.

c. Prior statement of identification. [§14.613]

Out-of-court statement was one of identification of a person made after perceiving the person.

2. ADMISSION BY PARTY OPPONENT. [§14.62]

At common law, admissions by a party opponent are considered exceptions to the hearsay rule. The FRE and most state codes now define admissions as non-hearsay.

F. OTHER HEARSAY PROBLEMS. [§14.7]

1. MULTIPLE HEARSAY. [§14.71]

When evidence contains at least two separate out-of-court statements, each of which is offered for its truth.

2. APPROACH TO MULTIPLE HEARSAY. [§14.713]

Analyze each statement separately. (1) Determine whether each is hearsay; (2) look for an exception for each hearsay statement. Multiple hearsay is admissible only if you have a hearsay exception for each layer of hearsay.

G. LIMITED ADMISSIBILITY. [§14.72]

A single statement may be hearsay if offered for one purpose and not hearsay if offered for another purpose. If this happens, court may admit the statement, instructing jury to consider it only for the non-hearsay purpose.

H. SILENCE. [§14.73]

Silence is a form of non-verbal conduct. Thus, under FRE, if intended as an assertion, it is hearsay (Category 2); if not intended as an assertion, it is not hearsay (Category 3). Under common law, more easily viewed as hearsay (since jury is asked to infer that silence betokens person's belief about something and that the belief is correct). But once a common law court concludes silence is sufficiently probative, it rarely excludes it on hearsay grounds.

VII. HEARSAY EXCEPTIONS

A. HEARSAY EXCEPTIONS IN GENERAL. [§15.0]

Numerous exceptions to the hearsay rule, most justified on ground that particular classes of statements possess inherent guarantees of reliability.

1. MNEMONIC DEVICE: "BAD SPLITS, PEPPI". [§15.1]

B - Business records
A - Admission by party opponent
D - Dying declaration

S - Spontaneous statements (excited utterance and present sense impress'
P - Past recollection recorded
L - Learned treatise
I - Interest, Declaration against
T - Testimony, Former
S - State of mind or condition

P - Public records
E - Equivalency (residual, catch-all)
P - Prior inconsistent statement
P - Prior consistent statement
I - Identification

> **NOTE:** Admissions by a party opponent and certain prior statements by a witness (the last three "exceptions" listed in PEPPI) are defined in FRE and many state codes as non-hearsay.

B. ADMISSION BY PARTY OPPONENT. [§16.0]

Any statement made by opposing party.

1. NOT AN EXCEPTION. [§16.1]

At common law, admissions by a party opponent were considered a hearsay exception. FRE and many state codes define admissions as non-hearsay.

2. NOT BASED ON RELIABILITY. [§16.2]

Justified on responsibility or estoppel ground, not reliability. Party is estopped from objecting to own statements on the ground that he can't cross-examine the declarant (i.e., himself). Two consequences:

a. Limited Admissibility. [§16.21]
Admissions are admissible only against the party who made the statement. Important in multi-party litigation.

b. Personal Knowledge Not Required. [§16.22]
Admissions are admissible even if party had no firsthand knowledge of facts asserted.

3. ANY STATEMENT MAY BE AN ADMISSION. [§16.3]

Any statement of a party opponent falls within this exception even if party wasn't admitting (i.e., confessing) to anything at time statement was made.

4. THREE DIFFERENT KINDS OF ADMISSIONS. [§16.4]

(1) party's own statements; (2) adoptive admissions; and (3) vicarious admissions.

a. Party's Own Statements. [§16.41]
Anything a party says may be offered over a hearsay objection by his opponent.

b. Adoptive Admissions. [§16.42]
Party can adopt a statement made by another person as her own, either explicitly or tacitly, and that other person's statement will be treated as an admission of the party.

(1) Tacit Admissions. [§16.422]
When a statement is made in a party's presence and contains an assertion that a reasonable person would, under the circumstances, deny if it were not true, failure to deny is construed as adoption of the assertion. Called a "tacit," "adoptive" or "implied" admission, or "admission by silence."

(a) Silence Must Equal Assent. [§16.4221]
Tacit admission found only when it is reasonable to view party's silence as constituting assent to the truth of the assertion.

c. Vicarious Admissions. [§16.43]
Statements by a non-party may be attributed to and used against a party under certain circumstances because of special relationship between the party and the declarant.

(1) Vicarious Admissions by Agents and Employees. [§16.431]
Statement by a party's agent or employee.

(a) Common Law View. [§16.4311]
Only if agent was authorized to speak on behalf of the party.

(b) Federal Rules. [§16.4312]

Statements made by someone authorized by a party to speak . Also, statements by a party's agent or employee if the statement (a) concerned a matter within the scope of his agency or employment, and (b) was made while speaker was still an agent or employee.

(2) Co-Conspirator Admissions. [§16.432]

Statement made by a party's co-conspirator if proponent shows (a) that declarant and party were co-conspirators; and statement was made (b) during pendency and (c) in furtherance of conspiracy.

(a) Proof of Conspiracy. [§16.4321]

Many common law courts require proof of existence of conspiracy through independent evidence. Supreme Court has held co-conspirator's statements may be considered in deciding whether proponent has made necessary showing. Court has also held that existence of conspiracy need only be established by preponderance of the evidence.

C. HEARSAY EXCEPTIONS: AVAILABILITY IMMATERIAL. [§17.0]

FRE 803 lists hearsay exceptions that apply regardless of whether the declarant is available to testify at trial.

1. SPONTANEOUS STATEMENTS. [§18.0]

Two related exceptions based on spontaneity: (a) excited utterances and (b) present sense impressions.

a. Excited Utterances. [§18.1]

Statements (a) made while the declarant was under stress of excitement caused by startling event or condition (b) that relate to the event or condition.

(1) Rationale. [§18.11]

Stress ensures spontaneity and precludes possibility of fabrication.

(a) Must Relate to Startling Event. [§18.11]

Encompasses not only statements that describe or explain the event, but statements that relate to it in any way.

(b) While Under Stress of Excitement. [§18.13]

Statement must be made before declarant has had time to reflect. Usually made soon after exciting event, but no time requirement.

b. Present Sense Impression. [§18.2]

Statements that (a) describe or explain an event or condition (b) made while declarant was perceiving the event or condition or immediately thereafter.

(1) Rationale. [§18.21]

Spontaneity ensures declarant will not have had time to think about what to say.

Sum & Substance QUICK REVIEW of Evidence

(2) Time Factor. [§18.22]

Must be made while the event or condition is being perceived or immediately afterwards.

(3) Must Describe or Explain the Event. [§18.23]

Limited to statements that "describe or explain" the event.

2. STATE OF MIND: MENTAL OR PHYSICAL CONDITION. [§19.0]

Statements by declarant relating to her then existing mental, emotional, or physical condition. Related exception covers statements made for the purpose of medical diagnosis or treatment.

a. Present State of Mind. [§19.1]

Statements of intent, belief ("I think my brakes are bad"), attitude, mental feeling, pain and bodily health.

(1) Rationale. [§19.11]

No problems of memory or perception. Also, since person's state of mind often difficult to prove, frequently a need for such direct evidence.

(2) Proper Uses of Present State of Mind: To Prove State of Mind Itself. [§19.12]

Where person's intent, knowledge, belief, attitude, or physical condition is itself a relevant issue.

(3) Proper Uses of Present State of Mind: To Prove Conduct of the Declarant. [§19.13]

Statement of existing intent to do something in the future admissible to prove declarant actually carried through with plans.

(4) Improper Use of Present State of Mind: To Prove Truth of Underlying Facts. [§19.14]

May not be used to prove the truth of the facts remembered or believed or underlying the belief.

(a) Exception: Statements Relating to a Will. [§19.141]

Statement of memory or belief admissible to prove fact remembered or believed if it relates to execution, revocation, identification, or terms of declarant's will.

(5) Controversial Use of Present State of Mind. [§19.15]

Courts divided as to whether declarant's statement may be used to prove someone else's conduct.

(6) State of Mind Exception Distinguished From State of Mind Non-Hearsay. [§19.16]

If out-of-court statement used as circumstantial evidence of declarant's mental state, it is not hearsay because not offered for its truth. If person makes direct assertion of his mental state, it is hearsay if used to prove existence of that state of mind but admissible under the state of mind exception.

b. Statements Made for Purpose of Medical Diagnosis or Treatment. [§19.2]

(1) Statements of Present Symptoms, Etc. [§19.21]

Statements of present symptoms, pain, sensations, or physical condition. FRE and most states admit statements even if made to consulting physician.

(2) Statements of Past Symptoms, Etc. [§19.22]

Statements as to person's medical history, past symptoms, pain or physical condition if made either for diagnosis or treatment. Common law does not allow.

(3) Statements of Cause. [§19.23]

FRE and most states allow statements as to cause or external source of pain, symptom, condition, etc. insofar as pertinent to diagnosis or treatment.

3. BUSINESS RECORDS. [§20.0]

Written record qualifies for business records exception if it was (a) the regular practice of the business to keep such records; and the records were made (b) in the regular course of the business; (c) at or near the time of the event or condition recorded; and (d) by an employee with personal knowledge of the event or upon information provided by someone with a business duty to report the information. But court should exclude record if the source of information or the method or circumstances of its preparation indicate a lack of trustworthiness.

a. Mnemonic Device: "KRAP". [§20.1]
Keep; Regular course; At or near the time; Personal knowledge.

b. Rationale. [§20.2]
Business records qualify for a hearsay exception because of their reliability.

c. Analysis of Elements. [§20.3]
(1) Personal Knowledge. [§20.31]

(a) Analysis: Entrant Has Personal Knowledge. [§20.312]

Personal knowledge requirement fulfilled if maker of record has personal knowledge of recorded facts.

(b) Analysis: Information From Someone With Business Duty to Report. [§20.313]

Personal knowledge requirement fulfilled even if maker of record lacks personal knowledge of recorded facts if the information comes from someone else with business duty to report the information.

(c) Analysis: Information From Someone Without Business Duty to Report. [§20.314]

If maker of record lacks personal knowledge of recorded facts and the information comes from someone not under obligation to report, record is inadmissible unless another hearsay exception can be found for reporting person's statement.

(2) Regular Course of Business. [§20.32]
Must be type of record regularly kept by business. Must have been recorded in routine fashion.

(a) Records Made in Contemplation of Litigation. [§20.321]
Courts suspicious of records made with eye toward litigation.

(3) Lack of Trustworthiness. [§20.33]
If four requirements (KRAP) shown, record admitted unless opponent shows source of information or method or circumstances indicate a lack of trustworthiness.

d. Laying the Foundation. [§20.4]
May be done by any person who knows how record is made and kept. May, but need not, be maker or custodian of record.

4. PUBLIC RECORDS AND REPORTS. [§21.0]
FRE and many states have expansive exception for public records. Rationale: public officials will perform duties properly. FRE admits records and reports of a government agency setting forth information falling within four categories.

a. Activities of the Agency. [§21.1]
Records setting forth the agency's own activities.

b. Matters the Agency is Required to Observe and Report. [§21.2]
Records setting forth matters that agency is required by law to observe and report. Involves recording of public officials' own first-hand observations.

(1) But Not in Criminal Cases. [§21.21]
Excludes in criminal cases, matters observed by police officers and other law enforcement personnel.

c. Factual Findings. [§21.3]
Reports setting forth factual findings that result from authorized governmental investigation admissible (a) in civil cases and (b) against government in criminal cases.

(1) Includes Conclusions As To Fault. [§21.31]
Supreme Court has rejected attempts to give narrow reading to "factual findings."

(2) Excluded If Not Trustworthy. [§21.32]
Public report setting forth factual findings inadmissible if opponent shows that sources of information or other circumstances indicate lack of trustworthiness.

d. Vital Statistics. [§21.4]
Covers public records of births, deaths, and marriages.

5. LEARNED TREATISES. [§22.0]

Common law allows cross-examiner to impeach expert by pointing out discrepancies between witness's testimony and statements made in a treatise or article that witness has relied on. FRE and many states have hearsay exception for statements contained in published treatises, periodicals, or pamphlets concerning history, medicine or any other science or art.

a. Three Restrictions. [§22.1]
(1) Admissible only to extent called to attention of expert on cross-examination or relied upon by expert in direct exam. (2) Work must be established as reliable authority by (a) the witness (b) another expert or (c) judicial notice. (3) Statements may be read into evidence but not introduced as exhibits.

6. PAST RECOLLECTION RECORDED ("PRR"). [§23.0]

Allows statement previously recorded by witness to be used at trial when witness cannot remember what happened.

a. Elements of PRR. [§23.1]
Six requirements: declarant (a) testifies at trial; (b) once had personal knowledge about matter; (c)insufficient recollection to testify fully and accurately; (d) made or adopted statement; (e) while event fresh in memory; and (f) accurately reflected his knowledge.

b. Rationtale. [§23.2]
Reliability and necessity.

c. May Only Be Read Into Evidence. [§23.3]
PRR is only a substitute for the witness's testimony; proponent may only have PRR read to jury. Opposing party is entitled to examine the memo and introduce it.

d. Availability of the Declarant Required. [§23.4]
PRR requires that declarant be a witness.

e. Present Recollection Refreshed Distinguished. [§23.5]
Past Recollection Recorded: a hearsay exception which allows use of a previously written statement by a witness who can no longer remember what happened. Present Recollection Refreshed: technique and procedures surrounding attempt by counsel to jog a forgetful witness's memory. Present Recollection Refreshed does not involve hearsay.

7. CATCH-ALL EXCEPTION: EQUIVALENT TRUSTWORTHINESS. [§24.0]

Under FRE, even if hearsay statement does not fall within specific hearsay exception, admissible if it possesses "equivalent circumstantial guarantees of trustworthiness." Four additional requirements.

a. Must Be Material. [§24.1]
Offered as evidence of material fact.

b. Must Be Necessary. [§24.2]
Statement more probative on point for which offered than any other evidence which proponent can reasonably be expected to come up with.

c. Must Serve Justice. [§24.3]
Admission must best serve interests of justice.

d. Notice Requirement. [§24.4]
Proponent must give adverse party notice of (a) intent to u
exception; and (b) particulars of statement.

D. HEARSAY EXCEPTIONS: UNAVAILABILITY REQUIRED. [§2

Four hearsay exceptions apply only if declarant is unavailable: **"DAFT"**: **D**ying declarations; **A**gainst interest declarations; **F**amily and personal history statements; **T**estimony, former.

1. UNAVAILABILITY DEFINED. [§25.1]

Declarant is "unavailable" if (a) too ill to testify or dead; (b) validly asserts privilege; (c) refuses to testify despite court order; (d) lacks memory; or (e) is absent and proponent cannot procure her attendance or testimony.

a. Definition of Unavailability Mnemonic: "PRIMA". [§25.11]
Privilege; **R**efusal to testify; **I**ll or dead; **M**emory; **A**bsent.

2. DYING DECLARATIONS. [§26.0]

Statements made by a person who believes death is imminent. Said to be reliable because person would not want to go to his maker "with a lie on his lips."

a. Common Law Version. [§26.1]
Requires (a) declarant believe his death is imminent (b) statement concern causes and circumstances of the impending death. In addition, dying declarations admitted (c) only in the homicide prosecution of the declarant's killer, so (d) declarant must be dead.

b. Federal Rules. [§26.2]
Under FRE, statement qualifies if (a) declarant made statement while believing death was imminent; (b) statement concerns causes or circumstances of impending death; (c) declarant is unavailable and (d) statement is offered in a civil case or any homicide prosecution.

3. DECLARATION AGAINST INTEREST. [§27.0]

a. Rationale. [§27.1]
People don't say things adverse to their own interest unless true.

b. Analysis of Elements. [§27.2]
(1) Unavailability. [§27.21]
Declarant must be unavailable.

(2) When Made. [§27.22]
Against declarant's interest at time statement was made.

(3) Pecuniary or Proprietary Interest. [§27.23]
Person acknowledges facts that might adversely affect financial well-being or limit property rights.

(4) Civil Liability. [§27.24]

FRE and many states include statements that would tend to subject declarant to civil liability.

(5) Criminal Liability. [§27.25]

FRE and many states allow statements that tend to subject the declarant to criminal liability. But FRE require corroboration of declarations against penal interest offered to exculpate an accused.

(6) Mixed Motives. [§27.27]

The United States Supreme Court has ruled that the declaration against interest exception reaches only those parts of a statement that are disserving to the declarant. It does not sanction admission of neutral or self-serving statements made in the course of a broader, and generally disserving, narrative.

4. FORMER TESTIMONY. [§28.0]

Out-of-court statement now being offered was itself made as testimony.

a. Other Hearing or Deposition. [§28.1]

Given under oath at earlier trial, a deposition, or some other proceeding.

b. Unavailability Required. [§28.2]

Declarant must be unavailable.

c. Opportunity and Motive to Develop the Testimony. [§28.3]

Admissible only if party against whom it is now being offered had (a) opportunity and (b) similar motive to develop the testimony in the former hearing.

(1) Predecessor in Interest Okay for Civil Cases. [§28.31]

Under FRE, in civil cases, admissible if predecessor in interest of the party had the opportunity and similar motive to develop the testimony.

d. Common Law Approach. [§28.4]

Admissible only if identity of issues and parties in former and current proceedings.

5. STATEMENTS OF PERSONAL OR FAMILY HISTORY [§29.0]

(See §32.0 et seq.)

E. PRIOR STATEMENTS OF A WITNESS. [§30.0]

Three kinds of statements previously made by a witness exempted from the hearsay rule. Defined as non-hearsay.

1. DECLARANT MUST TESTIFY AND BE SUBJECT TO CROSS-EXAMINATION. [§30.1]

Exemptions cover only out-of-court statements made by someone who testifies at current trial and is subject to cross-examination about prior statement. They are as follows:

a. Certain Prior Inconsistent Statements. [§30.2]

Prior inconsistent statement of witness made (a) under oath, (b) subject to penalty of perjury, (c) at earlier trial, hearing, or other proceeding, or deposition, is defined as non-hearsay and may be used for its truth. Grand jury testimony meets these requirements.

b. Certain Prior Consistent Statements. [§30.3]

Prior statement of witness if (a) consistent with witness's trial testimony and (b) offered to rebut charge of recent fabrication or improper motive or influence.

c. Prior Statements of Identification. [§30.4]

Witness's out-of-court identification of a person made after perceiving him.

F. MISCELLANEOUS EXCEPTIONS. [§31.0]

1. PERSONAL OR FAMILY HISTORY. [§32.0]

Number of hearsay exceptions to prove matters relating to someone's personal or family history.

a. Statements Regarding Personal or Family History. [§32.1]
Unavailability required.

b. Records of Vital Statistics. [§32.2]

c. Records of Religious Organizations. [§32.2]

d. Marriage, Baptismal, and Similar Certificates. [§32.4]

e. Family Records. [§32.5]

f. Reputation. [§32.6]

g. Judgments. [§32.7]

2. ANCIENT DOCUMENTS. [§33.0]

Statements contained in documents at least 20 years old.

3. PROPERTY INTERESTS. [§34.0]

Several exceptions may be used to prove facts relating to property or interests in property.

a. Records of Documents Affecting Property Interests. [§34.1]

b. Statements Contained in Documents Affecting Property Interests. [§34.2]

c. Reputation. [§34.3]

d. Judgments. [§34.4]

4. MARKET REPORTS AND COMMERCIAL PUBLICATIONS. [§35.0]

Market quotations, tabulations, lists, etc. generally used and relied upon by the public or by persons in particular occupations.

5. REPUTATION. [§36.0]

May be used to prove: personal or family history; land boundaries and customs; events of general history important to the community, state or nation; a person's character.

6. JUDGMENT OF PREVIOUS CONVICTION. [§37.0]

Felony conviction is admissible to prove any fact essential to sustain the judgment if the judgment was entered after a trial or upon a guilty plea. But (a) does not apply if conviction entered upon nolo contendere plea; (b) may not be used by government in a criminal case, except for impeachment purposes.

G. CONFRONTATION CLAUSE. [§38.0]

Sixth Amendment guarantees criminal defendant right "to be confronted with the witnesses against him." Extent to which it limits prosecution's ability to introduce hearsay against accused far from certain.

1. NO CONFRONTATION CLAUSE PROBLEM IF HEARSAY DECLARANT TESTIFIES. [§38.1]

If declarant testifies at trial and can be cross-examined about hearsay statements, no Confrontation Clause problem.

2. IF DECLARANT DOES NOT TESTIFY: EARLY TWO-PART TEST. [§38.2]

In *Ohio v. Roberts*, 448 U.S. 56 (1980), the Court stated that the Confrontation Clause demanded first, that if the prosecution did not produce the declarant at trial it must demonstrate that (1) the declarant was **unavailable** to testify at trial and (2) the hearsay is **reliable**.

3. IF DECLARANT DOES NOT TESTIFY: MORE RECENT CASES. [§38.3]

More recently, the Court has indicated that the hearsay (other than that offered as former testimony) may be admitted even if the prosecution does not produce the declarant and he is available to testify.

a. Hearsay Must Be Reliable. [§38.31]
If the declarant does not testify, the hearsay must be reliable. Reliability established in either of two ways.

(1) Firmly Rooted Hearsay Exception. [§38.311]
If the hearsay falls within firmly rooted hearsay exception, it is deemed reliable.

(2) Particularized Guarantee of Trustworthiness. [§38.232]

If the hearsay does not fall within firmly rooted hearsay exception, prosecution must show it possesses particularized guarantees of trustworthiness.

VIII. WITNESSES

A. COMPETENCY OF WITNESSES. [§39.0]

FRE drop almost all restrictions on witness competency; common law jurisdictions have dropped many.

1. NO MENTAL OR MORAL REQUIREMENTS UNDER FRE. [§39.1]

Every person is competent to be a witness except for judges and jurors.

2. COMMON LAW: CAPACITY TO OBSERVE, RECALL, AND RELATE. [§39.2]

Witness incompetent if lacks sufficient mental capacity to accurately observe, recall or relate facts.

a. Age. [§39.21]
No minimum age limits.

b. Insane Persons May Testify. [§39.22]
Adjudication of incompetency or insanity not conclusive of person's competency to testify.

3. DEAD MAN'S STATUTE. [§39.3]

Can arise in federal court only when state law claim being adjudicated; little uniformity among states.

a. Basics of the Dead Man's Statute. [§39.31]
(1) In cases brought by or against the personal representative of a deceased (2) a party (3) may not testify as to a transaction (4) with the deceased.

4. COMPETENCY OF JUDGES AS WITNESSES. [§39.4]

A judge may not testify in a case over which the judge is presiding.

5. COMPETENCY OF JURORS AS WITNESSES. [§39.5]

a. At the Trial. [§39.51]
A juror may not testify in a case in which the juror is sitting.

b. At Hearing Challenging Validity of Verdict. [§39.52]
After verdict is reached, juror may not testify about (a) any matter or statement that occurred during the jury's deliberations or (b) anything that influenced any juror's mental processes in arriving at a verdict. Rationale: desire to protect jurors from harassment and promote finality of judgments.

(1) Exceptions. [§39.521]

Jurors may testify as to whether (a) extraneous prejudicial information was improperly brought to jury's attention or (b) any outside influence was improperly brought to bear on a juror.

6. COMPETENCY AND HYPNOSIS. [§39.6]

Some courts do not allow witnesses who have been hypnotized to testify. Others allow such witnesses if certain procedural safeguards are followed. Some states permit such testimony on an ad hoc basis.

B. OATH OR AFFIRMATION. [§40.0]

Witnesses required to declare that they will testify truthfully, by an oath or affirmation.

C. PERSONAL KNOWLEDGE. [§41.0]

With the exception of experts, witnesses may not testify unless they have personal knowledge of the matter about which they are testifying.

D. EXCLUSION OF WITNESSES: INVOKING "THE RULE." [§42.0]

Party may ask court to exclude all witnesses from the courtroom so they cannot hear what other witnesses say.

1. THREE EXCEPTIONS. [§42.1]

Three types of witnesses exempt from exclusion: (a) party who is a natural person; (b) officer or employee of a non-natural party who is designated as its representative; and (c) person whose presence is shown to be essential to presentation of the party's cause.

E. EXAMINATION OF WITNESSES: INTRODUCTION. [§43.0]

Cross-examination refers to a stage of questioning; leading questions refers to the form in which a question is asked; and impeachment refers to the attempt to attack a witness's credibility.

1. STAGES OF EXAMINATION. [§44.0]

a. Direct Examination. [§44.1]
The initial round of questions put to a witness by the calling party.

b. Cross-Examination. [§44.2]
After the calling party completes direct examination, the opposing party conducts cross-examination of the witness.

c. Redirect- and Recross-Examination. [§44.3]
After cross-examination, the calling party may conduct a redirect exam, followed by opponent's recross-exam.

d. Calling and Questioning Witnesses by the Court. [§44.4]
Under FRE, trial judge is authorized to call witnesses on its own motion. All parties entitled to cross-examine such witnesses. Judge permitted to interrogate any witness, whether called by the court or a party.

2. OBJECTIONS AS TO FORM OF QUESTION. [§45.0]

a. Questions Calling for Narrative. [§45.1]

Open-ended questions calling for an undirected narrative by the witness are objectionable.

b. Leading Questions. [§45.2]

One that suggests the answer the witness is to give. "Isn't it true that . . ." or "Didn't you then . . ."

(1) General Rule: Leading Questions Allowed on Cross, But Not on Direct. [§45.21]

Leading questions generally not allowed on direct examination but may be asked on cross-examination.

(2) Leading Questions Sometimes Allowed on Direct. [§45.22]

A few instances in which leading questions may be asked on direct examination:

(a) Preliminary Matters. [§45.221]

About preliminary matters not in dispute, such as name, address, and occupation of witness.

(b) Where Necessary. [§45.222]

When witness has difficulty testifying in response to non-leading questions, e.g., witness with language problem, child, weak-minded witness, and witness unable to remember.

(c) Witnesses Unlikely to Follow Lead. [§45.223]

When the witness is (a) an adverse party; (b) a witness identified with an adverse party; or (c) hostile.

c. Argumentative Questions. [§45.3]

Questions used to make or emphasize some point or to argue to the jury.

d. Questions Assuming Facts Not in Evidence. [§45.4]

e. Compound Questions. [§45.5]

Question that contains two inquiries but calls for only one answer.

f. Ambiguous or Unintelligible Questions. [§45.6]

g. Questions Calling for Speculation. [§45.7]

h. Repetitive Questions: Asked and Answered. [§45.8]

i. Non-Responsive Answers to Proper Questions. [§45.9]

Questioner may object to non-responsive answer, but most jurisdictions do not allow opposing counsel to object on other grounds. Opposing counsel may object if testimony is otherwise inadmissible and ask court to instruct witness to answer only questions asked.

3. REFRESHING A WITNESS'S MEMORY. [§46.0]

Attempt to jog witness's memory, to refresh his recollection. Anything that will help trigger the witness's memory may be used.

a. If the Witness Remembers, No Hearsay Problem. [§46.1]

If witness's memory is refreshed, he testifies from memory and no hearsay problem exists.

b. Refreshing Item is Not Evidence. [§46.2]

It is only a device used to jog the witness's memory and is not itself being offered as proof. Thus, no need to authenticate, comply with Best Evidence Rule, fall within a hearsay exception, or meet any other requirement of admissibility.

c. But Procedural Safeguards Exist. [§46.3]

When a document is used to refresh a witness's memory, some procedural safeguards apply.

(1) Memory Refreshed While Witness is Testifying. [§46.31]

If a witness's memory is refreshed while on the stand, opposing counsel entitled to inspect the document, cross-examine the witness about it, and introduce relevant portions of the document.

(2) Memory Refreshed Before Trial. [§46.32]

If witness reviews document to refresh memory before he testifies, FRE 612 gives court discretion to order counsel to turn over the document to his opponent for inspection, cross-examination, and introduction of relevant portions. Common law does not authorize judge to do this.

4. NATURE AND SCOPE OF CROSS-EXAMINATION. [§47.0]

a. Form of Questioning. [§47.1]

Cross-examiner has broad leeway in using leading questions and repeating the same question, but trial court given great deal of control over such matters.

b. Scope of Cross-Examination. [§47.2]

FRE adopts majority rule: cross-examination limited to the subject matter of direct examination and matters affecting witness's credibility. But trial court has discretion to permit inquiry during cross-examination into "additional matters as if on direct examination."

(1) Minority Rule. [§47.21]

Wide-open cross-examination (i.e., questioning as to any relevant issue in the case).

c. Redirect- and Recross-Examination. [§47.3]

Redirect ordinarily limited to matters brought out in preceding cross-examination. Recross-examination ordinarily limited to matters explored in preceding redirect exam.

5. RIGHT TO CONFRONTATION. [§48.0]

Confrontation Clause issues arise in two settings.

a. Right to Cross-Examine Adverse Witnesses. [§48.1]

Right to cross-examine considered so important that direct testimony will be stricken if witness cannot be subjected to full cross-examination

due to sickness, death, or a refusal to answer. But reasonable li
be placed on method and extent of cross-examination.

b. Right to Face Accuser. [§48.2]
Confrontation Clause limits ability of the state to have its w
testify outside the presence of accused.

F. IMPEACHMENT IN GENERAL. [§49.0]

An attack on witness's credibility, i.e., an attempt to show that witness is lying,
mistaken, or both.

1. IMPEACHING ONE'S OWN WITNESS. [§49.1]

a. Common Law Voucher Rule. [§49.11]
Common law ordinarily forbids a party from impeaching its own
witness. Exception: when witness unexpectedly testifies in a manner
injurious to the calling party.

b. Federal Rules: No Voucher Rule. [§49.12]
FRE 607 and many state codes allow a party to impeach its own witness.

2. FIVE TECHNIQUES OF IMPEACHMENT: "BICCC". [§49.2]

Bias, Inconsistent Statements, Capacity, Character, Contradiction.

a. Capacity. [§50.0]
Showing defects in witness's ability to see, hear, recall, or recount the
facts.

(1) Physical or Mental Disabilities. [§50.1]
Insanity or other relevant psychological abnormalities; drug or
alcohol use at the time witness perceived the event.

(2) Memory. [§50.2]
Test memory by questions concerning details of events about which
the witness has testified.

(3) No Foundation Requirement. [§50.3]
No foundation before asking a witness questions that reveal a lack
of capacity nor before introducing extrinsic evidence of lack of
capacity.

(4) Extrinsic Evidence Allowed. [§50.4]
Extrinsic evidence admissible to prove lack of capacity.

b. Bias. [§51.0]
Showing witness has reason, independent of merits of case, to give
testimony favoring one side or the other: e.g., personal relationship with
a party, animosity, financial interest, intimidation, desire to curry favor
with the prosecution, or witness is being paid by a party to testify.

(1) Ability to Show Bias Important. [§51.1]
Supreme Court has held that undue limits on an accused's ability
to show bias of a prosecution witness is unconstitutional.

(2) Foundation Requirement. [§51.2]

Some jurisdictions: witness must be asked about alleged bias before extrinsic evidence may be offered. FRE: no foundation requirement.

(3) Extrinsic Evidence. [§51.3]

Admissible to prove bias under general relevancy principles.

c. Prior Inconsistent Statements ("PINS"). [§52.0]

Fact that witness has previously made statements inconsistent with his trial testimony.

(1) Theory: Why Prior Inconsistent Statements Are Not Hearsay When Offered to Impeach. [§52.1]

A witness's own out-of-court statements are hearsay if offered for the truth of the matter asserted. But the fact that the witness previously made a statement that is inconsistent with his testimony at trial tends to detract from his credibility. It demonstrates that he "blows hot and cold," telling one story one time and another story another time. In theory, the impeaching party is not asking the jury to believe that the witness's previous statement is true. All it wants to show is that the witness is not credible.

(2) Limiting Instruction. [§52.11]

When a party impeaches a witness with his prior inconsistent statement (PINS), its opponent is entitled to a limiting instruction.

(3) Some Prior Inconsistent Statements are Better Than Others. [§52.12]

Recall: FRE declare that a prior inconsistent statement made (a) under oath, (b) subject to penalty of perjury, (c) at an earlier trial, hearing, or other proceeding, or deposition is not hearsay. Thus, it can be used for its truth as well as to impeach.

(4) Foundation Requirement. [§52.2]

(a) Common Law. [§52.21]

Foundation must be laid to impeach a witness with his PINS. First, witness must be asked about the PINS before extrinsic evidence may be offered. Second, the question asking witness about the PINS must include (a) identity of person to whom made, (b) time and place made, and (c) substance of statement.

(b) Federal Rule. [§52.22]

Abandons the common law foundation requirement, as have many states.

(5) Extrinsic Evidence of Prior Inconsistent Statements ("PINS"). [§52.3]

Watch for two factors: (a) procedures (foundation requirement) and (b) whether the PINS relates to a collateral matter.

(a) Procedure. [§52.31]

Common law: extrinsic evidence of a PINS only if the witness first refuses to admit having made the statement. FRE: extrinsic evidence of a PINS admissible if (a) witness is given opportunity to explain or deny the statement and (b) opposing counsel is given chance to question witness about the statement.

(b) Collateral Matter. [§52.32]

If the PINS relates to a collateral matter, extrinsic evidence is not permitted.

d. Character for Truthfulness. [§53.0]

Evidence of witness's poor character for truthfulness offered for inference that witness is acting in conformity with that character trait, i.e., is testifying untruthfully.

(1) Three Ways to Prove Untruthful Character. [§53.1]

May be established through (a) opinion or reputation testimony, (b) specific acts not resulting in conviction, and (c) convictions.

(2) Opinion or Reputation. [§53.2]

To impeach Witness 1, the attacking party may call Witness 2 to testify to her opinion of Witness 1's honesty or to Witness 1's reputation in the community. Witness 2 may not cite specific instances of dishonest conduct.

(a) Evidence of Good Character Allowed After Attack. [§53.21]

No evidence of Witness 1's good character for truthfulness until his character attacked. Then, proponent of Witness 1 may call own good reputation or opinion witnesses.

(b) But at a Price. [§53.211]

Witness 1's opinion or reputation witnesses are subject to cross-examination with "Did you know" and "Have you heard" questions. Rules are the same as for other opinion and reputation witnesses: questions may be asked, but questioner is bound by the answer.

(3) Specific Acts Not Resulting in Conviction. [§53.3]

In discretion of court, Witness 1 may be asked on cross-examination about specific things he has done that bear on his truthful disposition.

(a) Act Must Relate to Truthfulness. [§53.31]

The cited conduct must be probative of untrustworthy character.

(b) Bound By Answer. [§53.32]

The questioner is bound by the witness's answer. No extrinsic evidence to prove witness actually engaged in the conduct.

(c) Minority Rule. [§53.33]

Some jurisdictions do not permit a witness to be impeached this way.

(4) Convictions. [§53.4]

Fact that witness has been convicted of certain crimes may be used to prove witness's untruthful character.

(a) FRE: Crimes Involving Dishonesty or False Statement. [§53.41]

Witness may be impeached by showing he has been convicted of crime involving dishonesty or false statement, regardless of punishment. Court may not balance probative value of conviction against danger of unfair prejudice.

(b) FRE: Felonies Not Involving Dishonesty or False Statement. [§53.42]

Witness may be impeached with a felony that did not involve dishonesty or false statement. But court must balance probative value of the conviction against the danger of unfair prejudice. One balancing test for criminal defendants; another for other witnesses.

(i) Witness is Criminal Defendant. [§53.421]

Felony not involving dishonesty or false statement may be used to impeach accused only if the court determines that probative value outweighs prejudicial effect.

(ii) Witness is Anyone Else. [§53.422]

Felony not involving dishonesty or false statement admissible to impeach other witnesses unless court determines that probative value is substantially outweighed by danger of unfair prejudice.

(c) Special Balancing Test For Remote Convictions. [§53.43]

If conviction is remote, it may be used only if court finds that its probative value substantially outweighs prejudicial effect.

(5) Warning: These Rules Apply Only to Attacks on the Witness's Character for Truthfulness. [§53.5]

e. Contradiction. [§54.0]

Issue: when will impeaching party be allowed to offer extrinsic evidence to contradicting some aspect of witness's testimony.

(1) The Collateral Matter Rule. [§54.1]

If the extrinsic evidence is relevant solely because it tends to discredit the witness, it is collateral and inadmissible. If it is also relevant to prove or disprove a substantive fact in dispute, it is not collateral and admissible.

(2) Really a Matter of Balancing. [§54.2]

Federal and most state rules say nothing about collateral matter test. Therefore, courts exclude this evidence on the basis of FRE 403.

(3) Apply This Rule with Prior Inconsistent Statements ("PINS") Also. [§54.3]

Extrinsic evidence of a PINS not admissible if it relates only to collateral matter.

3. SUPPORTING A WITNESS'S CREDIBILITY. [§55.0]

Bolstering and rehabilitation seek to build up the credibility of a witness.

a. Bolstering. [§55.1]

Oft-stated general rule that bolstering is not permitted is not quite accurate. Courts routinely allow some bolstering with evidence about witness's background, perception, and lack of bias. Rules against bolstering really are directed toward preventing evidence of (a) a witness's good character for truthfulness and (b) a witness's prior consistent statements.

(1) Witness's Truthful Character. [§55.11]

Evidence of a witness's truthful character may be offered only after attack has been leveled at the witness's character for truthfulness.

(2) Witness's Prior Consistent Statements. [§55.12]

A witness's prior consistent statements may be used if (a) they are independently admissible under a hearsay exception or exemption or (b) to rehabilitate the witness in certain circumstances.

b. Rehabilitation. [§55.2]

Attempt to rebuild witness's credibility after it has been attacked. Rehabilitation allowed, but technique must match the impeachment technique.

(1) Truthful Character. [§55.21]

Witness whose character for truthfulness has been attacked may be rehabilitated with reputation or opinion evidence of her truthful character, in accordance with the rules stated above.

(2) Prior Consistent Statements: Recent Fabrication, Yes; PINS, No. [§55.22]

General rule: witness who impeached with her PINS may not be rehabilitated by showing that she previously made statements consistent with her trial testimony. But prior consistent statements admissible to rebut a charge that witness changed her story or recently fabricated her testimony if the prior statements were made before the motive to change the story or fabricate the testimony arose.

IX. OPINIONS AND EXPERT TESTIMONY

A. OPINION TESTIMONY IN GENERAL. [§56.0]

There is one set of rules for "expert" witnesses and another for non-expert ("lay") witnesses.

1. LAY WITNESS OPINIONS. [§56.1]

A witness not testifying as an expert.

a. Common Law Rule. [§56.11]
Lay opinion testimony not allowed.

(1) Numerous Exceptions. [§56.112]
Lay witnesses allowed to testify to "short-hand renditions of fact" or "collective facts."

b. Modern Approach. [§56.12]
FRE and many states abandon common law. Lay witnesses may testify in form of opinion or inference if (a) opinion is rationally based on witness's perception; and (b) helpful to clear understanding of witness's testimony or determination of a fact in issue.

B. EXPERT TESTIMONY. [§56.2]

1. SUBJECT MATTER. [§56.21]

FRE and many modern formulations allow expert testimony regarding scientific, technical, or other specialized knowledge if it will assist the factfinder to understand the evidence or determine a fact in issue.

a. Common Law Rule. [§56.211]
Some courts allowed expert testimony only as to matters beyond the common knowledge and experience of the factfinder. Modern approach is more expansive.

2. QUALIFICATIONS. [§56.22]

Expert must be shown to possess requisite specialized knowledge. Knowledge may come through formal education, informal study, self-study, or experience.

a. Voir Dire. [§56.221]
Proponent of witness must prove her qualifications. Opposing party has right to "take witness on voir dire" to cross-examine her about qualifications.

b. Preliminary Question. [§56.222]
Admissibility of expert testimony is a preliminary question for the judge to decide.

3. BASIS OF EXPERT OPINIONS. [§56.23]

Experts need not base their opinions on personal knowledge.

a. Common Law. [§56.231]
Common law allows expert to base opinion on (1) personal knowledge, (2) facts in evidence, or (3) combination of the two.

(1) Hypothetical Question. [§56.2311]
Used to provide facts to expert who does not have personal knowledge.

b. Modern Approach. [§56.232]
Under FRE, an expert may base his opinion on facts "perceived by or made known to the expert at or before the hearing."

(1) Goes Beyond Common Law. [§56.2322]
Allows expert to base an opinion solely on facts outside his personal knowledge and not in the record if they are of a type reasonably relied upon by experts in the same field.

(2) Hypothetical Question Not Required. [§56.2323]
FRE allow expert to state his opinion without prior disclosure of the underlying facts.

4. EXAMINATION OF EXPERT WITNESSES. [§56.24]

Expert may be questioned as to: (a) qualifications; (b) bases of opinion; (c) compensation; and (d) discrepancies between opinions expressed by the expert and statements contained in treatises and articles.

5. OPINIONS ON ULTIMATE ISSUES. [§56.3]

FRE and most states reject "ultimate issue" as a valid objection. But courts still frequently exclude opinions as to mixed questions of law and fact because they tend to mislead jury.

6. NOVEL SCIENTIFIC EVIDENCE. [§56.4]

Use of a special threshold (the *Frye* test) test has been greatly criticized and has been abandoned in the federal courts and in many states.

a. The *Frye* Test. [§56.41]
Proponent of novel scientific evidence must demonstrate that proffered test, theory, or principle has gained general acceptance in scientific community.

b. Federal Rules. [§56.42]
Supreme Court has rejected the *Frye* test. Admissibility of scientific evidence is governed by the standards set forth in Rule 702. The evidence must be (a) scientifically valid and (b) must have a valid scientific connection to the pertinent inquiry. Court uses multi-factor approach to make this determination.

c. Establishing Validity. [§56.43]
Regardless of test used, proponent of scientific evidence will have to establish the validity of the underlying scientific test, theory, or principle.

X. AUTHENTICATION

A. AUTHENTICATION. [§57.0]

Proponent must establish that item is what it purports to be.

1. CONDITIONAL RELEVANCE STANDARD. [§57.1]

Proponent need only introduce enough evidence for a reasonable juror to find that the item is what it purports to be.

2. REAL AND DEMONSTRATIVE EVIDENCE. [§57.2]

Real evidence refers to tangible items that actually played a role in the matter in dispute. Demonstrative evidence refers to tangible items that did not actually play a role in the matter in dispute, but are used for illustrative purposes. Proponent of demonstrative evidence must establish that it is a fair and accurate representation of what it purports to depict.

B. AUTHENTICATION OF WRITINGS. [§58.0]

Several ways to authenticate a writing.

1. PERSONAL KNOWLEDGE. [§58.1]

By a person who has personal knowledge that the writing is what it is claimed to be.

2. AUTHENTICATION BY CIRCUMSTANTIAL EVIDENCE. [§58.2]

Some standard techniques of authentication by circumstantial evidence.

a. Handwriting. [§58.21]
(1) Lay Witness. [§58.211]
Under FRE, lay witness's familiarity with handwriting must not have been acquired for purposes of litigation.

(2) Expert Witness. [§58.212]
Expert may compare genuine sample of the purported author's handwriting with the writing in question.

(3) Comparison by the Trier of Fact. [§58.213]
Exemplar and contested writing may be submitted directly to the factfinder for comparison.

b. Reply-Message Doctrine. [§58.22]
If contents of writing indicate it is in reply to a previous communication addressed to the purported author and it is unlikely that anyone other than the purported author would have sent the response, writing will be authenticated.

c. Ancient Documents. [§58.23]
Writing authenticated if (a) in condition creates no suspicion as to authenticity; (b) found where likely to have been kept; and (c) at least 20 years old (common law at least 30 years old.

d. Public Records or Reports. [§58.24]
Recorded or filed in public office.

e. Content. [§58.25]

Authentication if contents include information known only by purported author.

C. AUTHENTICATION OF OBJECTS. [§59.0]

Authentication by showing item is what it purports to be.

1. PERSONAL KNOWLEDGE. [§59.1]

Witness recognizes the object based on unique markings, properly affixed labels, etc.

2. AUTHENTICATION BY CIRCUMSTANTIAL EVIDENCE. [§59.2]

Some standard techniques of authentication by circumstantial evidence.

a. Distinctive Characteristics. [§59.21]

Distinctive characteristics, appearance, contents, or internal patterns may be used.

b. Chain of Custody. [§59.22]

Authentication by proving an unbroken chain of custody from the time item came into proponent's possession until its submission into evidence.

3. PHOTOS, MAPS, MODELS. [§59.3]

May be used to illustrate testimony so long as witness testifies that exhibit is fair representation of what it purports to be.

D. AUTHENTICATION OF VOICES. [§60.0]

Ways of establishing that a voice heard or recorded belonged to a particular person.

1. PERSONAL KNOWLEDGE. [§60.1]

2. AUTHENTICATION BY CIRCUMSTANTIAL EVIDENCE. [§60.2]

a. Contents. [§60.21]

Identity of speaker may be shown if contents of statement include information known only by the purported speaker. The reply-message doctrine also applies.

b. Distinctive Characteristics. [§60.22]

Identity of speaker may be shown by distinctive characteristics of speaker.

c. Voice Prints. [§60.23]

The courts are split as to whether voice prints may be used to identify a speaker.

d. Special Rules for Telephone Communications. [§60.24]

(1) Personal Identity. [§60.241]

Witness testifies that he dialed the listed number and circumstances show person answering to be the one listed and called.

(2) Business. [§60.242]

Witness testifies that she dialed the listed number and conversation related to type of business commonly transacted over the telephone.

E. SELF-AUTHENTICATION. [§61.0]

Likelihood of forgery or tampering so small that proponent not required to present any evidence to establish that the item is what it purports to be. **"CONTAC"**: **C**ommercial paper; **O**fficial publications; **N**ewspapers and periodicals; **T**rade inscriptions; **A**cknowledged documents; **C**ertain public records.

1. COMMERCIAL PAPER. [§61.1]

Commercial paper, signatures on commercial paper, and related documents are self-authenticating. [FRE 902(9)].

2. OFFICIAL PUBLICATIONS. [§61.2]

3. NEWSPAPERS AND PERIODICALS. [§61.3]

4. TRADE INSCRIPTIONS AND THE LIKE. [§61.4]

Ownership, control, or origin established by an inscription, sign, tag, or label affixed in course of the business and indicating ownership, control, or origin.

5. ACKNOWLEDGED DOCUMENTS. [§61.5]

Document already been acknowledged before a notary public.

6. CERTAIN PUBLIC RECORDS. [§61.6]

Requirements vary, depending on whether document is foreign or domestic, under seal or not, and whether certified as correct or not.

XI. BEST EVIDENCE RULE

A. BEST EVIDENCE RULE. [§62.0]

The Best Evidence Rule requires only that when a party seeks to prove the contents of a writing, recording, or photograph, the party must use the original writing, recording, or photograph.

1. RATIONALE. [§62.1]

The BER is a product of the days when documents were hand-copied and the risk of error in transcription was significant.. and so the law developed a preference for the original of a writing. With technological advances law of evidence has created exceptions to the BER.

B. ANALYSIS OF A BER PROBLEM. [§62.2]

1. PROVING THE CONTENTS OF A WRITING. [§62.21]

Three situations where party seeks to prove the contents of a writing, recording, or photograph.

a. Category 1: Writings with Independent Legal Significance. [§62.211]

Where rights or obligations arise directly from a writing, the precise words (i.e., the contents) of the writing possess independent legal significance.

(1) Types of Actions. [§62.2111]

Litigation directly involves a writing such as a contract, lease, will, written libel, photograph, or book.

b. Category 2: Writing Offered in Evidence. [62.212]

If a party physically offers a writing in evidence, she thereby puts the terms of the writing in issue (by asking the trier of fact to rely on it).

c. Category 3: Testimony Relying Upon a Writing. [§62.213]

Testimony in which the witness relies totally upon a writing.

2. WRITING, RECORDING, PHOTOGRAPH DEFINED. [§62.22]

Defined broadly: every tangible process of recording words, pictures or sounds.

3. ORIGINAL DEFINED. [§62.23]

Typically, the writing or recording itself. But other things count as "originals."

a. Counterparts. [§62.231]

If person executing the writing intends a counterpart to have the same effect, it will be considered an original.

b. Photographs. [§62.232]

Includes the negative or any print made from the negative.

c. Computer Printouts. [§62.233]

Any printout shown to reflect the data accurately.

4. EXCEPTIONS. [§62.24]

a. Duplicate. [§62.241]

May be used in lieu of the original unless a genuine question is raised about the authenticity of the original.

b. Public Records. [§62.242]

Certified copy of a public record or a copy that is testified to be correct may be used in lieu of the original.

c. Summaries. [§62.243]

If original is voluminous, its contents may be presented in the form of a chart, summary, or calculation. Opponent must be given reasonable opportunity to inspect and copy original.

d. Unavailability of Original. [§62.244]

If the original is unavailable through no fault of proponent, any evidence may be used.

(1) Lost or Destroyed. [§62.2441]

(2) Original Not Obtainable. [§62.2442]

Original cannot be obtained by judicial process or procedure.

(3) Original in Opponent's Possession. [§62.2443]

Opponent has control of the original and is on notice that contents would be the subject of proof.

e. Collateral Matters. [§62.245]

If contents relate to a collateral matter, BER is inapplicable.

XII. PRIVILEGES

A. PRIVILEGES IN GENERAL. [§63.0]

Law recognizes privileges because the cost incurred by the loss of reliable evidence is outweighed by social benefits that accrue from having privileges. But because cost is high, privileges are construed narrowly.

1. TWO KINDS OF PRIVILEGES. [§63.1]

(a) A group that protects confidential communications, and (b) a group of miscellaneous privileges.

2. FEDERAL RULES. [§63.2]

FRE 501, the only privilege rule in the FRE, provides that privileges are to be "governed by the principles of the common law" as interpreted by the courts "in light of reason and experience." In diversity cases, federal courts apply state privilege law.

3. VARIATION AMONG STATES. [§63.3]

Much diversity exists among jurisdictions regarding privileges, but certain basic rules are common.

B. CONFIDENTIAL COMMUNICATION PRIVILEGES: OVERVIEW. [§64.0]

Generally accepted confidential communication privileges: attorney-client; physician-patient; psychotherapist-patient; husband-wife; and communications to a clergyman. Scattered states recognize privilege for communications between: accountant-client; parent-child; and social worker-client.

1. RATIONALE. [§64.1]

Guaranteeing confidentiality necessary to foster what society deems an important relationship. Benefits gained outweigh the harm caused by shielding the communication from disclosure.

2. SCOPE OF PRIVILEGE. [§64.2]

Allows holder (a) to refuse to disclose, and (b) to prevent others from disclosing the protected communication.

3. IMPORTANT: COMMUNICATIONS ARE PRIVILEGED; INFORMATION IS NOT. [§64.3]

Communication privileges protect communications, but not the underlying information.

4. ATTACK PLAN. [§64.4]

Ask yourself following six questions.
1. **Relationship.** Is there a privileged relationship?
2. **Communication.** Was there a germane communication?
3. **Confidentiality.** Was the communication confidential?
4. **Holder.** Is the holder asserting the privilege?
5. **Waiver.** Did the holder waive the privilege?
6. **Exceptions.** Is there an exception to the privilege?

C. ATTORNEY-CLIENT PRIVILEGE. [§65.0]

Allows (a) a client (b) to refuse to disclose and to prevent others from disclosing (c) confidential (d) communications (e) made between the attorney and client or their representatives (f) for the purpose of facilitating the rendition of legal services.

1. ATTORNEY-CLIENT RELATIONSHIP. [§65.1]

a. Lawyer. [§65.11]
Someone licensed to practice law. Reasonable mistake that person is licensed does not destroy relationship.

b. Client. [§65.12]
An individual or entity such as a corporation who consults a lawyer with the idea of obtaining legal services.

c. Representatives of Lawyers and Clients. [§65.13]
Confidential communications may pass through representatives of lawyers and clients.

(1) Representative of Lawyer. [§65.131]
Someone employed by the lawyer to assist in the rendition of legal services.

(2) Representative of Client. [§65.132]
When a client is a corporation, several tests advanced for determining who is representative of corporation.

(a) Control Group Test. [§65.1321]
Only members of the control group of a corporation (e.g., officers and directors).

(b) Diversified Industries Test. [§65.1322]
Protects communication made by an employee outside control group if (a) communication made at the behest of superior; (b) superior made request so corporation could secure legal advice; and communication (c) made for purpose of securing legal advice, (d) concerned a matter within scope of

employee's duties, and (e) was not disseminated beyond those persons who needed to know its contents.

(c) Supreme Court Rejects Control Group Test. [§65.1323]

In *Upjohn*, Supreme Court rejected the control group test but declined to set forth a test for courts to follow. Nevertheless, the Court cited factors consistent with the criteria set forth in *Diversified Industries*.

2. COMMUNICATION. [§65.2]

a. Must Be Germane. [§65.21]
A communication is privileged only if made for the purpose of facilitating the rendition of legal services.

(1) Lawyer in Non-Lawyer Capacity. [§65.211]
Not privileged when made to a lawyer acting in non-legal capacity.

b. Communication. [§65.22]
Generally are verbal, either oral or written. Non-verbal statements intended to communicate information also qualify.

(1) Observations. [§65.221]
Observations made by the lawyer during the relationship are generally not considered communications.

(2) Writings. [§65.222]
Writing that did not originate as a communication to the lawyer is not privileged, even if client subsequently turns it over to the lawyer. If client writes down for the lawyer the history of a dispute, the privilege applies.

3. CONFIDENTIALITY. [§65.3]

a. Presence of Third Persons. [§65.31]
Presence of someone other than the lawyer, client, and their representatives for a person reasonably necessary for the transmission of information (e.g., an interpreter), destroys confidentiality.

b. Intent to Maintain Confidentiality Decisive. [§65.32]
Communication is confidential if client intended that it would be disclosed only to (a) lawyer and (b) anyone else to whom disclosure was necessary to help provide legal services.

(1) Eavesdroppers. [§65.321]
Most jurisdictions: overheard communication retains confidentiality so long as client intended that it remain confidential.

4. CLIENT IS HOLDER. [§65.4]

Client is holder of privilege: entitled to assert it or waive it. Lawyer may assert on client's behalf. Privilege survives client's death.

5. PRIVILEGE MAY BE WAIVED. [§65.5]

If client (a) fails to timely assert it or (b) voluntarily reveals a significant part.

6. EXCEPTIONS. [§65.6]

a. Crime or Fraud. [§65.61]
Communications made by client seeking lawyer's advice to enable client to commit what he knew or should have known was a crime or fraud.

b. Breach of Duty. [§65.62]
Communications relevant to an issue of breach of duty between lawyer and client.

c. Joint Clients. [§65.63]
Where two or more clients consult a lawyer upon a matter of common interest.

d. Document Attested By Lawyer. [§65.64]

e. Claimants Through Deceased Client. [§65.65]

7. PRIVILEGE v. WORK PRODUCT v. OBLIGATION TO MAINTAIN CONFIDENTIALITY. [§65.7]

Attorney-client privilege allows client to refuse to reveal and to prevent someone else from revealing attorney-client communications. Work product shields from discovery certain information obtained by lawyer in anticipation of litigation or preparation for trial, including information obtained from third parties. Professional obligation to maintain confidentiality is imposed by professional rules of ethics and forbids lawyers from voluntarily disclosing information about their clients.

D. PHYSICIAN-PATIENT PRIVILEGE. [§66.0]

Federal courts do not recognize; many states do. Even where recognized, riddled with exceptions.

1. PHYSICIAN-PATIENT RELATIONSHIP. [§66.1]

Patient must consult doctor for purposes of diagnosis or treatment. The physician must be licensed to practice medicine.

2. COMMUNICATIONS. [§66.2]

Protected communications include medical and hospital records, direct communications between doctor and patient, and information observed by doctor through physical examinations and tests.

3. CONFIDENTIALITY. [§66.3]

The presence of necessary third parties (nurses, attendants, consultants, and the like) does not destroy confidentiality.

4. PATIENT IS HOLDER. [§66.4]

Patient is holder; physician may assert privilege on patient's behalf. Privilege survives patient.

5. WAIVER. [§66.5]

Same way as the attorney-client privilege.

6. EXCEPTIONS. [§66.6]

Different states have different exceptions. The most common:

a. Criminal Proceedings. [§66.61]
In many states, the privilege does not apply in criminal proceedings.

b. Patient-Litigant. [§66.62]
No privilege if patient puts her physical or mental condition in issue.

c. Breach of Duty. [§66.63]
In fee disputes or malpractice actions between physician and patient.

d. Court-Appointed Physician. [§66.64]
When patient is examined by court-appointed physician.

E. PSYCHOTHERAPIST-PATIENT PRIVILEGE. [§67.0]

Recognized by every state and in federal court.

1. PSYCHOTHERAPIST-PATIENT RELATIONSHIP. [§67.1]

Definition of psychotherapist (e.g., whether therapists other than psychiatrists and psychologists included) varies from state to state. Supreme Court includes communications made licensed social workers in the course of psychotherapy.

2. EXCEPTIONS. [§67.2]

Those applicable to the physician-patient privilege often applicable to psychotherapist-patient privilege as well. Supreme Court has not articulated what exceptions will apply in federal court.

F. COMMUNICATIONS TO CLERGYMEN. [§68.0]

Most states recognize a privilege for communications made to a member of the clergy. Some apply only to confessions made to a priest. Others are much broader and apply to confidential communication made to a clergyman in his or her capacity as a spiritual adviser. No generally accepted exceptions.

G. ACCOUNTANT-CLIENT PRIVILEGE. [§69.0]

Most states do not recognize.

H. MARITAL COMMUNICATION PRIVILEGE. [§70.0]

Distinguish this privilege — for confidential communications made during marriage — from the testimonial privilege, which permits a person to refuse to testify against her spouse in a criminal case.

1. MARITAL RELATIONSHIP. [§70.1]

Must be legally married at time communication is made.

a. Effect of Divorce. [§70.11]
The privilege survives divorce but relates only to communications made during the marriage.

b. Married But Separated. [§70.12]
Federal courts are increasingly unwilling to apply privilege where spouses are separated.

2. COMMUNICATION. [§70.2]

Courts split. Some courts: only verbal statements and non-verbal acts intended to be communicative are protected. Others: protect private observations made during marriage if spouse, relying upon confidential nature of marital relationship, allowed other spouse to observe.

3. CONFIDENTIALITY. [§70.3]

Must be made privately.

4. BOTH SPOUSES ARE HOLDERS. [§70.4]

In most states, either one may assert privilege.

5. WAIVER. [§70.5]

Same way as other communication privileges. Some states, however, vest privilege only in the communicating spouse.

6. EXCEPTIONS. [§70.6]

Vary from jurisdiction to jurisdiction.

a. Actions Between Spouses. [§70.61]
E.g., a divorce proceeding.

b. Crime or Fraud. [§70.62]
Communications made by a spouse in furtherance of a crime or fraud.

c. Crime Against Family Member. [§70.63]
When spouse is charged with a crime against a family member (e.g., wife beating, child abuse).

I. PARENT-CHILD. [§71.0]

Both federal courts and overwhelming majority of state courts reject such a privilege.

J. MISCELLANEOUS PRIVILEGES. [§72.0]

Privileges for matters other than confidential communications: Spousal testimonial; voter's; trade secrets; informer's identity; and state secrets. Constitution provides basis for journalist's and executive privilege and privilege against self-incrimination.

K. SPOUSAL TESTIMONIAL PRIVILEGE. [§73.0]

Applies in criminal cases only.

1. COMMON LAW RULE. [§73.1]

Criminal defendant has right to prevent his spouse from testifying against him.

2. MODERN TREND. [§73.2]

The modern trend gives witness spouse the right to refuse to testify against a criminal defendant spouse. The Supreme Court adopted this approach in Trammel.

3. RATIONALE. [§73.3]

Usually justified on ground that forcing spouse to give testimony that could result in her spouse's conviction is too destructive of the marital relationship.

4. END OF MARRIAGE, END OF PRIVILEGE. [§73.4]

Right of a spouse to refuse to testify against defendant spouse terminates with end of marriage.

5. EVEN IF SPOUSE TESTIFIES, COMMUNICATION PRIVILEGE STILL EXISTS. [§73.5]

Even in a jurisdiction that allows wife to choose to testify against her husband, husband may prevent her from revealing confidential communications made during marriage.

6. EXCEPTIONS. [§73.6]

(a) Crime Against Family Member. [§73.61]
When spouse is charged with a crime against a family member (e.g., wife beating, child abuse).

(b) Marrying the Eyewitness. [§73.62]
In some jurisdictions, does not apply to events that occurred before the marriage.

7. MARITAL COMMUNICATION DISTINGUISHED FROM SPOUSAL TESTIMONIAL PRIVILEGE. [§73.7]

Communication privilege protects (a) confidential communications (b) made during marriage. Survives marriage and applies in both civil and criminal cases. Spousal testimonial privilege (a) applies only in criminal cases and (b) allows spouse to refuse to testify against her criminal defendant spouse. Terminates upon end of the marriage.

L. POLITICAL VOTE. [§74.0]

A person may refuse to reveal how he voted in a secret ballot unless he voted illegally.

M. TRADE SECRETS. [§75.0]

Qualified privilege allowing person to refuse to disclose (and prevent others from disclosing) a trade secret owned by him.

N. IDENTITY OF INFORMER. [§76.0]

Government may refuse to disclose identity of person who has furnished information to law enforcement officials regarding illegal conduct. If court informer can give testimony necessary to a fair trial and government still refuses to disclose, court must dismiss the relevant charges.

O. STATE SECRETS. [§77.0]

Privilege for matters such as military secrets and other classified information.

P. EXECUTIVE PRIVILEGE. [§78.0]

Protects confidential communications between president and his immediate advisers.

Q. JOURNALIST'S PRIVILEGE. [§79.0]

First Amendment does not create a privilege that allows journalists to refuse to divulge information about the sources of their stories, but many states have enacted statutory privileges with varying coverage and exceptions.

R. PRIVILEGE AGAINST SELF-INCRIMINATION. [§80.0]

Two components: (1) Protects individual from being (a) compelled to engage (b) in testimonial conduct (c) that would tend to incriminate himself. (2) Gives criminal defendant right not to take the stand.

1. ACTIVITY MUST BE COMPELLED. [§80.1]

Only protects individual from being compelled from engaging in testimonial activity. Contents of voluntarily created written materials (e.g., a diary) are not privileged.

2. ACTIVITY MUST BE TESTIMONIAL. [§80.2]

If the compelled activity is non-testimonial, privilege is inapplicable.

a. Testimonial Activity Defined. [§80.21]
"Testimonial" if individual is being forced to reveal, directly or indirectly, his knowledge of facts or his belief about a matter.

3. MUST TEND TO INCRIMINATE. [§80.3]

Information tends to incriminate if it would constitute link in chain of evidence that might lead to person's conviction.

a. Immunity. [§80.33]
The danger of incrimination may be removed by granting the witness use of immunity.

4. RIGHT NOT TO TESTIFY. [§80.4]

Prosecution may not call defendant and force him to assert this privilege or comment upon the defendant's failure to take the stand.

5. WAIVER. [§80.5]

If a party voluntarily testifies, he waives right to refuse to answer questions on cross-examination that are related to the testimony.

XIII. JUDICIAL NOTICE

A. JUDICIAL NOTICE. [§81.0]

An evidentiary shortcut. Allows courts to accept certain facts or propositions of law as true without requiring formal proof.

1. RATIONALE. [§81.1]

(1) Save time and expense in proving facts not subject to reasonable dispute and (2) avoid disrespect for court system that would result if trials resulted in obviously erroneous factual findings.

B. THREE TYPES OF JUDICIAL NOTICE: "L.A. LAW". [§81.2]

 Courts may judicially notice (1) legislative facts, (2) adjudicative facts, and (3) law. (Mnemonic: L.A. Law). Federal rules address only judicial notice of adjudicative facts.

1. ADJUDICATIVE FACTS. [§81.3]

Facts that relate to the immediate parties or event. Judicial notice may be taken of **indisputable** adjudicative fact. Two situations in which this occurs:

a. Facts in Common Knowledge. [§81.31]
Facts that well-informed persons in the community generally know and accept.

b. Readily Verifiable Facts. [§81.32]
Facts not generally known, but which can be easily verified by resort to sources whose accuracy cannot reasonably be questioned.

c. Effect of Judicial Notice. [§81.33]
Depends on whether it is a civil or criminal case.

(1) Civil. [§81.331]
Court instructs jury to accept the truth of that fact. Once fact is noticed, evidence to disprove its truth is inadmissible.

(2) Criminal. [§81.332]
Under federal rules and in many jurisdictions, court in a criminal case is permitted only to instruct jury that it may, but is not required to, accept truth of judicially noticed fact.

2. LEGISLATIVE FACTS. [§81.4]

Facts that a court considers in making policy decisions in course of interpreting common-law doctrines, statutes, and the constitution.

a. Not Codified. [§81.41]
Neither the federal rules nor most state evidence rules contain provisions governing judicial notice of legislative facts. Courts may

Sum & Substance QUICK REVIEW of Evidence

notice legislative facts without regard to whether they are indisputable and without following any particular procedure.

3. JUDICIAL NOTICE OF LAW. [§81.5]

Judges ordinarily may take judicial notice of the law. Two exceptions: foreign law and municipal ordinances.

4. PROCEDURES. [§81.6]

Court may take judicial notice of adjudicative facts on its own motion. Upon request by party, court must take judicial notice if supplied with necessary information by the party.

a. Hearing. [§81.61]
Party may request a hearing regarding propriety of taking judicial notice and tenor of matter noticed.

5. WHEN NOTICE MAY BE TAKEN. [§81.7]

Judicial notice may be taken at any time.

XIV. BURDENS OF PROOF AND PRESUMPTIONS

A. BURDENS OF PROOF. [§82.0]

Sometimes refers to burden of production (burden of going forward with the evidence). Sometimes refers to burden of persuasion (risk of non-persuasion).

1. WHO BEARS THE BURDEN OF PERSUASION. [§82.1]

Substantive law determines.

a. Civil Cases. [§82.1]
Plaintiff has burden of persuasion as to elements of its claim; defendant bears burden of persuasion as to any defenses.

b. Criminal Cases. [§82.12]
Prosecution has burden of persuasion as to every element of the crime charged. Burden of persuasion as to an affirmative defense may constitutionally be placed on defendant.

2. HOW HEAVY IS THE BURDEN OF PERSUASION. [§82.2]

Varies with type of case.

a. Preponderance of the Evidence. [§82.21]
Ordinarily, the party with the burden in a civil case must prove its case by preponderance of the evidence.

b. Clear and Convincing Evidence, [§82.22]
In some cases, burden is "clear and convincing evidence."

c. Beyond a Reasonable Doubt. [§82.23]
In criminal cases, prosecution must meet its burden as to each element of the crime by presenting proof that satisfies the jury "beyond a reasonable doubt."

3. BURDEN OF PRODUCTION. [§82.3]

A party that fails to meet its burden of production will lose without getting to the jury; judge will grant a directed verdict against the party.

a. Meeting the Burden of Production. [§82.31]
Party meets burden of production if it produces enough evidence so that a reasonable juror could find for the party.

B. PRESUMPTIONS IN CIVIL CASES. [§83.0]

A presumption is a procedural device which requires the jury to draw a particular conclusion from certain proved facts.

1. BASIC AND PRESUMED FACTS. [§83.1]

Basic fact: the proved fact from which the prescribed conclusion must be drawn. Presumed fact: the prescribed conclusion.

2. HOW PRESUMPTIONS WORK IN GENERAL. [§83.2]

Distinguish between treatment of basic facts and presumed facts.

a. Basic Facts. [§83.21]
Presumptions come into play only if proponent proves basic facts. Opponent of presumption may always try to show that basic facts don't exist.

b. Effect of Triggering the Presumption. [§83.22]
If basic facts found to exist, presumption is triggered. Effect of the presumption varies with type of presumption.

3. IRREBUTTABLE (CONCLUSIVE) PRESUMPTIONS. [§83.3]

If basic facts proved, presumed fact is conclusively established.

4. REBUTTABLE PRESUMPTIONS. [§83.4]

If basic facts of a rebuttable presumption proved, jury is required to find the presumed fact unless opponent of presumption rebuts it. How much evidence the opponent must produce to negate the effect of the presumption depends on the jurisdiction's approach to rebuttable presumptions. Two basic approaches.

a. Presumption Shifts Burden of Persuasion. [§83.41]
Morgan-McCormick approach: shift the burden of persuasion. If proponent triggers presumption by establishing basic facts, **jury must find that presumed fact exists unless opponent** persuades it that presumed fact does not exist.

b. Presumption Shifts Production Burden: The Bursting Bubble Approach. [§83.42]
Sometimes referred to as Thayer-Wigmore approach. Presumption acts merely to shift the burden of production to the opponent. Opponent may negate its effect merely by producing evidence that would allow a juror to find that the presumed fact does not exist. If opponent does this, the presumption disappears.

(1) Presumption is Gone, But Logical Inference Remains. [§83.422]

Although procedural effect of the presumption may be overcome, any logical inference that flows from the basic facts remains.

c. Determining Which View to Apply. [§83.43]

FRE shifts burden of production and not the burden of persuasion. In diversity and other cases in which state law governs, the FRE defer to the state law of presumptions.

d. Jury Not Told Directly About "Presumption." [§83.44]

Jury not told directly about existence of presumption. Judge instructs jury as to the consequence of finding basic facts.

5. SUMMARY OF PRESUMPTIONS IN CIVIL CASES. [§83.5]

Focus on three things: (a) type of presumption involved; (b) whether basic facts have been contested; and (c) whether evidence has been introduced that disputes existence of the presumed facts.

6. PRESUMPTIONS IN CRIMINAL CASES. [§84.0]

Constitution requires the state to prove each element of the crime beyond a reasonable doubt. This limits the ability of the state to use a presumption to prove an element of a crime.

a. Permissive Inferences. [§84.1]

Court tells jury that it may infer the "presumed" fact from proof of the basic fact. Jury is free to accept or reject the inference. A permissive inference is constitutional if (a) under the facts of the case, the connection between the basic fact and the presumed fact is rational and (b) the presumed fact more likely than not flows from the basic fact.

b. Mandatory Inferences. [§84.2]

Court tells jury that if it finds the basic fact, it must find the presumed fact unless the defendant comes forward with evidence to rebut the presumed fact. A mandatory inference is permissible only if the court finds, independent of the facts of the particular case, that the proof of the basic facts establishes the existence of the presumed fact beyond a reasonable doubt.

I. INTRODUCTION

About the Author —

Professor Steven Goode is the Fulbright & Jaworski Professor of Law at the University of Texas, where he is a popular teacher and prolific writer on the law of evidence. A winner of the Texas Excellence Teaching Award, Professor Goode is co-author of *Courtroom Handbook on Federal Evidence* (West Publishing 1995) as well as *Courtroom Handbook on Texas Evidence* (2d ed. West Publishing 1995) and the two volume *Guide to the Texas Rules of Evidence: Civil and Criminal* (2d ed. West Publishing 1993). A graduate of Williams College and Yale Law School, Professor Goode practiced law in Washington, D.C. before entering teaching.

From the Author —

1. What's It All About? A typical trial involves questions about both law and facts. Before the relevant substantive law can be applied, a factfinder (the jury or, in a bench trial, the judge) must determine what happened. Once the factfinder decides what happened (that is, decides what the facts are), the factfinder applies the law to the facts and arrives at a verdict. **The law of evidence is concerned with the factfinding part of a trial. It tells us what is and what is not admissible evidence.** Looked at one way, it tells the lawyers what information they will be able to present to the jury in their efforts to establish that their respective version of the facts is the correct one. Looked at another way, it tells us what information we will allow jurors to consider as they perform their factfinding function.

2. Rules, Rules, and More Rules. If you are one of the many law students who bemoaned the abundance of ambiguity in your first year of law school, cheer up. The law of evidence is chock full of rules. No matter how much your professor insists that he or she is going to emphasize the policy behind the rules, you can be sure you are going to be tested on your knowledge of these rules. Regardless of the type of exam — essay, short answer, or multiple choice — you must know how the rules of evidence operate. Of course, this is not good news for everyone. If you are the type who really knows how to "wing it" and can easily ace trendy courses with names like "Quick Weight Loss and the Law," Evidence is likely to pose more of a challenge to you. Evidence, however, can be one of the more interesting courses you take in law school. It can be quite timely; some highly publicized case that is being tried as you study Evidence may raise some difficult evidentiary issues.

3. Do the Problems. A word of advice. Do the problems — both the review problems in the text and the multiple choice and essay questions following the text. More than any other area of law, evidence is learned by doing it. Hearsay, for example, is tricky, but eventually you will develop a knack for it, and once you do, it's like riding a bike. But you can't learn to ride a bike merely by reading about it, and the same holds true for hearsay (and much of the rest of evidence). So, in the words of one well-known advertisement, "Just do it."

The materials in **Quick Review** are designed to allow you to maximize your performance on your Evidence examination. They do not, and cannot, replace the insights and information imparted in your class. These materials should be used as a supplement to classroom notes and casebook materials. By no means do we suggest that you begin your preparation a mere 10 hours before your exam. The law of evidence is far too complicated to learn in such a short period of time.

Before You Begin the 10-5-2 Hour Countdown

Not all Evidence courses are the same. Professors stress different topics, so, **be sure to know what areas were emphasized in class.** Spend a couple of hours reviewing your professor's past exams. Professors tend to test on the same subjects time and time again.

Before you get down to the final 10 hours of study time, you should **thoroughly review your class notes** at least once. As you go through your notes, you should begin to see where you are having difficulty. Resolve any areas of difficulty through discussions with friends, study group members, your professor, or by reference to **Quick Review**.

In reviewing your notes, try to see how the evidence rules relate to each other. Be aware of general issues that arise again and again, such as the balance of probative value and prejudicial effect and the policies underlying the various rules. Most of all, **get a good grasp as to how each rule works. Quick Review** can be of great use to you here as it provides a concise survey of the law and a clear statement of the pertinent rules, exceptions, policies, and important cases.

10 Hours of Study Time Before the Final Examination

___ Review class notes with close attention to (a) areas emphasized in class and (b) your professor's areas of interest and opinions.

___ Review **Quick Review** as a means of reinforcing substantive rules and policies gleaned from class notes.

___ Answer objective questions at the rear of **Quick Review** as a means of checking your understanding of the rules and policies.

___ Undertake one final review of the major cases assigned and examined in class, filling in any gaps in your understanding with the **Case Squibs** provided in that section. Ask yourself: What issue was raised in this case? What rule, exception, and/or policy was applied?

___ Review any model answers of past exams given by your professor. Also do some practice essay questions at the rear of **Quick Review** to test your knowledge and skills in an essay format.

5 Hours of Study Time Before the Final Examination

___ Quickly scan through your class notes, emphasizing those areas with which you are still having difficulty.

___ Review and highlight the **Capsule Outline** in **Quick Review**.

You may wish to annotate the Capsule Outline with your class notes.

___ Make a list of your mnemonic devices or create a summary checklist of all the concepts in your annotated capsule outline. Try to limit the main concepts of the entire subject to one piece of paper.

Then spend time reviewing and memorizing it. This process of condensing is a way of organizing the information in your head so that ultimately you only need to remember a few concepts which will "trigger" all of the information you will need for the exam.

2 Hours of Study Time Before the Final Examination

___ Review your highlighting of the **Capsule Outline** in **Quick Review** or your summary checklist/flowchart.

___ Quickly review your notes for your professor's favorite areas that you believe are most likely to be tested.

___ Review the "Analytical and Exam Approach" sections in **Quick Review**.

___ Create a final 10-12 word checklist of the main concepts that you will memorize as "trigger" words. When you get into the exam, you can write these down on your scratch paper before you start preparing your essay outline (also useful for multiple choice questions). This will remind you of issues to discuss as necessary.

___ Relax! Take a break at least a few minutes before exam time.

III. ANALYTICAL AND EXAM APPROACH

A. EVIDENCE AS AN OBSTACLE COURSE. [§1.0]

There are numerous grounds upon which a court may exclude a particular piece of evidence. In thinking about the admissibility of any piece of evidence, picture an obstacle course. At the starting line stands the piece of evidence that a party is seeking to introduce. At the finish line is the jury box. That piece of evidence must be able to hurdle any number of a series of obstacles that its opponent puts up (by way of objections) in its path to the jury box. For example, the opponent may object that this piece of evidence is inadmissible because it is (a) irrelevant, (b) hearsay, (c) presented through an incompetent witness, (d) privileged, (e) impermissible opinion, and (f) in violation of the best evidence rule. **Each one of these is an independent obstacle (objection). Each one will have to be hurdled before the evidence can be deemed admissible and be heard by the jury.**

B. APPROACHING EVIDENCE PROBLEMS: "HEAR PA BROWN." [§1.1]

This book divides the law of evidence into ten subject areas. (This corresponds with the way the Federal Rules of Evidence, many casebooks, and evidence courses divide up the law.) When you approach an evidence problem you need to think about all the obstacles (objections) that can possibly be raised to its admission. The mnemonic **HEAR PA BROWN** will clue you in to the various grounds for objection.

HEAR — Hearsay

P — Privileges
A — Authentication

B — Best evidence rule
R — Relevance
O — Opinion testimony
W — Witnesses
N — Notice (judicial notice)

1. ANSWERING AN EXAM QUESTION. [§1.11]

Almost every evidence problem you get will fall into one or more of these areas. On an essay question, you are typically asked to discuss all the plausible grounds for exclusion. Run through HEAR PA BROWN in your mind. Relevance is usually addressed first in an essay question. If there is a hearsay problem, discuss it. If the evidence raises a privilege problem, discuss that. Don't stop simply because you conclude the evidence is inadmissible hearsay. Within the time constraints, discuss all plausible issues. The idea, after all, is to show off all you know that is pertinent to the question.

2. STATE THE OBJECTION, THEN STATE THE RESPONSE. [§1.111]

With respect to a particular piece of evidence, state the objection that is most likely to be raised; if it is not obvious, state why the objection is appropriate. Then discuss the arguments for admission that can plausibly be raised in response to the objection and reach a conclusion as to the validity of the objection. Be sure to discuss both sides of the argument.

Next, if there is another ground for objecting to the piece of evidence, discuss it in the same way. If not, go on to the next piece of evidence that might be objectionable and discuss it in the same manner.

3. DISCUSS EACH OBJECTION SEPARATELY AND COMPLETELY. [§1.112]

Do not raise all the objections at once. Take them one at a time and fully resolve each one before moving on to the next. This will make your answer clearer and more effective.

> **NOTE: What's Missing From HEAR PA BROWN.** You may have noticed that although this book contains ten subject matter areas, HEAR PA BROWN covers only eight. Don't worry. One of the omitted subject areas is "General Provisions," which deals mostly with procedural matters. The other is "Presumptions." You don't have to keep a look-out for presumption issues. They are red-flagged in the question. If there is a presumption issue, you will see it.

C. THE FEDERAL RULES AND THE COMMON LAW. [§1.2]

Throughout most of this century, the vast majority of states (with California as an important exception) followed the common law in dealing with questions of evidence. Despite differences in detail from state to state, a majority common law rule could be discerned in most areas of evidence law. The enactment of the Federal Rules of Evidence in 1975 marked a dramatic change. Although the federal rules embraced many common law rules, they also departed from the common law in many respects. Since their enactment, 34 states (plus Puerto Rico and the military) have adopted codes of evidence based on the federal rules. Due to the dominant position they have assumed, this book focuses on the federal rules. However, it also pays attention to the common law for two reasons. First, sometimes it is necessary to understand the common law in order to understand a federal rule. Second, some professors like to test on the common law. So throughout the book you will find references both to the law under the federal rules (FRE) and the common law.

IV. GENERAL PROVISIONS

A. LIMITED ADMISSIBILITY. [§2.0]

One of the most important general principles in the law of evidence is that **a piece of evidence may be admissible for one purpose but not another, or admissible against one party but not another.** Such evidence may be admitted under the doctrine of limited admissibility.

> **1. EXAMPLE: Limited Purpose. [§2.1]** Evidence that Tenant told Landlord, "The carpeting in the hall is loose," is hearsay and not admissible if offered to prove the carpeting was loose. However, it is not hearsay and is admissible if offered to prove Landlord had notice of the defect.

> **2. EXAMPLE: Limited To Party. [§2.2]** Defendant and Co-Defendant are on trial for bank robbery. Prosecution offers Co-Defendant's confession. It is admissible against Co-Defendant but not against Defendant.

B. LIMITING INSTRUCTIONS. [§2.3]

When evidence is admissible only for a limited purpose, the judge must, upon request, instruct the jury to consider the evidence only for its admissible purpose. For instance, in the example above, the court would tell the jury that it may consider Tenant's statement as proof that Landlord had notice but not as proof that the carpeting was loose.

1. WHEN COURTS MAY EXCLUDE. [§2.31]

The trial court may exclude evidence with limited admissibility if it believes that the limiting instruction is inadequate to protect the objecting party against unfair prejudice. The court may feel that the danger that the jury will consider the evidence for the forbidden purpose far outweighs its probative value as to the permissible purpose. For instance, in Example 2 above, the court might conclude that even with a limiting instruction, the jury would consider Co-Defendant's confession as evidence against Defendant as well. In such a case the court might (a) **exclude** the statement entirely; (b) order references to Defendant **excised** redacted from the statement; or (c) order **separate trials** for Defendant and Co-Defendant.

C. PRESERVING ERROR FOR APPEAL. [§3.0]

Litigants must be sure to take all required steps in order to preserve for appeal erroneous rulings by the trial judge regarding the admission or exclusion of evidence.

1. GENERAL PRINCIPLE: THE DECK IS STACKED IN FAVOR OF THE TRIAL JUDGE. [§3.1]

The system is designed to affirm the trial judge's ruling whenever possible. **Whichever party complains on appeal that the judge erred must have done everything necessary to inform the judge of the evidence rule in question and its application to the evidence in question.** If you remember this basic rule, you will be able to handle all questions regarding whether a party acted properly to preserve an evidentiary ruling for appeal.

2. ERRONEOUS ADMISSION OF EVIDENCE. [§3.11]

If a party complains on appeal that the trial judge erroneously admitted evidence, it must show that (a) it **specifically objected** to the evidence; (b) it did so in a **timely fashion**; (c) the evidence was inadmissible **on the stated grounds**; and (d) admission of the evidence affected a **substantial right** of the appellant. [FRE 103(a)(1)].

a. Specific Objection. [§3.111]

The objection must be stated with enough specificity to put the judge on notice as to its legal basis and give the proponent of the evidence an opportunity to respond. Thus, merely stating "Objection, your honor" is insufficient. The objecting party must explicitly identify the particular basis for claiming the evidence is inadmissible (e.g., hearsay, impermissible character evidence, probative value is substantially outweighed by danger of unfair prejudice).

b. Timely Fashion. [§3.112]

The objection must be made at the first reasonable opportunity. Failure to do so constitutes waiver of the objection.

(1) Motions in Limine. [§3.1121]

A motion **in limine** ("at the threshold") is a motion made prior to trial seeking a ruling on some evidentiary issue that is likely to arise. The effect of the court's ruling on a motion in limine is a point of some controversy. Some courts view the motion in limine ruling merely as a preliminary ruling: the party that lost the motion must still raise the question again at trial (out of the presence of the jury) in order to preserve the issue for appeal. Other courts view the motion in limine ruling as sufficiently final so that the issue need not be raised again at trial. Still other courts look at the facts of the particular case, with special emphasis on the nature of the issue, the degree to which the issue was fully presented, and the extent to which the court's ruling was equivocal.

c. Erroneously Admitted Evidence: Affirm Unless Inadmissible on Stated Grounds. [§3.113]

If the objection failed to state a proper legal basis for excluding the evidence, the trial judge's decision to admit the evidence will be upheld **even if the evidence should have been excluded for some other reason.** In other words, it is the responsibility of the party, not the trial judge, to find the right ground for exclusion.

> **(1) EXAMPLE. [§3.1131]** The trial court overrules defendant's hearsay objection and admits the evidence. If the court correctly ruled on the hearsay point, defendant will not prevail on appeal even if the evidence could have been excluded on privilege grounds.

3. ERRONEOUS EXCLUSION OF EVIDENCE. [§3.12]

If a party complains on appeal that the trial judge erroneously excluded evidence, it must show that (a) it made an **offer of proof** at trial; (b) the evidence could not have been excluded **on any ground;** and (c) exclusion of the evidence affected a **substantial right** of the appellant. [FRE 103(a)(2)].

a. Offer of Proof. [§3.121]

If the court excludes proffered evidence, the proponent must make an offer of proof to insure that the trial and appellate courts are aware of the substance of the proffered evidence.

(1) Excluded Evidence is Witness Testimony. [§3.1211]

If the court excluded a witness's testimony, the offer of proof may be made by (a) counsel relating to the court the substance of the witness's testimony; or (b) taking the witness's testimony (outside the presence of the jury) in question and answer form.

(2) Excluded Evidence is Exhibit. [§3.1212]

If the excluded evidence is a document, chart, or some other form of tangible exhibit, it should be marked for identification and made part of the record.

b. Erroneously Excluded Evidence: Affirm If Inadmissible on Any Ground. [§3.122]

Even if the judge excluded the evidence in response to an objection that raised an invalid ground for exclusion, the judge's ruling will be affirmed if there exists any valid reason for excluding the evidence. The reason for this is simple. It would make little sense for the appellate court to remand the case for a new trial so that the evidence could once again be excluded, this time on the proper ground.

> **(1) EXAMPLE. [§3.1221]** The trial judge excludes evidence upon a hearsay objection. Even if the evidence was not objectionable as hearsay, the decision to exclude will be upheld if the evidence could have been excluded under some other rule of evidence.

4. LIMITED ADMISSIBILITY REVISITED: MORE DECK-STACKING. [§3.13]

Suppose Tenant offers his statement to Landlord, "The carpeting in the hall is loose." As we will see later, this statement is inadmissible hearsay if offered to prove the carpeting was loose, but is not hearsay if offered to prove that Landlord had notice of the defect. Landlord objects on hearsay grounds. If the judge overrules the objection, the ruling will be affirmed. The appellate court will tell the complaining party (Landlord) that it was his responsibility to narrow his objection to the hearsay use of this evidence. Further, Landlord should have requested a limiting instruction that the statement could be used only as proof of notice. If, however, the court sustains the objection, the trial court's ruling **will still be affirmed.** In this instance the appellate court will tell the complaining party (now Tenant) that it was his responsibility to narrow his offer of the evidence to its non-hearsay use (i.e., to have stated at trial, "I'm only offering this to prove notice"). This is just another example of the basic principle that the party complaining on appeal must have taken the appropriate steps at trial to object (Landlord) or respond to a valid objection as to why the evidence was admissible (Tenant).

OUTLINE

D. PRELIMINARY FACT QUESTIONS FOR THE COURT. [§4.0]

The admissibility or inadmissibility of a piece of evidence sometimes turns on the existence or non-existence of some preliminary fact. In some instances, the court must be satisfied that the preliminary fact does or does not exist before ruling on admissibility. In other instances, the court will leave it to the jury to decide.

1. GENERAL RULE: COURT DECIDES WHETHER PRELIMINARY FACT PROVED. [§4.1]

The trial judge decides any factual issues related to questions such as whether:

(a) a witness is qualified as an expert, (b) a statement is hearsay, (c) a hearsay statement falls within an exception, or (d) a statement is privileged.

The judge must resolve such factual issues under a **preponderance of the evidence** standard. In resolving these issues, the judge may consider evidence (other than privileged matter) that is not itself admissible under the rules of evidence. [FRE 104(a)].

> **a. EXAMPLE. [§4.11]** Defendant objects to certain testimony on the ground that it is a privileged communication he made to his wife during their marriage. The proponent argues (a) the statement was not made in confidence, and (b) Defendant was not legally married to "wife" at the time the statement was made. The trial court should uphold the privilege claim only if it is satisfied by a preponderance of the evidence that (a) the statement was made in confidence, and (b) that Defendant was legally married to "wife" at the time. In deciding these issues, the court may consider evidence that would not be admissible under the rules of evidence (such as inadmissible hearsay).

2. JURY GETS TO DECIDE A FEW: "BARK". [§4.2]

Four preliminary fact issues are left to the jury. These can be remembered by the mnemonic **BARK: B**est Evidence Rule; **A**uthenticity; **R**elevance; **K**nowledge.

a. Best Evidence Rule. [§4.21]

Most "best evidence" issues are decided by the judge. However, if there is an issue as to (a) whether the writing ever existed; (b) which of two or more writings is the original; or (c) whether some secondary evidence accurately reflects the contents of the original (e.g., a claim that the original was altered, as in the movie, *The Verdict*), the jury, not the judge, decides.

b. Authenticity. [§4.22]

The jury decides whether a writing or document has been authenticated. (See §57.1).

c. Relevance. [§4.23]

The jury decides issues of conditional relevancy. (See §5.5).

d. Knowledge. [§4.24]

The jury decides whether or not a witness has personal knowledge. (See §41.0).

(1) During trial, counsel for Defendant elicits from a witness an answer that includes inadmissible hearsay. About thirty seconds later, counsel for Plaintiff realizes what has happened and objects. The witness is already answering the next question. What should the judge do?

Answer: Overrule the objection. Counsel for Plaintiff failed to object to the hearsay in a timely fashion.

(2) Prosecutor calls Stooge to testify against Defendant. In response to one of Stooge's answers, defense counsel states, "I object, Your Honor. The testimony is irrelevant." The court overrules the objection. Defendant is convicted. While working on the appeal, defense counsel realizes that although the answer was relevant, it contained inadmissible character evidence. Defense counsel argues on appeal that the evidence should have been excluded.

Answer: The appellate court will uphold the trial court's decision. Defense counsel failed to state the proper ground for exclusion.

V. RELEVANCY

A. BASIC PRINCIPLES OF RELEVANCY. [§5.0] Evidence must be relevant to be admissible. However, not all relevant evidence is admissible. In fact, most of the rules of evidence address the question of when relevant evidence is and is not admissible.

1. DEFINITION OF RELEVANCY. [§5.1]

A piece of evidence is relevant if it has any tendency to make the existence of any fact of consequence to the case more probable or less probable than it would be without that piece of evidence. [FRE 401]

2. TWO ASPECTS OF RELEVANCY: [§5.2]

This definition of relevancy has two components. First, the proffered piece of evidence must **logically** tend to prove the fact that it is offered to prove. Second, the evidence must be offered to prove a fact that is **material** to the case. That is, the fact that the party is attempting to esatblish must relate to an issue that the substantive law deems of consequence to the outcome of the case.

> **a. EXAMPLE: [§5.21]** Defendant is charged with rape. He seeks to testify that the Complainant invited him to her bedroom. This evidence is **relevant**. The testimony logically may tend to prove that Complainant consented, and her consent is an issue that the substantive criminal law deems of consequence to the case. If Defendant were charged with statutory rape, the testimony would be **irrelevant**. Although it still might tend to prove **consent**, the substantive law says that consent is not a defense to a statutory rape charge.

3. RELEVANCY vs. SUFFICIENCY. [§5.3]

A common error in relevancy analysis is to confuse the question of whether evidence is **relevant** with the question of whether the evidence, taken alone, is **sufficient to justify a verdict.** A piece of evidence may be relevant even though it does not prove its proponent's case. Indeed, most pieces of evidence are, by themselves, inadequate to sustain a verdict. A piece of evidence is relevant so long as it makes the existence of a material fact more (or less) probable than it would be without the evidence.

> **a. EXAMPLE: [§5.31]** In the example immediately above, Defendant's testimony is relevant, although it does not by itself prove consent. C may have invited Defendant to her room to show him something, without the slightest intention of having sexual relations with him, or Defendant may be lying. In either case, if the jury believes the testimony, it may logically think it more likely that C consented than it did before it heard the evidence. That is all the test of relevance demands.

4. DIRECT vs. CIRCUMSTANTIAL EVIDENCE. [§5.4]

a. Direct Evidence. [§5.41]

Direct evidence proves a consequential fact directly. No inference has to be drawn from the evidence to the consequential fact.

b. Circumstantial Evidence. [§5.42]

Circumstantial evidence requires the factfinder to draw inferences from the evidence in order to conclude that some consequential fact exists.

> **c. EXAMPLE. [§5.43]** Eyewitness testimony that the defendant shot the victim is "direct evidence" of defendant's assault, but testimony establishing that the defendant had a motive to shoot the victim, or that the defendant was seen leaving the victim's apartment with a smoking gun, is "circumstantial evidence" of the defendant's assault.

5. CONDITIONAL RELEVANCY. [§5.5]

Sometimes the relevancy of a proffered piece of evidence depends on the existence of another fact that has not yet been proved. Such evidence is said to be **conditionally relevant.** A court should admit such evidence either (a) upon the introduction of evidence sufficient to support a finding of the existence of the other fact or (b) subject to the introduction of such evidence. [FRE 104(b)].

> **a. EXAMPLE. [§5.51]** Defendant is on trial for extortion. The prosecution calls Victim to testify that Bruiser visited him in his office and said, "You better give that contract to the right person, if you know what's good for you." Because this testimony tends to prove Defendant's guilt only if Bruiser can be linked to Defendant, it is conditionally relevant. The court (a) can refuse to admit it until the prosecution introduces evidence sufficient to support a finding of a link between Defendant and Bruiser, or (b) can admit it subject to evidence of a link between Defendant and Bruiser being introduced later on in the trial. If the court chooses the latter option and the prosecution subsequently fails to offer evidence linking Defendant and Bruiser, the trial judge will strike from the record the evidence of Bruiser's visit and order the jury to disregard it.

B. REASONS FOR EXCLUDING RELEVANT EVIDENCE. [§6.0]

There are **two basic reasons** for excluding relevant evidence. First, evidence may be excluded because of **extrinsic social policies**, even though exclusion will hinder the factfinder's efforts to determine what happened. Second, even though it is relevant, the evidence may be excluded because admitting it would lead to **less accurate factfinding.**

1. EXTRINSIC SOCIAL POLICIES. [§6.1]

In some instances, accurate factfinding is subordinated to the goal of promoting some other social concern. For example, evidence may be excluded because it is privileged, or is evidence of a subsequent remedial measure. (See §10.0).

2. ACCURACY IN FACTFINDING. [§6.2]

Although relevant, evidence may lead to less accurate factfinding because its probative value is outweighed by the danger that it will confuse or prejudice the jury. It may also be excluded because its probative value simply is not worth the time it would take to present the evidence. (See §10.0).

a. Discretionary exclusion. [§6.21]

FRE 403 requires the court to exclude relevant evidence when its **probative value is substantially outweighed** by countervailing concerns such as the danger of **unfair prejudice, confusion of issues, or misleading the jury,** or by considerations of **judicial efficiency** (such as undue delay or presentation of cumulative evidence).

b. Specific evidence rules. [§6.22]

Some evidence rules deal with specific categories of evidence, setting forth when such evidence is admissible and when it is not. For example, specific rules deal with the admissibility of character and habit evidence, evidence of liability insurance, and proof of prior sexual conduct. These rules are discussed below.

NOTE: Legal vs. logical relevance. [§6.23]
Some courts and professors still speak of logical and legal relevance. By logical relevance, they mean evidence that meets the definition of relevance set forth in §5.1. By **legal relevance,** they mean relevant evidence whose probative value is not outweighed by the countervailing concerns set forth in the immediately preceding section.

C. DISCRETIONARY EXCLUSION: GENERAL PRINCIPLES. [§7.0]

Courts have broad discretion to balance the probative value against the danger of unfair prejudice, confusion, etc., but rarely exercise it to exclude evidence possessing significant probative value.

1. FACTORS IN EXERCISING DISCRETION. [§7.1]

a. Nature of Case. [§7.11]

The court is most likely to exercise its discretion to exclude evidence when it is offered against a criminal defendant.

b. Importance of Issue. [§7.12]

The more directly the evidence tends to prove issues central to a case, the less likely the court is to exclude it.

c. Efficacy of Limiting Instruction. [§7.13]

The court will generally exclude evidence on this ground only when it concludes that a cautionary limiting instruction will not provide sufficient protection.

D. DISCRETIONARY EXCLUSION: SIMILAR HAPPENINGS EVIDENCE ("SHE"). [§8.0]

Because courts exercise their power of discretionary exclusion on a case-by-case (indeed, issue-by-issue) basis, it is hard to draw bright-line rules about how courts (and professors) will rule on certain issues. Nevertheless, certain types of issues occur with some frequency and courts tend to approach them in the same way. One area in which courts are frequently called upon to rule is the admissibility of **similar happenings evidence ("SHE").**

1. "SHE": IN GENERAL. [§8.1]

Sometimes, as proof of the occurrence in issue, a party wishes to use evidence of **other events or transactions** between the parties now engaged in litigation or involving another party or parties similarly situated. For example, in a slip-and-fall case, a party might want to offer evidence that other people slipped and fell on defendant's premises. **Generally, courts are reluctant to admit such evidence.** Often the probative value of such evidence is suspect and substantially outweighed by the danger of confusing the jury or wasting time. **Nevertheless, under certain conditions courts are likely to admit similar happenings evidence.**

2. "SHE": PRIOR OR SUBSEQUENT ACCIDENTS. [§8.2]

Evidence of other accidents or injuries offered to prove the negligence of a party or the dangerousness of a condition may be admissible if its proponent shows that the other accidents or injuries **occurred under circumstances substantially similar to those surrounding the event in issue.** Without such a threshold showing, the probative value of the other accident or injury evidence will clearly be insufficient to outweigh the danger that it will confuse the jury or waste the court's time. Even when such a showing is made, the court may still determine that the probative value is substantially outweighed by the danger of confusion or waste of time, and exclude the evidence.

> **a. EXAMPLE. [§8.21]** To prove that a particular stairway in a theater was dangerous because the carpeting was loose, Plaintiff may attempt to offer evidence that two other persons tripped and fell at the theater. Normally, the court will require a showing that the other falls occurred at the same or a similar place, relatively proximate in time, and that the conditions surrounding the other falls were substantially similar in nature. If the crowd conditions, the lighting, the way the carpet was tacked, or any other material fact was different, the court may exclude the evidence. If, however, substantial similarity is shown, the court may admit the evidence as tending to prove the dangerous nature of the stairway. In addition, if the other falls occurred **prior** to Plaintiff's, they may be used to prove that Defendant was on notice that the stairway was dangerous.

3. "SHE": OTHER CONTRACTS OR DEALINGS TO PROVE TERMS. [§8.3]

Where the plaintiff and the defendant have a contract but there is a dispute as to the terms of that contract, evidence of other similar contracts **between them** is generally admissible.

a. Different Parties. [§8.31]

On the other hand, evidence of similar contracts with other persons is ordinarily inadmissible. Remember, however, that the court has broad discretion in this area.

> **b. EXAMPLE. [§8.32]** Plaintiff, a furniture manufacturer, contracts with Defendant, a retailer, to sell various items of furniture on July 1. The furniture is delivered and Defendant is billed $500 for freight charges. Defendant claims that the freight charges were to be included in the price and offers evidence that freight charges were included in a previous order from Plaintiff in May. Plaintiff claims that its freight policies have changed and offers evidence that since July 1 it has charged freight to all its other customers. Defendant's

evidence of prior dealings with Plaintiff is admissible to prove the terms of the July 1 transactions unless there were some substantial differences in material conditions (e.g., the May purchase was a special "close-out" deal). Plaintiff's evidence of subsequent dealings with other customers probably would be excluded since the parties were not the same. But remember, the court has broad discretion on such relevancy issues and could admit the evidence, especially if it admitted evidence of the May deal.

4. "SHE": OTHER CONTRACTS OR DEALINGS TO PROVE AGENCY. [§8.4]

When the authority of an agent to make a contract is disputed, evidence of similar contracts entered into by the purported agent ordinarily is admissible even if the parties are different.

a. EXAMPLE. [§8.41] Plaintiff enters into a contract with Agee, a salesman for Defendant, to purchase 5,000 cartons of bunting at $2 each, which is 30% off Defendant's regular price. After Defendant refuses to deliver, claiming that Agee had no authority to reduce the regular price, Plaintiff sues Defendant. Plaintiff may offer evidence that Agee had entered into contracts with Tribble and McGee in which he gave a 30% discount and that Defendant honored those discounts.

5. "SHE": NON-OBSERVATIONS AND NON-OCCURRENCES. [§8.5]

Using **evidence that an event or condition was not observed or that other injuries did not occur to prove the non-existence of the event, condition, or injury** raises relevance problems similar to those just discussed.

a. Non-Observation to Prove Non-Occurrence in General. [§8.51]

The probative value of such negative evidence is ordinarily deemed to be so slight as to render the evidence inadmissible. If, however, the proponent shows that the **event probably would have been observed had it occurred,** evidence of its non-observation will be admissible.

(1) EXAMPLE. [§8.511] Plaintiff slips on a broken ketchup bottle in Defendant Market. Defendant Market contends that the bottle must have fallen within five minutes of Plaintiff's injury and that it was not negligent in failing to discover and eliminate the danger. In response, Plaintiff seeks to testify that she was in the store for at least 30 minutes and that she did not hear the bottle fall. The court should admit the evidence if Plaintiff shows that she probably would have heard the bottle if it had fallen while she was in the store. If, on the other hand, the store was too large, too noisy, or too crowded to justify the conclusion that Plaintiff probably would have heard the bottle fall, the testimony is inadmissible.

b. Absence of Business Record to Prove Non-Occurrence. [§8.52]

Most states and the FRE permit a party to prove that an event or transaction did not occur by evidence that there is no business record of such an event or transaction. However, the proponent must show that it is the practice of the business to regularly record all events or transactions of the type in issue. [FRE 803(7)]. (See §20.6).

> **(1) EXAMPLE. [§8.521]** Plaintiff may prove that Defendant did not pay an outstanding debt by proving that Plaintiff's regular business records did not reflect any payment, and that Plaintiff regularly records all such payments.

c. Absence of Similar Accidents. [§8.53]

Evidence that a place, a particular product, or a similar product has been used over a period of time without any accident occuring similar to the one in issue is relevant to prove that the place or product is not dangerous. Such evidence of safety history is, however, inadmissible unless its proponent establishes that (1) the place or product involved was used a significant number of times under **conditions or circumstances substantially similar** to those involved in the accident in question, and (2) the **witness would have heard** of any previous accidents.

> **(1) EXAMPLE: No Similar Product Accidents. [§8.531]** Plaintiff is injured when a stone is thrown from Plaintiff's lawn mower into his eye. Plaintiff sues Defendant, the manufacturer of the mower, contending it was defectively designed because it provides no protection against such accidents. Defendant claims that the design is proper and that Plaintiff's injury was a freak accident. Defendant offers evidence that over 50,000 mowers of the same model used by Plaintiff have been sold over the last three years and that not one single complaint similar to Plaintiff's has been received. This evidence can be admitted if Defendant establishes that: (1) other customers used the mower under substantially similar conditions; and (2) Defendant probably would have received complaints if stones were thrown from the mower and injured the user.

6. "SHE": SALES OF SIMILAR PROPERTY TO PROVE VALUE. [§8.6]

Evidence of the selling price of a particular piece of property ordinarily may be used to prove the value of similar property. For example, a party may prove the value of a destroyed car by evidence of the recent selling price of a substantially similar car. Also, evidence of the selling price of a particular parcel of real property is admissible to prove the value of a similar tract of land. The proponent of such evidence must, however, satisfy the court that the properties are **substantially similar in nature** and that the other property was sold under **substantially similar market conditions.**

a. Unaccepted Offers. [§8.61]

Prior sale prices used to establish value must be genuine, and the price must actually have been paid. Unaccepted offers are generally inadmissible to prove value. A party may, however, introduce evidence of an unaccepted offer made by his opponent.

7. "SHE": PREVIOUS CLAIMS OR LAWSUITS TO IMPEACH PRESENT CLAIM. [§8.7]

In an effort to discredit a plaintiff's or complainant's charge, a defendant may seek to offer evidence of prior similar charges made by the plaintiff or complainant.

a. Chronic Litigant. [§8.71]

Evidence that tends to show only that the plaintiff or complainant is a chronic litigant (i.e., has been involved in numerous other suits) is inadmissible.

b. Prior Fraudulent Claims. [§8.72]

If the plaintiff or complainant has previously made similar fraudulent claims, such evidence can be used to prove the falsity of the present claim.

8. "SHE": CAUSATION [§8.8]

When causation issues are complex, evidence of what happened to other persons similarly situated may be admitted to establish causation.

> **a. EXAMPLE: [§8.81]** A plaintiff trying to establish that defendant caused his cancerous condition by dumping toxic wastes in a local river may introduce evidence of an unusually high cancer rate among those persons living near the river.

9. "SHE": BUSINESS CUSTOM TO PROVE CONDUCT. [§8.9]

Evidence of an established business practice may be used to show that the practice was followed in a particular case.

> **a. EXAMPLE. [§8.91]** Evidence that letters put in the "out basket" by 9:30 a.m. are routinely taken out and mailed by an employee before noon that day is admissible to prove that a particular letter put in the "out basket" was mailed.

E. DISCRETIONARY EXCLUSION: OTHER COMMON EXAMPLES. [§9.0]

Apart from evidence of similar happenings, there are other categories of evidence for which courts have developed certain basic approaches.

1. REENACTMENTS, DEMONSTRATIONS, AND EXPERIMENTS. [§9.1]

When a party seeks to prove a fact by **reenactment** (e.g., Plaintiff seeks to show the condition of Defendant's brakes by testimony of a police officer that he tried the brakes right after the accident and found them in good condition), **demonstration** (e.g., to prove Defendant could not have turned off a tape recorder while on the telephone, Plaintiff demonstrates the impossibility of trying to repeat the act), or **experiment** (e.g., a scientific test of a boiler's capacity to hold pressure), the evidence is admissible only if its proponent shows that the reenactment demonstration or experiment was conducted under conditions or circumstances **substantially similar** to those surrounding the event being replicated.

2. INDUSTRY STANDARD TO PROVE OR DISPROVE NEGLIGENCE. [§9.2]

A party may offer evidence of the standard in the industry as evidence of what reasonable conduct would be. Thus, evidence that a defendant's conduct fell short of the standard of care in the industry would tend to show negligence. Conversely, evidence that a defendant did comply with the industry standard would tend to show it did not act negligently. For example, evidence that all other manufacturers of batteries use a particular ventilation technique not used by defendant would be admissible as tending to show defendant's negligence in failing to ventilate its facilities properly.

a. Relevant, But Not Conclusive. [§9.21]

The industry standard, however, is not conclusive evidence of what constitutes reasonable conduct. Everyone in the industry may be negligent.

b. Medical Malpractice Cases. [§9.22]

In medical malpractice cases, however, the usual standard of care is that of doctors practicing in the defendant's local community. When specialists are involved, a national standard of care and knowledge will be applied.

3. STATISTICAL EVIDENCE. [§9.3]

Statistical evidence, if improperly used, presents a danger of unfair prejudice. Therefore, it is sometimes excluded, especially if the proponent of the statistical evidence is unable to prove the accuracy of the data underlying the statistical calculations. (See Case Squibs section, *People v. Collins.*) Where the proponent is able to do this, however, statistical evidence will be admitted. In race and sex discrimination cases, for example, statistical evidence often forms a major part of the plaintiff's case.

4. PHOTOGRAPHS AND REPULSIVE OBJECTS. [§9.4]

Photographs, frequently in color and often gruesome, and repulsive objects (e.g., a piece of skull, a glass eye, or a blood-splattered pair of panties), are often objected to on the ground that their prejudicial impact substantially outweighs their probative value. Courts must decide each objection on its own merits, so no hard-and-fast rule can be stated. More often than not, however, these objections are overruled. (See Case Squibs section, *State v. Poe.*)

5. JURY VIEWS. [§9.5]

The court has very broad discretion with respect to allowing in-court exhibitions (including demonstrations) and out-of-court jury views of matters and places in controversy.

a. Exhibition of Child. [§9.51]

In a paternity action, the plaintiff may seek to exhibit the child to the jury so the jurors can observe the baby's likeness to the defendant. Such exhibits can be highly misleading and prejudicial, and the courts are split on whether such evidence is proper. Some courts permit the jury to view the child if it is old enough to possess "settled features." Were it not for such constraints, Winston Churchill would undoubtedly have been held liable in countless paternity actions.

b. View of Scene. [§9.52]

A view of the scene may be helpful to the jurors, but it may expose them to information that is not evidence, such as a post-accident remedial measure (e.g., installation of a safety device). Thus, such views will be permitted only under strict safeguards and only where counsel and the parties are present.

PROBLEM 1. Pogo buys a new 1990 Flash sports car directly from Nero Motor's European factory and ships it to the United States. Immediately after delivery of the car on June 1, he takes it to Dover's Auto Maintenance (DAM) for servicing. Dover promises to have the car ready by noon the next day. On June 2, Pogo goes to pick up the car, but since Dover is out to lunch, Pogo just takes the car. Later that evening Pogo drives into a tree, totally destroying the car. Pogo sues Nero Motors and DAM for the value of a new Flash alleging (a) that the steering mechanism jammed because of its defective design and (b) that DAM failed to discover and repair the defect. Defendants allege that the accident was caused by Pogo's own negligence and excessive speed. Consider the admissibility of the following evidence in terms of the relevancy principles discussed in the preceding sections.

(1) Pogo seeks to offer the testimony of two former Flash owners, each of whom is prepared to testify that after only 2,000 miles of driving a new Flash, the steering jammed causing an accident. Both Nero and DAM object.

Answer: Inadmissible against DAM without more foundation. The evidence is irrelevant with respect to DAM unless evidence is offered to prove that DAM serviced each car prior to the accident, thereby laying the foundation that DAM was responsible for the mechanics of each car up to that point.

Likewise, Nero's objection must also be separately considered, since evidence can be admissible against one party even if inadmissible against the other under the doctrine of limited admissibility.

This similar happenings evidence of prior accidents is also inadmissible against Nero unless Pogo can establish that each incident occurred under circumstances substantially similar to Pogo's accident. And since there is no evidence that the other two Flash cars were the same model or year and since each other car had been driven at least 2,000 miles (Pogo's car was brand new), the evidence is inadmissible in its present state.

(2) Nero offers evidence purporting to establish that the steering mechanism in the 1990 Flash was identical in all respects to those used in Flash models since 1985, that no other design changes were made since 1985 that could affect the steering, and that they have sold over 20,000 Flash models since 1985 and there have been no other suits claiming a defective steering mechanism. Pogo objects.

Answer: Probably inadmissible without additional foundation. Note that the evidence is in terms of times sued, not complaints received. Nero may have satisfied other claims out-of-court. Therefore, although the testimony does satisfy the substantial similarity requirement (i.e., the same design was used in all 20,000 cars with no other changes that would affect the steering), the court should require Nero to show either that it received no complaints of defective steering or that it would have been sued by other owners if the steering was defective.

(3) Dover offers the testimony of Wood that Wood saw Pogo driving his Flash about five minutes before the collision and that Pogo was driving "at least 80 miles an hour." Pogo objects.

Answer: Probably admissible. Is Pogo's speeding five minutes before the incident in question relevant circumstantial evidence of his conduct at the time of the collision? While the issue is discretionary, most judges would admit the testimony because of the proximity in time. It has some tendency in reason to prove Pogo was speeding at the time of the collision. If Pogo could point out some material difference in condition (e.g., if Wood saw Pogo driving on an expressway and the accident occurred on a residential street), the evidence might be excluded.

(4) Dover seeks to prove that Pogo is currently involved in three other personal injury actions: a products liability action against the manufacturer of a lawn mower; a slip-and-fall case against a motel he stayed in; and a suit in which he alleges he was injured when the defendant rear-ended him in his car.

Answer: Inadmissible. Dover has merely offered evidence that tends to show Pogo is a chronic litigant. Absent a showing that these claims are fraudulent, the evidence is inadmissible.

(5) Pogo seeks to prove the amount of his damages by offering evidence of the current price of a 1991 Flash as asked by a local dealership. Nero objects.

Answer: Inadmissible. While evidence of the selling price (not the asking price) of similar property is admissible to prove value, there must be a substantial identity of material circumstances. Pogo's car was a 1990 model and there is no showing here that the 1991 model was equivalently priced or equipped.

F. SPECIFIC RELEVANCE RULES: GENERAL. [§10.0]

The preceding sections discuss the court's general power under FRE 403 to exclude relevant evidence. In addition, the Federal Rules (codifying common-law practice) contain **specific rules** that govern the admissibility of certain classes of relevant evidence. Some of these rules are based on **extrinsic social policies** (see §6.1 above), some are based on concerns about **accuracy in factfinding** (see §6.2 above), and some on a **combination** of these two concerns.

1. SUBSEQUENT REMEDIAL MEASURES ("SRM"). [§10.1]

Evidence that a party took remedial measures following the occurrence of an accident or injury is inadmissible to prove the party's negligence or culpable conduct. [FRE 407].

a. Elements. [§10.11]

This exclusionary rule applies only if (1) a **party** (2) took some **remedial measure** (3) **after** the accident or injury that is the subject of the suit.

b. Remedial Measure Defined. [§10.12]

Any measure that **would have made the accident or injury less likely to occur** if it had been in place before the accident or injury qualifies as a subsequent remedial measure. An SRM can take many forms, such as a **repair or improvement** (e.g., addition of handrails to a stairway), a **design change**, (e.g., a change in gas-tank placement), a **change in procedure** (e.g., a change in schedule for waxing floors),or a **policy change** (limiting the number of drinks that can be served to patrons of a bar).

c. Reason for Exclusion. [§10.13]

SRM evidence is excluded in order to promote an **extrinsic social policy**. The law wants to encourage parties to take safety measures and believes that they will be less likely to do so if they fear that such actions will be used as evidence against them in subsequent litigation.

d. Inadmissible Only to Prove Negligence. [§10.14]

FRE 407 excludes evidence of an SRM **only when it is offered to prove the party's negligence or culpable conduct.**

e. Proper Uses of Subsequent Remedial Measures. [§10.15]

If SRM evidence is offered **to prove something other than the party's negligence or culpable conduct,** it is admissible.

(1) Ownership or Control. [§10.151]

Evidence of an SRM may be used to prove ownership or control of the instrumentality if it is in dispute.

> **(a) EXAMPLE: [§10.1511]** Plaintiff sues Defendant, a general contractor, for injuries suffered at a construction site. Defendant denies liability, claiming that the sub-contractor was responsible for safety measures at the site. Plaintiff offers evidence that after his accident, the general contractor erected a fence around the site. This is admissible to prove safety measures were a matter in Defendant's control, although the evidence is not admissible to prove Defendant was negligent.

(2) Feasibility of Precautionary Measures. [§10.152]

If a party claims that the product, policy, site, etc. at issue could not have been manufactured or operated in a safer way, evidence of an SRM by that party will be admissible to show such a change was feasible.

(a) EXAMPLE: [§10.1521] Plaintiff is injured when a wood chip hit him in the eye as he was operating a power saw. He sues Defendant, the manufacturer of the saw, claiming that the saw was defectively designed. Defendant claims the saw could not feasibly be made safer. Plaintiff offers evidence that after his injury Defendant changed the design of its saws to shield users from flying wood chips. The evidence will be admissible to rebut Defendant's claim that such a change was not feasible.

---

(3) Impeachment. [§10.153]

Evidence of an SRM may be used to impeach a party's testimony at trial.

(a) EXAMPLE: [§10.1531] Plaintiff, who was accidentally shot when a shot-gun was being unloaded, sues Gun Manufacturer. The president of Gun Manufacturer testifies that the gun was "perfectly safe and we wouldn't want to make it any different." Plaintiff may impeach this witness by demonstrating that Gun Manufacturer changed the design of the gun to allow its safety to be in the on position when the gun is being unloaded.

---

f. Strict Product Liability Case. [§10.16]

Jurisdictions differ as to the admissibility of SRM evidence in **product liability cases brought on a strict liability theory.** The arguments for admissibility are that (a) neither negligence nor culpable conduct is an issue in such a case; and (b) regardless of the law of evidence, economic forces will compel manufacturers to make their products safer. Most federal courts reject these arguments and **exclude** SRM evidence in strict product liability cases. Many states, however, accept these arguments and admit SRM evidence in such cases.

2. COMPROMISES AND OFFERS TO COMPROMISE. [§10.2]

The fact that a party offered to settle a claim or actually settled the claim is inadmissible to prove the validity or invalidity of the claim or the value of the claim. [FRE 408].

---

a. EXAMPLE: [§10.21] P sues Driver for injuries suffered when Driver's car struck P's car. Driver offers to settle for $75,000. P may *not* introduce evidence of Driver's offer to settle as evidence either of Driver's liability or the amount of damages suffered.

---

b. EXAMPLE: [§10.22] P brings a slip and fall action against Store, seeking $2 million in damages. P offers to settle for $50,000. Store rejects the offer. Store may not introduce evidence of P's offer as proof of the invalidity of P's claim or the amount of damages.

> **c. EXAMPLE: [§10.23]** After an airplane crash, P1 sues Airline for $1 million. Airline settles the case for $900,000. P2, another injured passenger, sues Airline and seeks to offer evidence of Airline's settlement with P1 to prove Airline's liability. The evidence is inadmissible.

d. Reason for Exclusion. [§10.24]

Exclusion of settlement evidence is based on the **extrinsic social policy** of encouraging out-of-court settlements. At common law, there was also some feeling that such evidence was irrelevant because an offer to compromise a claim might result from the desire to avoid a lawsuit as much as a belief that one was not liable. Under modern notions of relevance, however, such evidence generally cannot be said to be irrelevant.

e. Express Admissions During Negotiations. [§10.25]

Evidence of conduct or statements made **during compromise negotiations** are also **inadmissible** under this rule. Thus, even express admissions made during negotiations (e.g., "I ran the red light. I'll pay you $500 to settle.") are inadmissible.

f. Dispute Requirement. [§10.26]

This rule protects settlement evidence only if the offer, settlement, or statement is **related to a claim that was disputed** either as to liability or amount of damages.

> **(1) EXAMPLE: [§10.261]** Plaintiff sues Defendant on a $500 note. Defendant tells Plaintiff, "I know I owe you the $500, but it will cost you that much to litigate it. I'll give you $250 to settle." This statement is admissible since Defendant disputes neither the validity of Plaintiff's claim nor the amount of damages involved.

g. Proper Uses of Compromise Evidence. [§10.27]

FRE 408 makes compromise evidence inadmissible **only when it is offered to prove the validity or invalidity of a claim or the amount of damages.** It, may, however, be **admissible when offered for another purpose.**

(1) Bias or Prejudice. [§10.271]

Compromise evidence may be used to prove the bias or prejudice of a witness. For example, a plaintiff may ask a witness, "Didn't defendant just pay you $10,000 [a generous amount] to settle your claim against her?" This question is being asked to show that the witness may be biased in favor of defendant as the result of defendant's generosity toward her.

(2) Undue Delay. [§10.272]

Compromise evidence may be used to rebut a contention of undue delay. For example, if Defendant asserts that Plaintiff delayed unduly in filing suit, Plaintiff may establish that he did not file sooner because he was negotiating a settlement with Defendant.

(3) Suit on the Compromise Agreement. [§10.273]

When a plaintiff brings an action to enforce the terms of a settlement agreement, evidence of the agreement will, of course, be admissible.

3. OFFERS TO PAY MEDICAL OR SIMILAR EXPENSES. [§10.3]

FRE 409 excludes offers to pay or actual payment of medical, hospital, or similar expenses occasioned by an injury. This is sometimes referred to (somewhat inaptly) as the Good Samaritan rule. However, while the federal rule bans use of the offer or fact of payment itself, **it does not ban other statements made in connection with the offer.** Thus, a statement of liability made in connection with an offer to pay medical expenses (e.g., "**It was all my fault**; I'll pay all your medical bills.") is admissible. Note that this rule applies to unilateral offers, i.e., offers that are not made in an effort to compromise a claim. If the offer to pay (or payment of) medical or similar expenses is made as part of settlement discussions (or a settlement), the rule on compromise offers (see §10.2) governs and the statement of liability would be inadmissible. The common law does not have a rule analogous to FRE 409.

4. OFFERS TO PLEAD. [§10.4]

To facilitate the plea bargaining process, certain pleas are inadmissible in either a civil or criminal proceeding against the defendant who made the plea. [FRE 410]. Neither a **guilty plea that is withdrawn** nor a **nolo contendere (no contest) plea,** whether or not withdrawn, may be used against the defendant. Evidence of a **guilty plea that is not withdrawn is not excluded** by this rule.

---

a. EXAMPLE: [§10.41] Plaintiff sues Defendant for injuries suffered in an auto accident. She attempts to prove that Defendant entered a nolo contendere plea in response to criminal reckless driving charges arising out of the accident. The evidence is inadmissible. If, however, Defendant had entered a guilty plea to the charges and the plea had not been withdrawn, the evidence would be admissible.

---

b. Statements Made During the Plea Process. [§10.42]

In addition to pleas, FRE 410 excludes evidence of certain statements made in the plea process. **Statements made during plea discussions** are protected (e.g., offers to plead guilty or statements of liability), as are **statements made during the actual plea proceeding** (where the defendant may have to acknowledge his guilt).

5. LIABILITY INSURANCE. [§10.5]

Evidence that a person was or was not insured against liability is not admissible to prove that the person acted negligently or wrongfully. It is admissible, however, to prove other things, such as agency, ownership, control, or the bias or prejudice of a witness. [FRE 411].

a. Reason for Exclusion. [§10.51]

Liability insurance evidence is excluded in an effort to promote **accuracy in factfinding.** If offered to prove negligence, it has little or no probative value, but may be quite prejudicial. When offered to prove something other than negligence, it may, however, have substantial probative value, as shown below.

b. Disputed Ownership or Control. [§10.52]

If the existence of an insurance policy is relevant to prove ownership or control of a vehicle or premises **and ownership or control is in dispute,** evidence regarding liability insurance is admissible because it is not being used to prove negligence. Thus, if Defendant claims he does not own a car, the fact that an insurance policy was taken out in his name is admissible to prove his ownership.

c. Showing Bias. [§10.53]

On cross-examination, counsel may show bias by eliciting the fact that a witness is employed by an insurance company that has a financial interest in the outcome.

d. Inseparable Reference to Insurance. [§10.54]

If a party makes a statement directly bearing upon liability or fault, the statement will be admissible notwithstanding a reference to insurance coverage (e.g., "I was driving too fast but all your damages will be covered by my insurance"). If it is possible to **sever** the insurance reference from the admission without lessening its evidentiary value, the court should strike the reference to insurance.

e. Evidence of No Insurance. [§10.55]

A defendant may not introduce evidence that she is **not** insured unless a plaintiff has falsely suggested that she **is** insured.

OUTLINE

PROBLEM 1. Plaintiff is injured when Defendant drives his car into the rear of her car. Plaintiff sues Defendant for $20,000.

(1) Plaintiff offers evidence that, right after the accident, Defendant said, "I'm sorry, I'll pay the hospital expenses. I was speeding."

> **Answer:** Although Defendant can prevent Plaintiff from offering evidence regarding Plaintiff's offer to pay hospital expenses, Defendant's statement about speeding is admissible.

(2) Plaintiff offers evidence that Defendant paid a $20 traffic fine without trial or protest in response to a citation for "following too close" given him at the scene of the collision.

> **Answer:** Admissible. The paying of a fine without a trial is construed as a plea of guilty. Naturally, Defendant can explain his motives for the plea, but pleas of guilty are admissible. Note, however, that some jurisdictions have a statute or special rule that treats an uncontested minor traffic offense as equivalent to a nolo contendere plea. In such jurisdictions, this evidence would be inadmissible.

(3) Plaintiff offers evidence that Defendant said, "The accident was my fault, but your damage claim is much too high. I'll give you $5,000 to settle."

> **Answer:** Inadmissible. Even express admissions made in connection with settlement offers are excluded by FRE 408 as long as there is a dispute either as to liability or the amount of damages.

PROBLEM 2. Plaintiff is injured when his automobile is struck by Defendant's train at a railroad crossing. Plaintiff offers evidence that after the accident, Defendant (a) installed new warning lights and (b) instructed its engineers to decrease their speed by twenty miles per hour when entering that crossing.

> **Answer:** Both the installation of new warning lights and the instruction to the engineers are inadmissible. Both qualify as subsequent remedial measures and are therefore inadmissible to prove Defendant's negligence.

G. CHARACTER EVIDENCE. [§11.0]

One of the trickiest areas of the law of evidence concerns the admissibility of evidence of a person's character or of a person's character trait. The common law developed a fairly complicated (some might say bizarre) set of rules to govern this question, which have for the most part been substantially incorporated into the Federal Rules. **Character evidence is always a favorite topic for exam questions. If you break down the question and follow the rules carefully, reaching the correct result is not that difficult.**

1. THE THREE STEP PROCESS. [§11.1]

Always analyze character evidence problems by asking the three following questions. (What-May-How?).

a. What is the evidence being offered to prove? b. May character evidence be used to prove this? If so, ask the third question. **c. How may character be proved?**

2. POSSIBLE USES OF CHARACTER EVIDENCE. [§11.2]

There are several purposes for which character evidence might be offered, and it is crucial to distinguish among them.

a. Character as an Element of a Claim or Defense. [§11.21]

A person's **character might itself be an element of a crime, claim or defense.** In such a case, evidence of the person's character will be **direct evidence** of a fact critical to the case. That is, the person's character will itself be an issue in the case. **When character is itself an element of a claim or defense, evidence of character is admissible. [FRE 404].** The following are examples of cases in which the substantive law makes character an element of a claim or defense, and therefore, admissible.

(1) Negligent Entrustment or Hiring. [§11.211]

Where Plaintiff claims that Defendant negligently entrusted his car to Driver, Plaintiff must establish as one of the elements of his cause of action that Driver was not the type of person to whom a car should be loaned (because, for example, he was a terrible driver). Thus, Driver's character is something that Plaintiff must prove to make out his claim. (Plaintiff will also have to establish that Defendant knew or should have known about Driver's character, but that is a separate element of his claim.)

(2) Defamation—Truth as a Defense. [§11.212]

In a libel or slander case, a defendant may assert the defense of "truth." If, for example, Defendant called Plaintiff a "liar and a thief," Plaintiff's character as a liar and a thief will be an element of Defendant's defense of truth.

(3) Entrapment. [§11.213]

Some versions of the entrapment defense to a criminal charge focus on the defendant's predisposition to commit the crime. Thus, Defendant's character may be an element of the entrapment defense.

(4) Custody Action. [§11.214]

In a child custody proceeding, the court may consider a party's character in deciding who should have custody of a child.

(5) Mental Condition or Competency. [§11.215]

In cases raising issues such as the sanity of the defendant, the competency of a testator to make a will, or the mental condition of the respondent to a civil commitment proceeding, character is an element of the claim or defense.

(6) Proving Character When It is an Element of a Claim or Defense. [§11.216]

When character is an element of a claim or defense, it may be proved through the use of **reputation** or **opinion** testimony [FRE 405(a)] or **specific instances of conduct.** [FRE 405(b)]. See §11.3 below.

b. Character Evidence Used to Prove Conduct. [§11.22]

A party might want to introduce evidence of someone's conduct in order to prove how that person acted on a particular occasion. That is, the character evidence will be offered as **circumstantial evidence:** the jury is to infer from the evidence of a person's character that the person acted in conformity with his character on the occasion in question.

(1) General Rule: Inadmissible to Prove Conduct. [§11.221]

The general rule is that character evidence is not admissible as circumstantial evidence that a person acted in conformity with his character on a particular occasion. [FRE 404(a)].

(a) EXAMPLE. [§11.2211] To prove Defendant murdered Victim, the prosecution seeks to prove that Defendant has a violent character. This is inadmissible.

(b) EXAMPLE. [§11.2212] Plaintiff sues Defendant for fraud. Plaintiff offers evidence that Defendant has committed numerous acts of dishonesty in the past to prove he committed fraud on this particular occasion. This is inadmissible.

---

(2) Rationale. [§11.222]

The reason for this is that character evidence is **not** considered **highly probative** on the issue of how a person acted on a particular occasion. On the other hand, such evidence may be **highly prejudicial.** The jury is likely to rule against Defendant because it has decided Defendant is a bad person.

c. Sounds Like Character Evidence But is Not. [§11.23]

Sometimes evidence is offered that looks and sounds a lot like character evidence, but is really not.

(1) Self Defense — Pre-Emptive Strike Theory. [§11.231]

One theory of self defense is that the defendant reasonably feared that the victim was about to inflict severe bodily harm on him and so struck the first blow to victim. **In such a case, it is not the victim's character that is the issue, but what the defendant reasonably believed about the victim.** For example, a defendant might have reasonably (but incorrectly) believed that the victim was a violent person who was about to kill him. (There is a second theory of self defense — that the victim was the first aggressor — which is discussed below at §11.421.)

(2) Injury to Reputation [§11.232]

In defamation cases, damages are measured according to injury to the plaintiff's reputation. Thus it is the plaintiff's **reputation,** before and after the tort, **not his character,** that constitutes the measure of damages. As we all know too well, a person's reputation can vary dramatically from his true character.

3. METHODS OF PROVING CHARACTER. [§11.3]

In theory at least, there are **three types of evidence** that might be used to prove a person's character: (a) **reputation;** (b) **opinion;** and (c) **specific instances of conduct. Which of these three types can be used under the rules depends on what the evidence is being offered to prove.**

a. Reputation. [§11.31]

Evidence of a person's reputation in the community might be offered to prove the person's character. For example, evidence that a person is known in the community as a violent person tends to prove that he is a violent person.

(1) Foundation Required for Reputation Testimony. [§11.311]

A witness called to testify as to another person's reputation in the community must first demonstrate that she has knowledge of the person's reputation in the community, although she need not actually know the person herself.

(2) Relevant Community. [§11.312]

Traditionally, reputation evidence related to the person's reputation in the community in which he or she lived. Courts now accept testimony relating to the person's reputation in other significant "communities," such as the place where the person works.

(3) Substance of Reputation Testimony. [§11.313]

When a witness gives reputation testimony, she is allowed to state only that the person's reputation in the community for the relevant trait is "good," "bad," "excellent," "terrible," etc., and may not give reasons why that reputation exists.

(4) Hearsay. [§11.314]

Reputation testimony calls for the recitation of hearsay, but an exception to the hearsay rule exists for such testimony. [FRE 803(21)].

b. Opinion [§11.32]

A witness may testify as to her opinion of another person's character. For example, a witness might testify in a defamation action that she knows the plaintiff and that in her opinion, the plaintiff is a liar and a thief. This method of proof is not permitted at common law, but is allowed under the federal rules [FRE 405] and in many states.

(1) Substance of Opinion Testimony. [§11.321]

As is the case with reputation testimony, an opinion witness may state only her opinion of the person's character. She may not give reasons as to why she holds that opinion.

c. Specific Instances of Conduct. [§11.33]

Evidence that a person has engaged in specific acts might tend to establish the person's character. For example, the fact that someone has committed four thefts tends to establish that he is the type of person who steals. This method of proof presents the greatest danger of unfair prejudice and so its use is limited. **Specific instances may be used when character is itself an element of a claim or defense (e.g., negligent entrustment) but may not be used when character is offered to prove conduct (e.g., as evidence of defendant's violent character to prove he committed the charged crime of violence).**

4. CHARACTER TO PROVE CONDUCT: EXCEPTIONS TO GENERAL RULE. [§11.4]

Recall that the general rule is that evidence of a person's character is not admissible to prove conduct (i.e., as proof that the person acted in conformity with that character on a particular occasion). [FRE 404(a)] **This general rule applies both in criminal and civil cases.** There are, however, **three important exceptions** to this rule:

a. Character of an Accused: Putting Character in Issue. [§11.41]

A criminal defendant may offer evidence of a pertinent trait of his character to prove his innocence. [FRE 404(a)(1)]. Thus, a defendant charged with murder (a crime of violence) may introduce evidence of his peaceable nature as evidence that he acted in accordance with his peaceable character on the occasion in question, and is therefore innocent. This is often referred to as "putting character in issue." **Do not confuse** this with those cases in which character is an issue (that is, when character is an element of a claim or defense).

(1) Must Be Pertinent Character Trait. [§11.411]

The accused may offer evidence only of a **pertinent character trait.** A murder defendant may not offer evidence of his honest character to prove he did not commit the murder.

(2) Method of Proof [§11.412]

The defendant may prove his character **only by reputation and opinion testimony.** He may not offer evidence of specific acts to prove his good character. [FRE 405].

(3) Prosecutor May Rebut. [§11.413]

If the defendant offers evidence of his good character, he is said to put "character in issue" and the prosecution may rebut. [FRE 404(a)(1)].

(a) Reputation and Opinion. [§11.4131]

The prosecution can call its **own reputation and opinion witnesses** to testify to the defendant's bad character for the relevant trait. [FRE 405(a)].

(b) Cross-Examination of Defendant's Witnesses. [§11.4132]

The prosecution may ask a reputation witness called by the defendant whether she "had heard" about specific acts of the defendant that

OUTLINE

would reflect badly on the defendant's reputation. The theory is that this tests how familiar the witness is with the defendant's reputation in the community. Similarly, the prosecution may ask an opinion witness called by the defendant whether she knows about specific acts of the defendant that might bear on her opinion. Again, the theory is that the prosecution is simply testing how well the witness knows the defendant. [FRE 405(a)].

(1) Form of Question. [§11.41321]

At common law, the precise form of a question put to a reputation witness on cross-examination was very important. (Remember, opinion witnesses were not permitted at common law.) The question had to be phrased in a manner that tested only the witness's knowledge of community reputation. The correct form was "Have you heard . . . .[that the defendant embezzled $10,000 from his daughter's Brownie troop]?" A question asking "Did you know . . ." was improper. Now that opinion witnesses are permitted under the federal rules and in many states, this distinction is of diminished importance and, according to some commentators and caselaw, has been abandoned in the federal courts.

(2) Pertinent Trait Only. [§11.41322]

The specific acts referred to in the prosecution's "have you heard" and "did you know" questions must relate to the character trait that the witness testified about on direct examination.

(3) Prosecution Bound by Answer. [§11.41323]

Although the prosecution may ask such "have you heard" and "did you know" questions, it **may not introduce evidence to prove that the specific acts actually occurred,** even if the witness answers in the negative. For example, if a defense witness testifies that the defendant has an excellent reputation for peaceableness, the prosecution may ask, "Have you heard that the defendant assaulted an 84 year-old lady in a wheelchair last year?" Even if the witness answers "no," the prosecution is barred from proving that the defendant actually committed the assault.

(4) Limiting Instruction. [§11.41324]

Because juries might well infer from the question that defendant did commit the specific act, the defendant is entitled to a limiting instruction that will explain to the jury (futilely) that the question is being asked only to test the witness's familiarity with defendant's reputation and is not evidence that the defendant committed the specific act.

(5) Good Faith Requirement. [§11.41325]

Because the jury is unlikely to understand the limiting instruction, "Have you heard" and "Did you know" questions are limited to instances of conduct that the prosecution believes in good faith actually occurred. (See Case Squibs section, *Michelson v. United States*.)

b. Character of Victim. [§11.42]

A criminal defendant may offer evidence of the character of his victim in order to prove the victim's conduct and his own innocence. [FRE 404(a)(2)]. This is usually offered to buttress a claim of self-defense.

(1) Self Defense: Victim as First Aggressor Theory. [§11.421]

In this second theory of self-defense [see §11.231 for the first theory], the defendant is arguing that the victim struck the first blow. Evidence of the victim's violent character is offered, therefore, as evidence that the victim acted in conformity with his violent nature on this occasion; that is, to prove that the victim started the fight.

(2) Method of Proof. [§11.422]

The defendant may use only **reputation and opinion** testimony to prove the victim's character. [FRE 405(a)]. In a few jurisdictions, the defendant may introduce specific acts by the victim.

(3) Prosecution May Rebut. [§11.423]

If the defendant offers evidence of the victim's bad character, the prosecution may rebut by **cross-examining defendant's witnesses** or by calling its **own reputation and opinion witnesses to testify to the victim's good character.** In addition, **in a homicide case,** if the defendant offers **any kind of evidence** that the deceased victim was the first aggressor, the prosecution may call reputation and opinion witnesses to testify to the victim's peaceable character. [FRE 404(a)(2)].

c. Applicability of Exceptions to Civil Cases. [§11.43]

These first two exceptions to the general rule prohibiting character evidence to prove conduct are, by their terms, applicable only in criminal cases. However, in a few instances, courts have allowed their use in civil cases that involved claims of criminal-like conduct. For example, in a civil rights case in which the defendants were accused of wrongfully killing the victim, the defendants were allowed to offer evidence of the victim's violent character.

d. Character to Attack or Support Credibility. [§11.44]

The third exception to the general rule prohibiting character evidence to prove conduct provides that evidence of a witness's character may be used to attack or support his credibility. [FRE 404(a)(3)]. That is, evidence that a witness has a truthful or untruthful character is offered to prove that the witness is testifying truthfully or untruthfully. A special set of rules governs when and how evidence of character may be used to attack or support credibility. (See §§53.0-53.51).

5. EVIDENCE OF PAST SEXUAL BEHAVIOR. [§11.5]

At common law, defendants accused of rape often introduced evidence of their victim's character. That is, they tried to prove that their victim was promiscuous to prove that she consented to sexual intercourse on this occasion. This resulted in a great deal of abuse, as rape victims frequently found themselves and their sexual histories the focus of the trial. As a result, **every jurisdiction has passed some form of "rape shield" law that**

strictly limits the admissibility of evidence of a victim's past sexual conduct. Many are similar to FRE 412.

a. Criminal Cases—General rule. [§11.51]

FRE 412 severely limits, in any criminal proceeding involving alleged sexual misconduct, the admissibility of evidence of an alleged victim's other sexual behavior or predisposition.

(1) Other sexual behavior. [§11.511]

Evidence that any alleged victim engaged in other sexual behavior is generally inadmissible. This includes evidence of actual physical sexual contact, activities that imply sexual contact (e.g., use of contraceptives), and reputation and opinion evidence. Note that the rule extends to any alleged victim and is **not restricted to the complainant** in the case. If, for example, Defendant is charged with sexually assaulting Victim, the prosecution might call Witness (another sexual assault victim of Defendant) to testify to Defendant's modus operandi. Witness is an alleged victim and evidence of her other sexual behavior is inadmissible.

(2) Sexual predisposition. [§11.512]

Evidence offered to prove an alleged victim's sexual predisposition (e.g., evidence of mode of dress, life-style) is likewise inadmissible.

(3) Not restricted to charges of sexual assault. [§11.513]

Although the rule will typically apply in cases in which the defendant faces charges of criminal sexual misconduct (e.g., sexual assault), it also reaches cases in which the defendant is charged with an offense that does not contain sexual misconduct as an element but where the defendant's sexual misconduct is relevant to prove motive or as background evidence. For example, evidence that the defendant sexually assaulted the victim might be relevant to establish his motive for kidnapping her.

b. Criminal cases—Exceptions. [§11.52]

FRE 412(b) enumerates three exceptions under which sexual misconduct or predisposition evidence may be admissible.

(1) Source of semen or injury. [§11.521]

The accused may offer evidence of specific instances of an alleged victim's sexual behavior to prove that someone other than the accused was the source of semen, injury, or other physical evidence. Of course, the other sexual behavior must have occurred at such a time that it actually tends to rebut or explain the prosecution's physical evidence.

(a) EXAMPLE. [§11.5211] Evidence that the alleged victim had intercourse with someone else three weeks prior to the alleged sexual assault will not tend to rebut prosecution evidence that the accused was the source of semen. On the other hand, evidence that the accused had intercourse with someone else the night before the alleged sexual assault would tend to rebut such evidence.

---

(2) Sexual behavior involving alleged victim and accused. [§11.522]

The accused may offer evidence of specific instances of sexual behavior between the accused and the alleged victim to prove consent. Thus, evidence that the accused and the alleged victim had previously had sexual relations would be admissible to prove that the alleged act of sexual assault was really consensual. The prosecution may also offer evidence of specific instances of sexual behavior between the alleged victim and the accused to the extent such evidence is admissible as other bad acts evidence.

(3) When constitutionally required. [§11.523]

Evidence of other sexual behavior or predisposition is admissible when exclusion would violate the accused's constitutional right to **confrontation** or **due process**. For example, in *Olden v. Kentucky*, 488 U.S. 227 (1988), the Supreme Court held that the defendant had a constitutional right to introduce evidence of the complainant's relationship with another man in order to show that she had a motive to falsely accuse the defendant of rape. (See Case Squibs section.)

c. Civil Cases—Generally [§11.524]

The general rule that ordinarily proscribes in criminal cases evidence of an alleged victim's other sexual behavior or sexual predisposition also applies in civil cases involving alleged sexual misconduct. [FRE 412(a)] This includes actions for sexual battery and sexual harassment.

d. Civil Cases—Exceptions [§11.525]

FRE 412(b) allows such evidence to be admitted if it (a) is **otherwise admissible** under the rules (e.g., it does not consist of inadmissible hearsay) and (b) a strict **balancing** test is met. The probative value of the evidence must **substantially** outweigh the danger of unfair prejudice to any party and the danger of harm to any victim. Evidence of an alleged victim's reputation is admissible only if it has been placed in controversy by the alleged victim.

e. Procedures. [§11.526]

A party that wishes to offer such evidence must file a **written motion** at least fourteen days prior to trial, unless the court for good cause relaxes the time limit. The motion must be served on all parties and must specifically describe the proffered evidence and the purpose for which it is being offered. The alleged victim (or the victim's guardian or representative) must also be notified. The court may not admit such evidence without first conducting an in camera hearing. The parties and alleged victim must be afforded the right to attend and be heard at the hearing.

6. THIRD EXCEPTION TO CHARACTER EVIDENCE RULE IN SEXUAL ASSAULT AND CHILD MOLESTATION CASES. [11.6]

Federal Rules 413-415, which went into effect in 1995, create a third exception to the general rule excluding character evidence when offered to prove conduct. These rules apply in criminal cases in which the defendant is charged with **sexual assault or child molestation** or in civil cases in which a **damage claim is predicated on the commission of a sexual assault or act of child molestation.**

a. Criminal Cases. [11.61]

FRE 413-414 govern the criminal cases. They provide that the prosecution may offer evidence that the defendant has committed other such offenses (that is, **other acts of sexual assault or child molestation** respectively) for its bearing on any relevant matter. This means the evidence may be offered to prove defendant's character so that the jury may infer the defendant acted in conformity with his character on the particular occasion and committed the charged act.

b. Civil Cases. [11.62]

Similarly, FRE 415 governs the admission of such evidence in civil cases. It allows evidence that a party committed **other acts of sexual assault or child molestation** for its bearing on any relevant matter, including as evidence of the party's character.

c. Notice Requirement. [11.63]

If a party intends to introduce evidence under FRE 413-415, it must provide to its opponent the statements of its witnesses or a summary of the substance of their expected testimony at least fifteen days prior to trial. The court may, for good cause, allow disclosure at a later date.

H. HABIT AND ROUTINE PRACTICE EVIDENCE. [§12.0]

The law of evidence distinguishes between a person's character or character traits and a person's habits. Evidence of a person's habit is more probative of his conduct on a particular occasion than is character evidence. Thus, evidence that a person always ran a particular stop sign is good evidence that the person ran **that** stop sign on the occasion in question, although evidence that he is a "careless" driver is not. Therefore, FRE 406 specifies that **evidence of a person's habit is admissible to prove that the person acted in accordance with that habit on a particular occasion.**

1. HABIT AND CHARACTER EVIDENCE DISTINGUISHED. [§12.1]

Habit is typically regarded as **a regular response to a repeated, specific situation.** In contrast, character relates to a generalized description of dispositions or traits such as prudence, honesty, or cautiousness. Usually, the distinction is an easy one to draw: it is the difference, for example, between always locking a particular gate in the front of one's house (a habit) and being "safety-conscious" (a character trait). A habit may be observed whereas a character trait is a matter of opinion. Normally, the words **"invariably," "automatically," "without fail,"** or **"always"** will warn you of a habit issue on an exam.

2. CORROBORATION AND NECESSITY LIMITATIONS ABANDONED. [§12.2]

FRE 406 states that habit evidence is admissible "whether corroborated or not and regardless of the presence of eyewitnesses." The quoted language repudiates a restriction many jurisdictions formerly placed on habit evidence. At common law, such evidence had been limited to situations where the use of such evidence was necessitated by the absence of eyewitnesses, or where there was corroboration of the "habit" (routine practice) of a business.

3. ROUTINE PRACTICE. [§12.3]

The "habit" of an organization is referred to as its **custom or routine practice** and is admissible to prove that the organization acted in conformity with its routine practice on the occasion in question. For example, evidence that a business date-stamps incoming mail within three hours of receipt will be admissible to prove that a letter stamped "March 2" was received on March 2.

SUMMARY CHART OF CHARACTER EVIDENCE

S = Specific acts; R = Repudiation; O = Opinion

	1. WHAT	2. MAY	3. HOW
Prosecutor / Plaintiff	Element of claim / defense Conduct in Conformity FRE exception: sexual assault / child molestation	Yes No Yes	S,R,O[*] N/A S
Criminal defendant	Element of claim / defense Conduct in Conformity — own character Conduct in Conformity — Victim's Character	Yes Yes Yes[%]	S,R,O R,O R,O[#]
Prosecutor — rebuttal	Conduct in Conformity — Defendant's character Conduct in Conformity Victim's character	Yes Yes	R,O[@] R,O

[*] Opinion testimony allowed under FRE; not common law.
[%] Except character of rape victim.
[#] Some common law jurisdictions allow specific instances also.
[@] Prosecution may also cross-examine defendant's reputation witnesses with "Have you heard" questions; opinion witnesses with "Did you know" questions.

OUTLINE

PROBLEM 1. Plaintiff is injured in an auto accident with Speedy. Plaintiff sues Defendant, the car owner, on a negligent entrustment theory, claiming that Speedy's unsafe driving caused the accident and that Defendant knew or should have known that Speedy was a dangerous driver.

(1) Plaintiff offers evidence that Speedy had four speeding tickets in the six months prior to the accident.

Answer: Admissible to prove Speedy's character as an unsafe driver. Inadmissible to prove that Speedy was speeding on the occasion in question. Note, however, that Plaintiff must still prove that Defendant knew or should have known about Speedy's character as an unsafe driver.

(2) Plaintiff offers testimony of Willie that he has driven with Defendant for over a year and that Speedy "likes to drive very fast."

Answer: Admissible to prove Speedy's character as an unsafe driver.

(3) Defendant offers testimony of Winnie that she has driven the route of the accident with Speedy daily for one year and that Speedy always slowed down to 20 M.P.H. at the spot of the collision.

Answer: Admissible as habit evidence to show that Speedy slowed down at the spot of the collision on the day in question.

PROBLEM 2. Defendant is charged with the murder of Victim, his wife.

(1) The prosecution offers evidence that Defendant previously was convicted of manslaughter arising out of a barroom fight.

Answer: Inadmissible. Under the general rule, evidence of a person's character may not be offered to prove that he acted in conformity with that character on a particular occasion.

(2) The prosecution offers evidence that Defendant has a reputation in the community as a very violent man.

Answer: Inadmissible under the general rule that evidence of a person's character is not admissible to prove conduct.

(3) Defendant calls Witness to testify that Defendant has a reputation in the community as a peaceable and law-abiding person.

Answer: Admissible. Defendant can offer reputation or opinion evidence of his good character to prove his innocence.

(4) The prosecution offers, in rebuttal, evidence of Defendant's conviction for manslaughter arising from the barroom fight.

> **Answer:** Inadmissible. Although the prosecution may rebut Defendant's evidence of his peaceable character, it may do so only asking Defendant's reputation witness "have you heard" about the manslaughter and by calling its own reputation and opinion witnesses. It may not offer evidence of specific acts of conduct committed by Defendant.

I. "OTHER CRIMES, WRONGS, OR ACTS" EVIDENCE ADMISSIBLE FOR NON-CHARACTER PURPOSES. [§13.0]

Evidence of a person's character ordinarily is inadmissible if offered to prove that the person acted in conformity with his character on a particular occasion. Thus, evidence that a person lied on many previous occasions may not be offered to prove his dishonest nature from which the factfinder is to infer that he committed perjury on the occasion in question. But such evidence may be **admissible if it is offered to prove something other than character from which conduct on a particular occasion is to be inferred.**

1. RATIONALE. [§13.1]

Remember that evidence of a person's character is ordinarily excluded because its slight probative value as proof of conduct on a specific occasion is outweighed by the danger of unfair prejudice it presents. When evidence of other acts is offered **to prove something other than character,** however, we can no longer say categorically that the balancing of probative and prejudicial value tilts towards exclusion. However, since the danger still exists that the jury may take the evidence as bearing on character, such evidence must be treated with some care.

2. "MIAMI COP" [§13.2]

Purposes for which other crimes, wrongs, or acts evidence (sometimes referred to as "extrinsic offense" evidence) may be offered may be remembered by the mnemonic device "Miami Cop." **M**otive; **I**dentity; **A**bsence of **M**istake or accident; **I**ntent; **C**ommon plan or scheme; **O**pportunity; **P**reparation. Although this is not an exclusive list, it does cover most of the uses of other crimes evidence.

a. Motive. [§13.21]

If some act by the defendant tends to show that he had a motive for committing the crime in question, evidence of the act is admissible.

> **(1) EXAMPLE. [§13.211]** In Defendant's trial for murder of Victim, Prosecutor offers evidence that Victim was an eyewitness to another murder committed by Defendant. This is admissible to prove that Defendant had a motive to kill Victim.

b. Identity. [§13.22]

Where the identity of the person who committed the crime is an issue, evidence may be offered that the defendant committed other similar crimes using the same distinctive **modus operandi** as that used by the perpetrator of the charged crime. The theory is that a distinctive method of committing a crime is like the perpetrator's **signature** or **calling card.**

> **(1) EXAMPLE. [§13.221]** Defendant is charged with sexually assaulting Victim. Victim testifies that she is unable to identify her assailant because he wore a purple and green ski mask and quickly tied a red bandana around her eyes. Prosecutor calls Witness who testifies that she was sexually assaulted a few days after Victim by a man wearing a purple and green ski mask who tied a red bandana around her eyes, but that she was nevertheless able to get a glance at her assailant and that it was Defendant. This is admissible to prove that Defendant was Victim's assailant.

c. Absence of Mistake or Accident. [§13.23]

Evidence of a person's other crimes, wrongs, or acts may tend to prove that the person possessed knowledge of what he was doing or of the consequences of his act.

> **(1) EXAMPLE. [§13.231]** Defendant, charged with possession of marijuana, claims that he mistakenly believed the substance he possessed was oregano. To rebut, Prosecutor offers to prove that Defendant was convicted of marijuana possession three years ago. This is admissible.

d. Intent. [§13.24]

In many cases, the prosecution must prove not only that the defendant committed the physical elements of the crime, but that he had the requisite criminal intent. Evidence of other crimes, wrongs, or acts may thus be used to prove intent. However, because intent is an issue in many criminal cases, courts typically restrict other crimes evidence to those cases in which the defendant contends that he did not have the requisite intent. (See Case Squibs section, *United States v. Beechum*.)

> **(1) EXAMPLE. [§13.241]** Defendant is arrested while leaving a department store with a watch in his coat pocket. At trial, he admits possessing the watch but claims that he did not intend to steal it. He contends that, unbeknownst to him, it fell into his pocket. The prosecution may be permitted to offer evidence that Defendant has been caught shoplifting four times in the past two years.

> **(2) EXAMPLE. [§13.242]** Defendant is tried for the murder of Victim. He raises an alibi defense. The prosecution will not be permitted to offer evidence that Defendant has committed murder on two other occasions to prove that he intended to kill Victim. Unlike the defendant in Example 1, who conceded he had the watch but claimed he lacked the requisite intent to steal, Defendant here denies any involvement whatsoever with the crime. He does not claim that whoever killed Victim lacked the intent to kill; he simply claims that he was not the killer.

e. Common Plan or Scheme. [§13.25]

The prosecution may offer evidence that the defendant committed another crime, wrong, or act as part of a plan or scheme to commit the charged act.

> **(1) EXAMPLE. [§13.251]** Defendant is charged with killing his mother. The prosecutor offers evidence that Defendant previously killed all persons other than himself named in his mother's will as evidence of his scheme to inherit all his mother's wealth. This is admissible.

f. Opportunity. [§13.26]

Evidence of other crimes, wrongs, or acts may be used to prove the defendant had access to the scene of the crime, or the knowledge or capacity to commit the charged crime.

> **(1) EXAMPLE. [§13.261]** In Defendant's prosecution for burglarizing a house with a sophisticated burglar alarm, Prosecutor may offer evidence that Defendant had committed other burglaries which required him to neutralize sophisticated burglar alarms.

g. Preparation. [§13.27]

As with common scheme or plan, evidence of other crimes, wrongs, or acts may be proved to show defendant's preparation for the charged crime.

> **(1) EXAMPLE. [§13.271]** Defendant is charged with murdering elderly hospital patients by injecting them with morphine. Evidence that Defendant stole morphine from the hospital pharmacy may be offered to prove his guilt.

3. "EXCEPTIONS." [§13.3]

Although these uses of other crimes evidence are often referred to as "exceptions" to the general rule prohibiting character evidence, they typically are not. These uses of other crimes evidence do not violate the character rule because the evidence is not being introduced for the forbidden purpose, that is, as evidence of character from which conduct is to be inferred. It is being offered as proof of guilt that does not require an inference to be made about the defendant's character. Nevertheless, especially when the other crimes evidence is offered to prove intent, it is often probative only because an inference is made from the other crimes to the defendant's character. For example, in the shoplifting hypothetical above (§13.241), the evidence of Defendant's prior acts of shoplifting tends to prove his intent to steal the watch because it shows he is the kind of person who steals.

4. PROCEDURAL CONSIDERATIONS. [§13.4]

Because other crimes evidence may be highly prejudicial to the defendant, certain procedural considerations must be observed.

a. Quantum of Proof Required. [§13.41]

Other crimes, wrongs, or acts evidence is not restricted to acts for which the defendant has previously been arrested or convicted. Jurisdictions vary as to the strength of the proof necessary to establish that the defendant committed the other crime, wrong, or act. Some require the prosecution to produce **plain, clear and convincing evidence** that the defendant had committed the other crime. (See Case Squibs section, *Tucker v. State*.) Others adhere to a preponderance of the evidence standard. The United States Supreme Court has adopted a still lower standard. In *Huddleston v. United States*, (See Case Squibs Section), the Court held that the prosecution is required to introduce only **enough evidence so that a reasonable juror could find that the defendant committed the other crime**.

b. Discretionary Exclusion. [§13.42]

Courts may exclude other crimes evidence on the ground that the danger of unfair prejudice substantially outweighs its probative value.

c. Notice. [§13.43]

Some jurisdictions require prosecutors to give defendants notice of their intent to use other crimes evidence. Under FRE 404(b), in a criminal case, upon request by the accused, the prosecution must provide reasonable notice of the general nature of any other crimes evidence it intends to introduce at trial for any purpose. This notice requirement, however, does not apply to offenses that are inextricably intertwined with the charged offense (e.g., evidence that the accused, accused of bank robbery, commandeered a car to make his getaway).

d. Acquittal. [§13.44]

Evidence of another crime may be offered by the prosecution even if the defendant has already been tried and acquitted for that crime. Evidentiary use of the other crime does not offend the Double Jeopardy Clause. (See Case Squibs Section, *Dowling v. United States.*)

PROBLEM 1. Defendant is on trial for burglary. The victim testifies that she awoke in the middle of the night and saw a man enter through her window and put on a Warren Beatty mask. He carried a gun, went straight to her kitchen, and took her silver. She is unable to identify Defendant as the burglar.

(1) Prosecutor offers evidence that Defendant has twice before been convicted of burglary.

Answer: Inadmissible. This is impermissible character evidence, offered to show that Defendant is the kind of person who commits burglaries, acted in conformity with his character on this occasion, and committed the charged burglary.

(2) Prosecutor calls Witness to testify that a week before Victim's burglary, she awoke in the middle of the night and saw a man enter through her window and put on a Warren Beatty mask. He carried a gun, went straight to her kitchen, and took her silver. Witness testifies that she caught of glimpse of the burglar's face before he put on his mask, and identifies Defendant as the burglar.

Answer: Admissible. This evidence is being offered to show that Defendant committed another burglary using the same distinctive modus operandi that was employed by the person who committed the charged burglary. Therefore this is admissible to prove identity.

PROBLEM 2. Defendant is on trial for blowing up a building. The prosecution's theory is that Defendant destroyed the building so he could collect on the insurance policy he held.

(1) The prosecution offers evidence that, one month before the explosion, Defendant broke into a demolition company's warehouse and took some detonation devices.

Answer: Admissible. The theft of the detonation devices is part of Defendant's preparation for the charged crime.

(2) The prosecution offers evidence that Defendant had incurred gambling losses totalling $250,000 and was being pressured to pay them off shortly before the building was destroyed.

Answer: Admissible to prove that Defendant had a motive for blowing up the building.

PROBLEM 3. Defendant is on trial for murdering his very wealthy wife.

(1) The prosecution offers the testimony of Butler that a few days before Wife was killed he saw Defendant strike Wife and heard Wife say to Defendant, "I'm going to divorce you and cut you out of my will."

Answer: Admissible to prove Defendant had a motive for killing Wife.

(2) Wife died from blows to the head from a blunt object. The prosecution offers evidence that Defendant had killed Victim four years earlier by striking Victim on the head with a blunt object. Defendant had been tried for the murder of Victim but claimed self defense and was acquitted.

Answer: Inadmissible. This is forbidden character evidence. The only reason for offering it is to show Defendant's violent character. The method of killing (using a blunt object) is not sufficiently distinctive to qualify as modus operandi evidence. If the evidence were admissible for some other purpose, however, the fact that Defendant had earlier been acquitted would not bar its use. The prosecution would only need to present enough evidence for a reasonable juror to find that Defendant had killed Victim.

VI. HEARSAY

A. HEARSAY. [§14.0] Hearsay is probably the most important topic in an evidence course. Certainly, it is the one tested most often, and it is also one of the most confusing. The basic rule concerning hearsay can be stated simply: Hearsay evidence is inadmissible unless it falls within an exception to the hearsay rule. Therefore, it is crucial to understand (a) what constitutes hearsay, and (b) what constitutes the exceptions. This chapter deals with the first of these problems: what constitutes hearsay. Chapter VII covers the hearsay exceptions.

Although it is often relatively easy to tell whether a particular statement is hearsay, it is sometimes quite difficult. Therefore, the **analysis in this chapter** is broken down into **two parts.** The **first** part deals with **basic** hearsay problems. These account for most of the hearsay you are likely to encounter in practice. The **second** part deals with **more sophisticated** (complex, bizarre) hearsay problems. Unfortunately, these are likely to occupy a disproportionate place in your study of hearsay.

1. HEARSAY DEFINED [§14.1]

The federal rules define hearsay as: **"A statement, other than one made by the declarant while testifying at the trial or hearing, offered in evidence for the truth of the matter asserted."** [FRE 801(c)]. As definitions go, this is the pits. It is not very helpful; in fact, it can be downright misleading at times.

2. THE HEARSAY PROBLEM. [§14.2]

Whenever a witness testifies at trial, the witness is under oath and can be cross-examined by adverse parties. The witness's credibility can thus be tested, and the jury can decide whether or not to believe the witness's story. Suppose Witness testifies: "John killed Victim." The probative value of that testimony depends upon Witness's **sincerity** (is she lying?), **communicative ability** (does she really mean that John killed Victim?), **perception** (did she accurately observe that John killed Victim?), and **memory** (does she really remember what happened?). John's lawyer can cross-examine Witness in an effort to show that she is deficient in one or more of these respects (i.e., she's lying, near-sighted, has a terrible memory or an even poorer command of the English language). However, suppose Witness testifies: "My friend [who we'll call Declarant] told me John killed Victim." The cross-examiner's job becomes harder. He can cross-examine Witness to test whether Declarant really made that statement to her. But the probative value of the statement ultimately depends on Declarant's credibility — his sincerity, communicative ability, perception and memory — and he is not there to be cross-examined. Hearsay problems thus arise **when a witness testifies to an out-of-court statement and the probative value of the statement depends on the credibility of the person who made the out-of-court statement.**

3. BASIC HEARSAY. THREE-STEP ANALYSIS. [§14.3]

Most hearsay problems can be answered successfully if you follow these three steps. **(1) Is there an out-of-court statement? If so, (2) What is it** being offered to prove? (3) Does its probative value depend on the credibility of the declarant?

a. Is There an Out-of-Court Statement? [§14.31]

A statement may be (a) **oral** or (b) **written**, or (c) it may take the form of conduct intended as a substitute for words.

> **(1) EXAMPLES. [§14.311]** Witness testifies: (a) "My friend Declarant told me, 'John killed Victim.'" (b) "I received a letter from Declarant which says 'John killed Victim.'" (c) "I asked Declarant whether he knew who killed Victim and he nodded and pointed at a picture of John." In each of these examples, Witness is testifying (in court) to an out-of-court statement made by Declarant.

(2) Articulating the Statement. [§14.312]

In many cases, the statement of the declarant is explicit (e.g., it is placed in quotation marks). In other cases, however, the declarant's statement is masked in a paraphrase and you must try to figure out exactly what the declarant said.

> **(a) EXAMPLE. [§14.3121]** Witness testifies: "Denny complained of headaches." Witness can be cross-examined to be sure that Denny really complained. Denny, however, is the declarant and it is his statement that concerns us for hearsay purposes. Looking at the evidence, it appears that Denny actually said something like, "My head hurts," or "I have a headache." That is Denny's out-of-court statement.

b. What is the Statement Being Offered to Prove? [§14.32]

This is easy, but crucial. The question will either tell you what the statement is being offered to prove, or it will be apparent from the context.

c. Does the Probative Value of the Statement Depend on the Declarant's Credibility? [§14.33]

This is really another way of asking whether the statement is being offered for the truth of the matter asserted. **If all we care about is whether the statement was made by the declarant (i.e., we don't care whether the declarant was lying or mistaken), IT IS NOT HEARSAY. PERIOD. GO NO FURTHER.** Remember, not all out-of-court statements are hearsay. If, however, we do care about the declarant's credibility (i.e., the probative value of the statement depends on whether the declarant was lying or mistaken when he made the statement), it is hearsay — subject to the qualifications we will study concerning More Sophisticated Hearsay. (See §14.5 below.)

B. NOT ALL OUT-OF-COURT STATEMENTS ARE HEARSAY. [§14.34]

If an out-of-court statement is relevant simply because it was made (i.e., all we care about is whether the witness who is relating the out-of-court statement is accurate when he relates the statement), it is not hearsay. There are **several common situations** in which this is the case. You do not need to memorize these. They all have one thing in common: **the out-of-court statement derives its probative value from the fact that it was made, not from the credibility of the declarant.**

(1) Effect of Statement on Listener. [§14.341]

Where the importance of a statement derives from the effect it had on a person who heard it, it is not hearsay. For example, if the issue is whether Defendant acted in good faith in firing Plaintiff, Witness's testimony, "Police Chief told Defendant that Plaintiff had been caught embezzling from his previous employer" is not hearsay. The probative value of this statement does not depend on Police Chief's credibility (i.e., whether Plaintiff had actually been caught embezzling). Rather, the mere fact that this statement was made to Defendant tends to prove he was acting in good faith when he fired Plaintiff.

(2) State of Mind of Declarant. [§14.342]

If the state of mind of a declarant is relevant to the case, a statement made by him may be circumstantial evidence of his state of mind, regardless of its truth. For example, if the issue is whether Defendant and Friend were on good terms, evidence that Friend said to several people, "Defendant is a no-good liar. You can't believe a word he says" is not hearsay. This statement by Friend is circumstantial evidence of Friend's negative attitude toward Defendant. Whether Defendant is a liar or should not be believed is of no consequence. If Friend had been on good terms with Defendant, he would not go around making such statements.

(3) Legally Operative Facts. [§14.343]

The substantive law imbues some statements with legal significance. That is, the fact that the declarant made such a statement has legal significance, regardless of whether the declarant was lying or mistaken. For example, **transactional words,** such as words of contract (e.g., offers, rejections, acceptances, terms), **statements of donative intent** accompanying the delivery of a "gift" (e.g., "I want you to have this car"), and **statements indicating open or hostile possession** (as proof of adverse possession) are not hearsay. Similarly, statements that are themselves actionable, such as words of **libel** or **slander, publicly uttered obscenities,** and **copyrighted passages,** are not hearsay. These are also referred to as **"verbal acts"** or words of **"independent legal significance."**

(4) Impeachment and Rehabilitation. [§14.344]

The prior statements of a witness may be offered to impeach the witness's credibility (by showing he has previously told a different story) or to rehabilitate him (by showing he has told the same story before). In both instances, the prior out-of-court statements of the witness are not being offered for their truth and are not hearsay. There are, however, special rules dealing with the use of such prior statements. These are discussed at §30.0 et seq., §52.0 et seq., and §55.22.

C. SOME DEFINITIONS. 1. "OUT OF COURT". [§14.41]
[§14.4]

Any statement other than one made by a witness while testifying at the present hearing is an "out of court" statement, even if it was made at a previous court hearing. "Out of court" means out of **this** court. The term "extrajudicial statement" is synonymous with "out-of-court statement".

2. "DECLARANT". [§14.42]

The declarant is the person who made the out-of-court statement. **A witness and declarant may be the same person.** With a few exceptions discussed later, it makes no difference whether a witness is relating her own or some other person's out-of-court statements. The hearsay analysis is the same for both. Remember, hearsay is defined as a statement, "other than one made by the declarant while testifying at trial" offered for the truth of the matter asserted. You may think that it doesn't make a lot of sense to treat a witness's own out-of-court statements as hearsay. After all, the witness can be cross-examined about them. You're right — it doesn't make a lot of sense. But, with a few exceptions discussed later, that's the rule.

3. DECLARANT MUST BE A PERSON. [§14.43]

When a witness testifies that a bloodhound sniffed a hat dropped at the scene of a crime, then sniffed several men in a line-up and barked vigorously at the defendant, the witness is testifying to the dog's out-of-court statement. Similarly, when a police officer testifies that he pointed his radar gun at defendant's car and the radar gun flashed "77 mph", he is testifying to the radar gun's out-of-court statement. But neither is hearsay. **The hearsay rule reaches only statements made by persons.** This makes sense because it would do no good to call the bloodhound or radar gun into court for cross-examination. Before testimony about the barking may be introduced, however, evidence will have to be presented regarding the bloodhound's competence to track scents and his handler's competence in interpreting the dog's reactions. In the case of the radar gun, evidence will have to be presented that the gun was in good working order and was operated properly. (See §56.43).

Determine whether the following pieces of evidence are hearsay.

issue

(1) To prove that Defendant was driving while intoxicated the night of May 1, Plaintiff calls Witness to testify, "I saw Defendant down six double scotches and drive off that night."

> **Answer:** Not hearsay. There is no out-of-court statement. Witness is testifying in court as to her out-of-court observations, not as to any out-of-court statement.

(2) To prove that Defendant was driving while intoxicated the night of May 1, Plaintiff calls Witness to testify, "My husband told me he saw Defendant down six double scotches and drive off that night."

> **Answer:** Hearsay. Husband's out-of-court statement to wife is being offered to prove that Defendant was drunk on the night in question and the probative value of Husband's statement depends on his credibility (i.e., we care about whether he was mistaken or lying when he made the statement to his wife).

(3) To prove that Brother survived Sister, Witness testifies, "I saw the crash in which they were killed. I rushed over, saw that Sister was dead and then heard Brother say, 'I am alive.'"

> **Answer:** Not hearsay. Although Brother made the out-of-court statement, "I am alive," this is not hearsay because the probative value of the statement flows from the fact that Brother **spoke** (hence was alive and survived Sister) after Sister died. The **content** of what he said is unimportant. The statement would have been just as probative if Brother had said, "I am dead." This hypo illustrates why the definition of hearsay may be quite misleading. Brother's statement — "I am alive" — appears to be offered for the truth of the matter asserted (i.e., that Brother was still alive). However, it is not hearsay because the probative value of the statement derives solely from the fact that it was made and does not depend on Brother's credibility.

(4) To prove the existence of an oral contract between Plaintiff and Defendant, Witness testifies, "I heard Defendant say to Plaintiff, 'I will sell you this bike for $10.'"

> **Answer:** Not hearsay. Defendant's statement constitutes an offer and therefore qualifies as a legally operative fact.

(5) To prove that there was a puddle in the aisle of defendant supermarket, Witness testifies, "I heard Customer tell the store manager that she almost slipped in a puddle on Aisle 6."

> **Answer:** Hearsay. Because the statement is offered to prove there was a puddle, the probative value of Customer's out-of-court statement depends on her (Customer's) credibility.

(6) To prove that the store manager had been put on notice that there was a puddle in the aisle, Witness testifies, "I heard Customer tell the store manager that she almost slipped in a puddle on Aisle 6."

Answer: Not hearsay. Now this statement is offered to show its effect on the listener (store manager). Customer's statement puts him on notice, even if it turns out to be false.

(7) To prove Defendant committed a crime, Police Officer testifies that Victim pointed out Defendant in a line-up.

Answer: Hearsay. Victim's statement is conduct intended as a substitute for words, the probative value of which clearly depends on whether Victim is mistaken or lying. In other words, it is an out-of-court statement (conduct) offered to show that Defendant was the one who committed a crime, the truth of which depends on Victim's sincerity, perception or memory.

(8) To prove that Defendant ran a red light, Witness testifies, "I told my wife I saw Defendant run the light."

Answer: Hearsay. The witness is relating his own out-of-court statement. The fact that he is also the declarant and is available for cross-examination does not change the hearsay analysis. It is still an out-of-court statement offered to prove that what he said actually occurred.

D. MORE SOPHISTICATED HEARSAY PROBLEMS. [§14.5]

The three-step analysis outlined above will always identify statements that clearly are not hearsay. If the probative value of the statement does not depend on the declarant's credibility, it is not hearsay. Unfortunately, we cannot always say that a statement is hearsay simply because its probative value does depend on the declarant's credibility. Some statements whose probative value depends on the declarant's credibiltiy may not be hearsay. It all depends on the precise way in which hearsay is defined. The common law defined hearsay broadly; the federal rules (and many state codes) define it more narrowly. We can see how the common law and federal rules definitions of hearsay differ by categorizing various kinds of out-of-court statements or conduct. In each of the five categories below, the probative value of the declarant's out-of-court statement or conduct depends on the declarant's credibility. Under the common law definition of hearsay, all five categories of statements or conduct are hearsay. Under the federal rules (and many state codes), however, only the first two are hearsay; statements or conduct that fall in Categories 3, 4, and 5 are not included within the definition of hearsay.

1. CATEGORY 1: EXPLICIT VERBAL ASSERTIONS. [§14.51]

Verbal statements (oral or written) that assert directly what they are introduced to prove.

> **a. EXAMPLE. [§14.511]** To prove that it was raining, Witness testifies that Declarant said, "It is raining outside."

2. CATEGORY 2: NON-VERBAL CONDUCT INTENDED AS AN ASSERTION. [§14.52]

When a person chooses to communicate by a sign or gesture rather than a verbal statement and the act is offered as evidence of the fact the person intended to communicate.

> **a. EXAMPLE. [§14.521]** To prove that it was raining, W testifies, "I asked Declarant what the weather was like and he made a gesture as if he were opening an umbrella."

3. CATEGORY 3: NON-VERBAL CONDUCT NOT INTENDED AS AN ASSERTION. [§14.53]

People often act with no intent to communicate a message. Nevertheless, if an act is offered as evidence that the actor believed something and that his belief was accurate, its probative value depends on his credibility.

> **a. EXAMPLE. [§14.531]** To prove that it was raining, Witness testifies, "I saw Declarant open up his umbrella as he stepped out into the street." This tends to prove it was raining only if we believe that Declarant thought it was raining and was accurate in that belief.

4. CATEGORY 4: NON-ASSERTIVE VERBAL CONDUCT. [§14.54]

The declarant uses words but does not intend to make an assertion. Nevertheless, his statement is offered as evidence of something implicit in the statement.

> **a. EXAMPLE. [§14.541]** To prove that it was raining, Witness testifies, "Just before Declarant left he asked, 'Does anybody have an umbrella I can borrow?'" Although Declarant did not intend to assert it was raining, we may infer that it was raining. But the probative value of this inference flows from his belief that it was raining and the accuracy of that belief.

5. CATEGORY 5: VERBAL ASSERTIONS USED INFERENTIALLY. [§14.55]

Although the declarant makes a verbal assertion, his statement is offered to prove something implicit in his statement rather than the truth of the statement itself.

> **a. EXAMPLE. [§14.551]** To prove it was raining, Witness testifies, "Just before Declarant left he said, 'Damn. I forgot my umbrella.'" This statement is not being offered to prove he forgot his umbrella, but for the unspoken, implicit statement, "it's raining."

6. COMMON LAW VIEW. [§14.56]

It is frequently said that the common law view was that **hearsay comprised all five of the above categories.** This statement is usually based on the famous English case, *Wright v. Tatham.* (See Case Squibs section, *Wright v. Tatham.*)

7. FEDERAL RULES. [§14.57]

The federal rules take a **narrower view** of hearsay. Rule 801 states that **non-verbal conduct not intended as an assertion** is not a "statement" and thus is **not hearsay.** This eliminates Category 3 from the definition of hearsay. Moreover, since Rule 801 defines hearsay as a "statement . . . offered for the truth of the matter asserted," **if there is no assertion** (Category 4) **or** a statement is being **offered to prove something other than what was asserted** (Category 5), it is **not hearsay.** (See Case Squibs section, *United States v. Zenni.*)

8. PROBLEMS. [§14.58]

Unfortunately, it is not always so easy to tell whether there is an assertion (i.e., did the speaker intend to assert something) or exactly what the speaker intended to assert. For example, suppose that in response to the question, "Is defendant a bookie?" the declarant replied, "Is the Pope Catholic?" Presumably, the declarant intended this reply (non-assertive in form) as an assertion and it should be treated as hearsay. Or, to continue with popes, suppose evidence that testator frequently stated, "I am the Pope," is offered to prove the testator's mental incompetence. One could argue that it is not hearsay because it is not offered to prove the truth of what was asserted (i.e., that testator really was the Pope). If, however, you view the statement as asserting "I believe I am the Pope," it is being offered to prove the truth of the assertion. Courts (and evidence professors) are split as to whether such statements should be considered hearsay.

9. SUGGESTED ANALYSIS. [§14.59]

Start with the basic three-step analysis. If you conclude that the probative value of the out-of-court statement does not depend on the declarant's credibility, it is not hearsay, regardless of whether you are working under the common law or the federal rules. Complications arise only when the probative value of the statement depends on the declarant's credibility. In that case, if you are asked whether it is hearsay under the common law, the answer is yes. If you are asked whether it is hearsay under the federal rules, you must look to see if the statement is being offered to prove what the declarant actually said or intended to communicate. If so, it is hearsay. If not, it is not hearsay.

E. NON-HEARSAY BY EXEMPTION. [§14.6]

Recall that in the discussion of basic hearsay we saw that a witness's own out-of-court statements were considered hearsay if offered for the truth of the matter asserted. We said that this did not make a lot of sense. Consequently, some such statements have been exempted from the definition of hearsay. Thus the federal rules and most modern codes declare that **certain types of prior statements of current witnesses are not hearsay.** In addition, **admissions by party opponents** are defined as non-hearsay. These will all be briefly mentioned here, but discussed in greater detail in other sections.

1. PRIOR STATEMENTS OF WITNESSES. [§14.61]

The prior out-of-court statement of a trial witness is not considered hearsay if the witness is **subject to cross-examination** about the particular statement and it falls into one of the three following categories.

a. Prior inconsistent statements. [§14.611]

The witness's out-of-court statement is **inconsistent** with her trial testimony and the **statement was** (a) given under **oath,** (b) subject to the **penalty of perjury,** (c) at some **other trial, hearing, proceeding,** or in a **deposition.** [FRE 801(d)(1)(A)]. (See §§30.2, 52.12).

b. Prior consistent statements. [§14.612]

The witness's out-of-court statement is **consistent** with her trial testimony and is offered to **rebut a charge of recent fabrication or improper motivation or influence.** [FRE 801(d)(1)(B)]. (See §§30.3, 55.22).

c. Prior statement of identification. [§14.613]

The witness's out-of-court statement was one of **identification of a person** made after perceiving the person. [FRE 801(d)(1)(C)]. (See §30.4).

2. ADMISSION BY PARTY OPPONENT. [§14.62]

At common law, admissions by a party opponent are considered exceptions to the hearsay rule. The federal rules and most state codes now define admissions as non-hearsay. [FRE 801(d)(2)]. (See §16.0).

F. OTHER HEARSAY PROBLEMS. [§14.7]

1. MULTIPLE HEARSAY. [§14.71]

Multiple hearsay is sometimes referred to as "hearsay within hearsay" or "totem pole hearsay." This problem arises when evidence contains at least two separate out-of-court statements, each of which is offered for its truth.

> **a. EXAMPLE 1: Oral Assertions. [§14.711]** Witness testifies: "My neighbor, June, told me that her husband, Ward promised to fix the fence." Witness is the witness; there are two declarants and two out-of-court statements: (1) Ward is the declarant of the statement (to June), "I promise to fix the fence." (2) June is the declarant of the statement (to Witness), "Ward promised to fix the fence."

> **b. EXAMPLE 2: Writing. [§14.712]** Sometimes multiple hearsay comes in the form of a writing which incorporates an oral statement. Suppose Plaintiff offers a hospital record prepared by Dr. Feelgood which states: "Klutz says he fell off a scaffold." Again there are two declarants and two out-of-court statements: (1) Klutz is the declarant of the statement (to Dr. Feelgood), "I fell off a scaffold." (2) Dr. Feelgood is the declarant of the statement (made in the record), "Klutz said, 'I fell off a scaffold.'"

c. Approach to Multiple Hearsay. [§14.713]

In dealing with multiple out-of-court statements, you must **analyze each one separately.** First, determine whether each statement is hearsay. Thus, in Example 1, you would ask whether the probative value of Ward's statement to June ("I promise to fix the fence") depends on Ward's credibility. If so, it is hearsay. Then ask if the probative value of June's statement to Witness ("Ward promised to fix the fence") depends on June's credibility (i.e., did Ward really make the statement to June). If so, it is hearsay. **Multiple hearsay will be admissible only if you have a hearsay exception for each layer of hearsay.** Therefore, if both Ward's and June's statements are hearsay, you will need a hearsay exception for Ward's statement and one for June's; otherwise Witness's testimony is inadmissible.

G. LIMITED ADMISSIBILITY. [§14.72]

Whether a given statement is hearsay depends on what it is being offered to prove. Therefore, it should be clear that a single statement may be hearsay if offered for one purpose and not hearsay if offered for another purpose. Suppose Witness testifies, "Shortly before Plaintiff fell, I heard Customer tell Store Manager the floor was slippery on aisle 6." This statement is hearsay if offered to prove the floor was slippery, but not hearsay if offered to prove Store Manager was put on notice. If notice is an issue in the cases, the court will admit such testimony and instruct the jury to consider it only as evidence of notice.

H. SILENCE. [§14.73]

Whether a person's silence should be treated as hearsay is easy to analyze under the federal rules. Silence is a form of non-verbal conduct. Therefore, if it is intended as an assertion (e.g., silence in response to the statement, "Say something if I am wrong"), it falls within Category 2 and is hearsay. If it is not intended as an assertion, it falls within Category 3 and is not hearsay. Under the broader definition of hearsay at common law, it can more easily be viewed as hearsay since the jury is being asked to infer that the silence represents the person's belief about something and that the belief is correct. Nevertheless, once a common law court concludes that a person's silence is sufficiently probative, it rarely excludes it on hearsay grounds. (See Case Squibs section. *Silver v. New York Cent. R. Co.*)

Determine whether the following pieces of evidence are hearsay.

(1) To prove that Defendant assaulted Victim, a little girl, Plaintiff offers testimony that when Victim saw Defendant in a line-up she ran to her mother and clung to her skirt.

> **Answer:** Not hearsay under the federal rules. See Category 3. The girl did not intend by her conduct to make an assertion (i.e., to communicate "He's the one"). Hearsay under the common law.

(2) To prove that Defendant assaulted Victim, a little girl, Plaintiff offers testimony that when Victim saw Defendant in a line-up, she said, "Mommy, don't let that man near me."

> **Answer:** Not hearsay under the federal rules. See Category 4. The statement is not an assertion by Victim and is not being offered for the truth of the matter asserted. Hearsay under the common law.

(3) To prove that Dr. Defendant checked in on Patient Plaintiff earlier in the day, Nurse testifies, "I saw Dr. Defendant and he told me, 'Patient Plaintiff is doing fine.'"

> **Answer:** Not hearsay under the federal rules. This is a verbal assertion used inferentially. Dr. Defendant did not assert that he saw Patient Plaintiff, which is what the statement is being offered to prove. Thus, even though the probative value of Dr. Defendant's out-of-court statement depends upon his credibility (the accuracy of the **implied** statement "I checked in on Plaintiff"), it falls within Category 5 and is not hearsay. Under the more expansive common law view of hearsay, however, Dr. Defendant's statement would be considered hearsay.

(4) To prove that Defendant had run a red light, Plaintiff calls Witness to testify, "Friend told me that Bystander told her that Defendant ran the red light."

> **Answer:** Double hearsay (both federal rules and common law). Two out-of-court statements: Friend's statement to Witness (Bystander told me that Defendant ran the red light) and Bystander's statement to Friend (Defendant ran the red light). The probative value of each depends on the credibility of its declarant. Both are hearsay.

A. HEARSAY EXCEPTIONS IN GENERAL. [§15.0]

Hearsay is inadmissible unless it falls within one of the exceptions to the hearsay rule. [FRE 802]. In fact, there are **numerous exceptions** to the hearsay rule, some of which are obscure and rarely the subject of examination. **Most hearsay exceptions are justified on the ground that particular classes of statements possess inherent guarantees of reliability:** the circumstances are such that the declarant is unlikely to be lying and/or the dangers of misperception or faulty memory are significantly reduced. When a statement is made under such circumstances, the absence of cross-examination is less crucial to reliability and fairness.

1. MNEMONIC DEVICE: [§15.1]

You can remember all the important hearsay exceptions if you remember **"BAD SPLITS, PEPPI"**.

- **B** — Business records
- **A** — Admission by party opponent
- **D** — Dying declaration

- **S** — Spontaneous statements (excited utterance and present sense impression)
- **P** — Past recollection recorded
- **L** — Learned treatise
- **I** — Interest, Declaration against
- **T** — Testimony, Former
- **S** — State of mind or condition

- **P** — Public records
- **E** — Equivalency (residual, catch-all)
- **P** — Prior inconsistent statement
- **P** — Prior consistent statement
- **I** — Identification

Technically, not all of these are hearsay **exceptions.** As mentioned earlier (See §§14.61-14.62), admissions by a party opponent and certain prior statements by a witness (the last three "exceptions" listed in PEPPI) are defined in the federal rules and many state codes as non-hearsay. As a practical matter, however, it makes no difference whether the evidence gets in because it falls within a hearsay exception or because it is considered "non-hearsay."

B. ADMISSION BY PARTY OPPONENT. [§16.0]

This is the most important exception and the one you should **always look for** first. A party may not object on hearsay grounds when his **opponent offers** a statement made by the party. That is, Plaintiff may offer any statement made by Defendant without worrying about a hearsay objection; Defendant may offer any statement made by Plaintiff. There are several idiosyncrasies about the admissions "exception" which should be noted.

1. NOT AN EXCEPTION. [§16.1]

At common law, admissions by a party opponent were considered a hearsay exception. The federal rules [FRE 801(d)(2)] and many state codes now define admissions as non-hearsay.

2. NOT BASED ON RELIABILITY. [§16.2]

Unlike most hearsay exceptions, the admissions "exception" is not justified on the ground that such statements are reliable. Instead, party admissions are admitted because a party should not be allowed to object to his own statements on the ground that he can't cross-examine the declarant (i.e., himself). The theory is one of **responsibility or estoppel:** "you said it, you explain it." **Two consequences** flow from this.

a. Limited Admissibility. [§16.21]

An admission of a party opponent is admissible under this "exception" **only as evidence against the party who made the statement.** This is important in multi-party litigation.

> **(1) EXAMPLE. [§16.211]** In a prosecution against A and B for assault, A's statement, "B and I really roughed up Victim" may be offered by the prosecution against A as his admission, but it is not admissible against B under this "exception."

b. Personal Knowledge Not Required. [§16.22]

A party's statement is admissible even if he had no firsthand knowledge of the facts asserted.

3. "AN ADMISSION IS NOT AN ADMISSION IS NOT AN ADMISSION." [§16.3]

An admission by a party opponent does **not** have to be an actual admission. **Any statement of a party opponent** falls within this exception even if the party wasn't admitting (i.e., confessing) to anything at the time the statement was made. In fact, the statement may have been self-serving at the time it was made. Do not call this the admission against interest exception (there is no such animal) and do not confuse this with the declaration against interest exception. Think of it as the statement by party opponent exception. Remember, a party may offer his opponent's statements pursuant to this exception, but not his own statements.

4. THREE DIFFERENT KINDS OF ADMISSIONS. [§16.4]

There are three different kinds of admissions: (a) a party's **own statements;** (b) **adoptive** admissions; and (c) **vicarious** admissions.

a. Party's Own Statements. [§16.41]

Anything a party says may be offered by his opponent. This includes statements concerning matters about which the party lacked personal knowledge (e.g., Defendant's statement as to how an accident occurred is admissible against her even if it can be shown that Defendant did not see the accident) and expressions of opinion (e.g., "I'm sorry, I was careless, the accident was my fault.").

(1) Statements in Pleadings. [§16.411]

A party's superseded pleadings or pleadings in other actions are admissible against the party as admissions. Moreover, procedural rules dictate that matters admitted in the pleadings or stipulated to on the record are judicial admissions which are conclusive in the proceeding in which they are made. A defendant's plea in a criminal case will qualify as an admission by a party opponent if offered against him in subsequent collateral litigation (e.g., a civil damage action brought by the victim of a criminal assault). However, certain pleas (a withdrawn plea of guilty or a plea of nolo contendere) are rendered inadmissible against the defendant because of an independent rule of evidence that prohibits the use of such pleas on policy grounds. See §10.4 above.

(2) Admissions by Conduct. [§16.412]

When a party acts in such a way that an inference may be drawn that she believes herself to be criminally or civilly liable (i.e., manifests "consciousness of guilt"), the act is often deemed a party admission. Examples of such acts include: (a) flight after the commission of a crime; (b) assumption of a false name; (c) resisting arrest; (d) attempting to bribe an arresting officer, witness or juror; (f) fabrication or destruction of evidence; (g) attempting to commit suicide; and (h) refusing to take a breath test. Note, however, that none of these is really hearsay under modern notions, since none of this conduct was intended by the party to communicate her consciousness of liability. The real question is one of relevancy.

b. Adoptive Admissions. [§16.42]

A party can, in effect, adopt a statement made by another person as her own, and the other person's statement will be treated as the admission of the party. A statement may be adopted by a party either explicitly or tacitly.

---

(1) EXAMPLE: Explicit Adoption: [§16.421] Witness testifies that the defendant told him, "Ask Joe how the accident happened. He knows." Joe's statement to Witness would be considered an adoptive admission by the defendant.

---

(2) Tacit Admissions. [§16.422]

When a statement is made in a party's presence and contains an assertion that a reasonable person would, under the circumstances, deny if it were not true, the party's failure to deny is construed as an adoption of the assertion. This kind of admission is called a "tacit," "adoptive" or "implied" admission, or an "admission by silence."

(a) EXAMPLE: [§16.4221] To prove that Defendant failed to deliver goods by June 1 as promised, Plaintiff testifies,"When I called up Defendant on June 2 I said, 'those goods still haven't arrived and they were supposed to be here yesterday,' and Defendant said nothing in response."

(b) Silence Must Equal Assent. [§16.4222]

A tacit admission will be found only when it is reasonable to view a party's silence as constituting assent to the truth of the assertion made in his presence. Therefore, if there are other plausible reasons that explain the failure to deny, the party's silence does not amount to a tacit admission.

(c) EXAMPLE: [§16.4223] To prove that Defendant stole a lamp, Prosecution calls Witness to testify that she heard Stranger say to Defendant, "you stole my friend's lamp" and that Defendant walked away from Stranger without responding. The evidence shows that Defendant was in a hurry and did not know Stranger. Under these circumstances, it is not reasonable to view Defendant's silence as indicating assent to Stranger's statement.

(d) Constitutional Limitations on Tacit Admissions. [§16.4224]

The Supreme Court has held that an accused's failure to respond to accusations after being arrested and given his *Miranda* warnings cannot be used as a tacit admission against him. *Doyle v. Ohio,* 426 U.S. 610 (1978). As a constitutional matter, however, an accused's **pre-arrest silence** may be used against him. Thus, a defendant who claims self-defense at trial may be impeached by showing that he never raised any claim of self-defense in the two weeks between the killing and his apprehension. *Jenkins v. Anderson,* 447 U.S. 231 (1980). Post-arrest silence may also be used where the defendant has not been given his *Miranda* warnings. *Fletcher v. Weir,* 455 U.S. 603 (1982).

c. Vicarious Admissions. [§16.43]

Statements by a non-party may be attributed to and used against a party under certain circumstances. In these cases the party is **not** the declarant, but because of the special **relationship between the party and the declarant,** it is considered fair to require the party to explain or clarify the declarant's statement.

(1) Vicarious Admissions by Agents and Employees. [§16.431]

A statement by a **party's agent or employee** may be considered the admission of the party. The federal rules and most states have expanded the scope of this "exception."

(a) Common Law View. [§16.4311]

Under the common law, an agent's statement is considered the party's admission only if the agent was authorized to **speak** on behalf of the party. An agent's authority to speak is not necessarily congruent with his authority to act. For example, Driver may be authorized to drive Defendant Company's truck, but not authorized to speak for Defendant Co. about the mechanical condition of the truck. The proponent of this type of vicarious admission must establish Driver's express or implied authority to **speak** for Defendant Co.

(b) Federal Rules. [§16.4312]

The federal rules consider statements made by **someone authorized by a party to speak** to be the party's admissions. [FRE 801(d)(2)(C)]. In addition, under the federal rules, a statement by a party's agent or employee will be considered the party's admission if the statement (a) concerned a **matter within the scope of his agency or employment** and (b) was made while the **speaker was still an agent or employee.** No authority to speak is required. [FRE 801(d)(2)(D)].

(c) Personal Knowledge Requirement. [§16.4313]

Recall that a party may not object on the ground of lack of personal knowledge when it is his own statement that is being offered by his opponent. The law is unclear as to whether such an objection may be made when the statement offered is a vicarious admission. (See Case Squibs section, *Mahlandt v. Wild Canid Survival & Research Center, Inc.*)

(2) Co-Conspirator Admissions. [§16.432]

A statement made by a party's co-conspirator is admissible against the party as a vicarious admission. The proponent of such a statement must show (a) that the **declarant and the party were co-conspirators;** and that the statement was made (b) during the **pendency** of the conspiracy (i.e., while the conspiracy is ongoing) and (c) **in furtherance** of the conspiracy. [FRE 801(d)(2)(E)].

(a) Proof of Conspiracy. [§16.4321]

Many common law courts require that the existence of the conspiracy must be proved by evidence other than the co-conspirator's hearsay statements. In contrast, the Supreme Court has held that such hearsay statements may be considered by the court in deciding whether the proponent has established the requirements for this hearsay "exception." In addition, the Court has held that the existence of the conspiracy need only be established by a preponderance of the evidence. (See Case Squibs Section, *Bourjaily v. United States.*)

(b) Admissible in Non-Conspiracy Cases. [§16.4322]

Note that the admission by co-conspirator "exception" can be used even if the party is not being prosecuted for conspiracy. As long as the proponent of the evidence establishes the requirements for the "exception," it can be used regardless of the kind of case.

(c) Confessions to Police. [§16.4323]

A confession made by a member of a conspiracy to the police will not qualify for admission against fellow conspirators under this "exception." Remember: an admission by co-conspirator must be made in furtherance of the conspiracy. Confessions to police rarely further a conspiracy's goals.

(3) Admissions by Parties in Privity. [§16.433]

Although not included in the federal rules, many states treat statements made by someone in privity with the party as the vicarious admission of the party.

C. HEARSAY EXCEPTIONS: AVAILABILITY IMMATERIAL. [§17.0]

Federal Rule 803 lists several hearsay exceptions which apply regardless of whether the declarant is available to testify at trial.

1. SPONTANEOUS STATEMENTS. [§18.0]

Statements that the declarant makes spontaneously (i.e., before he has had an opportunity to think about what to say) are said to be reliable. **Two related hearsay exceptions** fall within this rationale: (a) **excited utterances** and (b) **present sense impressions.**

a. Excited Utterances. [§18.1]

Both the federal rules [FRE 803(2)] and the common law recognize the excited utterance exception. The exception covers statements (a) made while the declarant was **under the stress of excitement** caused by a startling event or condition (b) that **relate to the event or condition.** In the past, this was sometimes referred to as "res gestae," but that term is now in disfavor.

(1) Rationale. [§18.11]

The stress under which the statement is made is deemed to ensure spontaneity and thus preclude the possibility of fabrication.

(2) Must Relate to Startling Event. [§18.12]

The statement must relate to the startling event or condition. This encompasses not only statements that describe or explain the event, but statements that relate to it in any way. Suppose Declarant is involved in a wreck and blurts out, "I'm in a hurry. I'm trying to reach an important customer". This will be deemed to relate to the startling event (the accident) and will qualify as an excited utterance.

(3) While Under Stress of Excitement. [§18.13]

The statement must be made before the declarant has had time to reflect. Therefore, excited utterances are usually made soon after the exciting event. However, there is **no time requirement** for excited utterances. Thus, a statement made immediately after a period of unconsciousness may qualify as an excited utterance, even if the unconsciousness lasted for hours or days. Particularly in child abuse cases, some courts have been quite lenient in finding that statements made by the child victim several hours, and even days, after the event qualify as excited utterances. (See Case Squib Section, *United States v. Iron Shell.*)

(4) Spontaneity Requirement. [§18.14]

Under the common law, the statement must be "spontaneous" and not a "mere narrative." Thus, statements made in response to a question (e.g., "What happened?") are excluded. The federal rules and most modern courts, however, merely consider such an inquiry as one factor in determining whether the declarant had the opportunity to reflect.

(5) Identity of Declarant Immaterial. [§18.15]

The declarant often is, but need not be, involved in the startling event; he may be a bystander. In addition, the declarant need not be identified. Thus, Witness may testify, "Someone yelled, 'The blue car ran the red light.'"

b. Present Sense Impression. [§18.2]

The federal rules contain an exception for statements that (a) **describe or explain** an event or condition (b) **made while the declarant was perceiving** the event or condition **or immediately thereafter.** [FRE 803(1)]. Although this exception was not widely accepted at common law, a Texas court recognized it in 1942 and many courts have followed suit.

(1) Rationale. [§18.21]

The spontaneity of the statement ensures that the declarant will not have had time to think about what she was going to say, and thus guarantees sincerity. In addition, the danger of memory loss is negligible. Finally, some courts stress that the person who heard the statement is usually in a position to verify its accuracy.

(2) Time Factor. [§18.22]

The statement must be made **while** the event or condition is **being perceived or immediately afterwards.** Only a slight time lapse is allowed.

(3) Must Describe or Explain the Event. [§18.23]

Unlike excited utterances, which may "relate" to the exciting event, present sense impressions must "describe or explain" the event. Thus, present sense impressions are limited to statements like, "The blue car just ran the red light."

(4) Corroboration [§18.24]

Because the justification for the present sense impression is sometimes based in part on the ability of the person who heard the statement to verify its accuracy, some courts require the witness to have been in a position to corroborate the statement. Other courts, and the federal rules, impose no such requirement.

> **(a) EXAMPLE. [§18.241]** Witness testifies, "Victim and I were chatting on the phone. Victim said to me, 'I've got to go. Defendant's at the door.'" Courts that apply a corroboration requirement will exclude such testimony because Witness was not in a position to verify the accuracy of Victim's statement. (How many times have you said to an unwanted caller, "I've got to go. Someone's at the door."?) Federal courts and states that do not apply a corroboration requirement will not hold the statement inadmissible simply because it is uncorroborated. The trial judge may, however, consider the lack of corroboration in determining whether the proponent of the hearsay statement has established that the statement really meets the requirements of the present sense impression exception.

2. STATE OF MIND: MENTAL OR PHYSICAL CONDITION. [§19.0]

The common law and the federal rules recognize a hearsay exception for certain statements by the declarant **relating to her then existing mental, emotional, or physical condition.** [FRE 803(3)]. A **related exception covers statements made for the purpose of medical diagnosis or treatment.** [FRE 803(4)].

a. Present State of Mind. [§19.1]

The state of mind exception covers statements of **intent** ("I plan to go to the store tomorrow"), **belief** ("I think my brakes are bad"), **attitude** ("I don't like him"), **motive** ("I owe him one for that"), **mental feeling** ("I am bored studying evidence"), **pain** ("my head hurts") and **bodily health** ("I have the flu").

(1) Rationale. [§19.11]

A statement relating a present state of mind or physical condition raises no problems of memory or perception. Moreover, since a person's state of mind is often difficult to prove, there is frequently a need for such direct evidence.

(2) Proper Uses of Present State of Mind: To Prove State of Mind Itself. [§19.12]

Where a person's intent, knowledge, belief, attitude, or physical condition is itself a relevant issue, any statement made by the person that **directly** reveals the intent, knowledge, etc. is admissible. Note that the exception requires only that the statement express the declarant's state of mind at the time the statement is made.

> **(a) EXAMPLE. [§19.121]** In an alienation of affections case, to prove that Wife no longer loved Husband, Witness testifies, "Wife told me, 'I hate my Husband.'" This is admissible as a statement of her then existing state of mind toward Husband. Her statement could also be used to infer that she felt that way toward Husband earlier or later in time.

(3) Proper Uses of Present State of Mind: To Prove Conduct of the Declarant. [§19.13]

People follow through on their intentions with sufficient frequency to justify the inference that someone who annouces his intent to do something or go somewhere actually did that thing or went to that place. Therefore, **a statement of an existing intent to do something in the future is admissible under the state of mind exception to prove the declarant actually carried through with his plans.** (See Case Squibs Section, *Mutual Life Ins. Co. v. Hillmon.*)

> **(a) EXAMPLE. [§19.131]** To prove that he was in Cincinnati on June 12, Defendant calls Witness to testify, "On May 25, Defendant told me that he was planning to go to Cincinnati the morning of June 12." This is admissible as a statement of Defendant's existing intent to do something in the future.

(4) Improper Use of Present State of Mind: To Prove Truth of Underlying Facts. [§19.14]

A statement of a currently existing memory or belief may not be used to prove the truth of the **facts remembered or believed.** For example, the statement, "I believe my husband put poison in my drink" is not admissible to prove that the declarant's husband put poison in her drink. (See Case Squibs section, *Shepard v. United States*). Nor may a statement of a present state of mind be used to prove the truth of the **facts underlying the belief.** For example, Victim's statement, "I am afraid of Defendant" would not be admissible to prove that Defendant had actually done anything (such as make threats) to induce such a state of mind. It would, however, be admissible to prove Victim did not voluntarily go out alone with Defendant.

(a) Exception: Statements Relating to a Will. [§19.141]

A statement of memory or belief may be offered to prove the fact remembered or believed if it relates to the **execution, revocation, identification, or terms** of the declarant's will. Thus, Testator's statement "I disinherited my son because he flunked Evidence" would be admissible under this exception.

(5) Controversial Use of Present State of Mind. [§19.15]

It is clear that a declarant's statement of his intent to do something may be offered to prove that he did it. Courts are divided, however, as to whether a declarant's statement may be used to prove **someone else's** conduct. Thus, although Declarant's statement, "I am going downtown tonight to meet Sam" is clearly admissible to prove that Declarant went downtown, its admissibility as proof that Sam went downtown is problematic. (See Case Squibs section, *United States v. Pheaster*.)

(6) State of Mind Exception Distinguished From State of Mind Non-Hearsay. [§19.16]

An out-of-court statement may sometimes provide circumstantial proof of the declarant's state of mind. That is, the fact that the declarant made a particular statement may reveal how the declarant feels about something or someone, regardless of whether the statement is true. Such out-of-court statements are not hearsay because they are not offered for their truth. In contrast, if a declarant makes a direct assertion about her state of mind, and that assertion is being offered for its truth, (i.e., to prove that the declarant possessed the state of mind asserted), the statement is hearsay, but admissible under the state of mind exception.

(a) EXAMPLE. [§19.161] If a father says, "My son is a spendthrift bum," the statement is not hearsay if used only as circumstantial evidence that the father desires to disinherit the son. No one is trying to prove the son is a bum. The fact that the father made that statement tends to prove that he is not well disposed toward his son. On the other hand, if the father says, "I won't leave my son a dime," the statement is a direct assertion of his intentions and bears on the issue of the son's inheritance only if it is true. It is hearsay, but comes in as a statement of a present state of mind.

OUTLINE

b. Statements for Purpose of Medical Diagnosis or Treatment. [§19.2]

The federal rules and many states have departed from the common law in enacting a special hearsay exception for statements made for the purpose of medical diagnosis or treatment. The exception covers statements as to **present symptoms and sensations**, as well as statements regarding **medical history** and **past symptoms and sensations**. In addition, certain statements relating to the **cause of the condition** are admissible under this exception. [FRE 803(4)].

(1) Statements of Present Symptoms, Etc. [§19.21]

The state of mind exception [FRE 803(3)] generally covers statements of **present symptoms, pain, sensations,** or **physical condition.** Under common law, however, courts generally did not admit such statements if they were made to a **non-treating** physician (typically, a physician consulted for purposes of litigation). Nevertheless, juries often learned of such statements since doctors testifying as experts were allowed to refer to them to show the basis of their opinion. Consequently, the FRE and most states reject the common law rule and allow the statements to be admitted, even if made to a consulting physician. The danger that the litigant might make exaggerated claims of pain and symptoms to a non-treating physician may be considered by the jury in deciding what weight to give the evidence.

(2) Statements of Past Symptoms, Etc. [§19.22]

Statements as to a person's **medical history, past symptoms, pain** or **physical condition** ("My back hurt all last month") are admissible if made either for **diagnosis or treatment.** If made to a treating physician, reliability is ensured by the desire to obtain effective treatment. If made to a non-treating physician, admission is justified on the ground that the jury will learn about the statement anyway, since the physician will be able to refer to it in explaining the basis for her opinion. The common law rule does not allow this type of statement, whether made to a treating or non-treating physician.

(3) Statements of Cause. [§19.23]

The federal rule and most states also depart from the common law in allowing statements as to the cause or external source of the pain, symptom, condition, etc. insofar as it is **pertinent to the diagnosis or treatment.**

> **(a) EXAMPLE. [§19.231]** Patient's statement to Doctor, "My neck pains began after I was rear-ended by a blue '57 Chevy that went through a stop sign" will not be admissible to prove the identity of the car or negligence of the driver that rear-ended Patient. Neither the make of car nor the negligence of the driver is pertinent to Patient's diagnosis or treatment. The fact that Patient was rear-ended may, however, be pertinent and that part of the statement may be admissible.

The exception requires only that the statement be made for purpose of medical diagnosis or treatment. Thus, a parent's statement regarding a patient-child's medical history is admissible under this exception.

(5) Need Not Be Made to a Doctor. [§19.25]

The exception covers statements made to hospital attendants, ambulance drivers, nurses, etc. if they are made for the purpose of receiving medical diagnosis or treatment.

(6) Child Abuse Cases. [§19.26]

This exception has been interpreted liberally by many courts to embrace statements made by child abuse victims to physicians. Some courts have even held that statements regarding the **identity** of the assailant are pertinent to diagnosis and treatment and thus admissible. (See Case Squibs section, *United States v. Iron Shell.*)

3. BUSINESS RECORDS. [§20.0]

A written record qualifies for the business records exception if it was (a) the regular practice of the business to **keep** such records and the records were made; (b) in the **regular course** of the business; (c) **at or near the time** of the event or condition recorded; and (d) by an employee with **personal knowledge** of the event or upon information provided by someone with a business duty to report the information. Even if these four requirements are met, however, the record will not qualify if the source of information or the method or circumstances of its preparation indicate a **lack of trustworthiness**. [FRE 803(6)].

a. Mnemonic Device: "KRAP". [§20.1]

To remember the four elements of the business record exception, take the first letter of the first boldfaced word for each of the four requirements: **K**eep; **R**egular course; **A**t or near the time; **P**ersonal knowledge.

b. Rationale. [§20.2]

Business records qualify for a hearsay exception because of their **reliability**. If businesses rely upon such records in their day to day affairs, it is reasonable to assume that they have sufficient incentive to ensure their accuracy.

c. Analysis of Elements. [§20.3]

(1) Personal Knowledge. [§20.31]

This is the most common kind of business record problem tested in law school. Many business record statutes (especially those drafted pre-FRE) provide that the entrant's (i.e., the person who made the record) lack of personal knowledge of the facts recorded goes to the weight, not the admissibility, of the business record. But such language was designed to obviate the need to produce as witnesses every member of a business organization who might have had a part in gathering or transmitting the information entered in the record. As a result, such statutes are not read literally. Rather, it is now well accepted that if the maker of a business record obtains from another person the information recorded, a double hearsay problem arises. Whether the record is admissible depends on the source of the information recorded and the applicability of other hearsay exceptions. (See Case Squibs section, *Johnson v. Lutz*.)

(a) EXAMPLE: [§20.311] Plaintiff offers Police Officer's report, which states, "Shortly after the accident I spoke with Bystander. She told me that the motorcycle ran a red light." If offered to prove the motorcycle ran a red light, this report constitutes double hearsay: the police officer's written statement ("Bystander told me the motorcycle ran a red light") and Bystander's statement to Police Officer ("The motorcycle ran a red light"). This will be admissible only if a hearsay exception can be found for both Police Officer's written out-of-court statement and Bystander's out-of-court statement to Police Officer.

(b) Analysis: Entrant Has Personal Knowledge. [§20.312]

If the maker of the record has personal knowledge of the recorded facts, the personal knowledge requirement is fulfilled.

(i) EXAMPLE. [§20.3121] Police Officer files a report which states, "I saw the motorcycle run the red light and crash into the truck."

(c) Analysis: Information From Someone With Business Duty to Report. [§20.313]

Even if the maker of the record lacks personal knowledge of the recorded facts, if the information comes from someone else who has **a business duty to report the information,** the personal knowledge requirement is fulfilled. This is to align the business record exception with modern business practices in which information may be transmitted through several employees before it is actually recorded (e.g., sales clerk to manager to head of bookkeeping to entrant).

(i) EXAMPLE. [§20.3131] Police Officer files a report which states, "Officer Jones told me that she saw the motorcycle run the red light and crash into the truck."

(d) Analysis: Information From Someone Without Business Duty to Report. [§20.314]

If the maker of the record lacks personal knowledge of the recorded facts and the information comes from someone who is not under any obligation to report the information (e.g., a bystander), the evidence will be inadmissible **unless another hearsay exception can be found** for the other person's statement.

(i) EXAMPLES. [§20.3141] (1) Police Officer files a report which states, "Bystander came running up to me and screamed excitedly, 'The motorcycle ran the light.'" Although this is double hearsay if offered to prove the motorcycle ran the light, Bystander's statement qualifies as an excited utterance and Police Officer's statement qualifies as a business record. The report, therefore, is admissible. (2) Police Officer files a report which states, "Motorcyclist told me that he ran the light." If offered against Motorcyclist, this is admissible because Motorcyclist's statement is an admission by a party opponent and the officer's statement qualifies as a business record.

(e) Analysis: Recorded Information Not Offered For Its Truth. [§20.315]

The multiple hearsay problem arises only if the recorded information that comes from someone other than the entrant is offered for its truth. That is, **if the record is offered merely to show that the "informer" made the statement, there is only one level of hearsay.**

> **(i) EXAMPLE [§20.3151]** Police Officer files a report which states, "Bystander told me, 'The motorcycle ran the light.'" If this is offered merely to prove that Bystander made this statement (not to prove that the motorcycle ran the light), Bystander's statement is not hearsay. Police Officer's statement is hearsay, but qualifies as a business record.

(2) Regular Course of Business. [§20.32]

In order to assure reliability of the record, it must be the type of record regularly kept by the business and it must have been recorded in routine fashion.

(a) Records Made in Contemplation of Litigation. [§20.321]

Courts are suspicious of records that are made with an **eye toward litigation.** (See Case Squibs section, *Palmer v. Hoffman.*) Such records tend to lack the reliability that other, more traditional business records hold.

(3) Lack of Trustworthiness. [§20.33]

Once the proponent of the record shows that the four requirements of the business record exception are met, the record will be admitted **unless** the opponent can show that the **source of information** or the **method or circumstances** surrounding its making indicate a **lack of trustworthiness.** Thus, even if a court concludes that an accident report was made in the regular course of business, it is still likely to exclude it on the grounds of lack of trustworthiness. Occasionally, however, a court finds that an accident report was made under circumstances that betoken no lack of trustworthiness and admits it. (See Case Squibs section, *Lewis v. Baker.*)

(4) Act, Event, Condition, Diagnosis, Opinion. [§20.34]

Many pre-FRE business record statutes permitted business records that memorialized "acts, events, or conditions," and some courts interpreted this to exclude opinions or diagnoses contained in hospital records. **The federal rule and most states now provide that business records may include diagnoses and opinions.**

d. Laying the Foundation. [§20.4]

In order to qualify a record as a business record, the proponent must establish that the elements of the exception ("KRAP") are met. **This may be done by any person who knows how the records are made and kept. It may, but need not,** be done by the maker or the custodian of the record. In addition, the record must be authenticated. That is, it must be shown that the record is what it purports to be (e.g., **a record of the XYZ Corp.**).

OUTLINE

e. Definition of Business. [§20.5]

Business is defined broadly enough to include any organization, entity, or association, whether or not for profit.

f. Absence of Record to Prove Non-Occurrence. [§20.6]

The federal rules [FRE 803(7)] and most states allow reference to business records to **prove the non-occurrence of an event not recorded if it was the practice of the business to record such events.**

4. PUBLIC RECORDS AND REPORTS. [§21.0]

The federal rules and many states now have an expansive exception for public records. Such an exception is justified primarily by the assumption that public officials will perform their duties properly. Under FRE 803(8), the **records and reports of a government agency** are admissible if they set forth information falling within one of **three categories.**

a. Activities of the Agency. [§21.1]

Records setting forth the **agency's own activities** (e.g., Treasury Department records of receipts and disbursements) are admissible. [FRE 803(8)(A)].

b. Matters the Agency is Required to Observe and Report. [§21.1]

Records setting forth **matters that the agency is required by law to observe and report** (e.g., rainfall records of the Weather Bureau) are admissible. This involves the recording of public officials' own first-hand observations. [FRE 803(8)(B)].

(1) But Not in Criminal Cases. [§21.21]

Congress amended this part of the public records exception by **excluding in criminal cases matters observed by police officers and other law enforcement personnel.** [FRE 803(8)(B)]. Courts have tended to give a broad reading to the term "law enforcement personnel." (See Case Squibs section, *United States v. Oates.*)

(2) Well, Sometimes in Criminal Cases. [§21.22]

Notwithstanding the language of FRE 803(8)(B), the courts have admitted records of matters observed by law enforcement personnel in criminal cases **where the matters observed are ministerial in nature,** that is, routine, objective observations made as part of the everyday functioning of the office. For example, courts have admitted Customs Service computer records of license plate numbers of cars crossing the border, reports listing the serial numbers on firearms, and calibration reports of breathalyzer maintenance operators.

(3) Can't Slip It In Through Business Record Exception. [§21.23]

Courts do not allow prosecutors to use the business record exception to circumvent the provision of the public records exception excluding law enforcement records in criminal cases. Thus, if a court finds that a law enforcement record is inadmissible because of this provision in the public records exception, it will not allow the record to be offered under the business records exception. (See Case Squibs section, *United States v. Oates*).

c. Factual Findings. [§21.3]

Reports setting forth the **factual findings that result from an authorized governmental investigation** are admissible (a) in **civil cases** and (b) **against the government in criminal cases.** [FRE 803(8)(C)].

(1) Includes Conclusions As To Fault. [§21.31]

The Supreme Court has held admissible public records setting forth conclusions as to fault (e.g., that pilot error caused an airplane crash), thereby rejecting attempts to give a narrow reading to "factual findings." (See Case Squibs section, *Beech Aircraft Corp. v. Rainey*.)

(2) Excluded If Not Trustworthy. [§21.32]

The opponent of a public report setting forth factual findings may convince a court to exclude the report by demonstrating that the **sources of information** or **other circumstances** (e.g., bias or inexperience of investigator) **indicate a lack of trustworthiness.**

d. Vital Statistics. [§21.4]

A related hearsay exception covers public records of births, deaths, and marriages. [FRE 803(9)].

e. Absence of Record to Prove Non-Occurrence. [§21.5]

As is the case with business records, the absence of a public record about an event may be used to **prove the non-occurrence of the event if reports of such an event are regularly made.** [FRE 803(10)].

5. LEARNED TREATISES. [§22.0]

The common law allows a cross-examiner to impeach an expert witness by pointing out discrepancies between the witness's testimony and statements made in a treatise or article that the witness has relied on. See §56.24 below. The federal rules and many states now have a hearsay exception for statements contained in **published treatises, periodicals,** or **pamphlets** concerning history, medicine or any other science or art.

a. Three Restrictions. [§22.1]

FRE 803(18) contains three important restrictions. First, statements in learned treatises, periodicals and pamphlets may be used **only to the extent that they are called to the attention of an expert on cross-examination or relied upon by an expert in direct exam.** Second, the work must be **established as reliable authority** by:

(a) the witness, (b) another expert, or (c) judicial notice.

Third, statements admitted under this exception may be **read** into evidence but may **not be introduced as exhibits.**

6. PAST RECOLLECTION RECORDED. [§23.0]

The Past Recollection Recorded exception (PRR) allows **a statement previously recorded by a witness to be used at trial when the witness can no longer remember what happened.**

OUTLINE

a. Elements of PRR. [§23.1]

A **recorded statement** concerning a matter is admissible as PRR if the following six requirements are met:

(a) the **declarant testifies** at trial; (b) he once had **personal knowledge** about the matter; (c) he now has **insufficient recollection to testify fully and accurately** about it; (d) he **made or adopted** the statement; (e) while the event was still **fresh** in his memory; and (f) it **accurately reflected his knowledge** at the time. [FRE 803(5)].

(1) Insufficient Recollection. [§23.11]

PRR may be used only when it is necessary. Thus, the witness's ability to remember the facts in question must be exhausted. **If, after reading the statement, the witness states that his memory has been jogged and that he now remembers the facts, PRR cannot be used.** (At that point, the witness's recollection has been refreshed. See §23.5 below.)

(2) Made or Adopted the Statement. [§23.12]

Even if the witness did not create the writing himself, if it was created at his direction (e.g., dictation) or adopted by him (e.g., he reads over and approves the content of someone else's statement), it may qualify as PRR.

b. Rationale. [§23.2]

This exception is justified on the basis of **reliability** and **necessity.** The witness/declarant provides assurances that he recorded the information when it was fresh in his mind and that it is accurate. Given that the witness/declarant no longer remembers the facts, use of the PRR is necessary.

c. May Only Be Read Into Evidence. [§23.3]

A memo that qualifies as PRR may not be introduced as an exhibit. Since it is a substitute for the witness's testimony, the proponent may only have the PRR read to the jury. However, the **opposing party is entitled to examine the memo and introduce it** (e.g., to show that there are erasures or irregularities which cast doubt on its reliability).

d. Contrary to Advertising, Availability of the Declarant Really is Required. [§23.4]

Although PRR is included among the hearsay exceptions in FRE 803 for which the availability of the declarant is said to be immaterial, PRR requires that the declarant be a witness.

e. Present Recollection Refreshed Distinguished. [§23.5]

Past Recollection Recorded is often confused with the similar-sounding Present Recollection Refreshed. Remember, **Past Recollection Recorded** is a **hearsay exception** which allows the use of a previously written statement by a witness who can no longer remember what happened. **Present** Recollection **Refreshed** merely refers to the technique and procedures surrounding an **attempt by counsel to jog a forgetful witness's memory.** This often involves showing the witness a writing that he (or someone else) created, in the hope that the witness will say, "Oh yes. Now I remember." Present Recollection Refreshed does **not** involve a **hearsay** problem and is covered in §46.0 below.

7. CATCH-ALL EXCEPTION: EQUIVALENT TRUSTWORTHINESS. [§24.0]

The federal rules and about half the states include a **"catch-all"** or **"residual"** hearsay exception. Even if the hearsay statement does not fall within a specific hearsay exception, it will be admissible if it possesses **"equivalent circumstantial guarantees of trustworthiness."** (Hence, "equivalency" in the mnemonic. See §15.1 above). In addition to finding "equivalency," the court must find that **four requirements** are met.

a. Must Be Material. [§24.1]

The statement is offered as evidence of a **material fact.** (Since evidence must be relevant to be admissible, this adds nothing.)

b. Must Be Necessary. [§24.2]

The statement must be **more probative** on the point for which it is offered than any other evidence which the proponent can reasonably be expected to come up with.

c. Must Serve Justice. [§24.3]

Admission of the statement must best serve the general purposes of the rules and the interests of justice. (If the other requirements are met, what are the odds that this requirement won't be met?)

d. Notice Requirement. [§24.4]

The proponent must give the adverse party **notice** of (a) the **intention to offer** hearsay under this exception; and (b) the **particulars** of the statement, including the **name and address of the declarant.** The notice must be given sufficiently in advance of trial to afford the opponent a fair opportunity to meet the evidence.

> **NOTE: TWO CATCH-ALL EXCEPTIONS. [§24.5]** Both FRE 803 (availability of declarant immaterial) and FRE 804 (declarant must be unavailable) contain a "catch-all" exception. [FRE 803(24); FRE 804(b)(5)]. Since FRE 803(24) applies even when the declarant is unavailable, it is questionable whether the second "catch-all" exception is necessary.

D. HEARSAY EXCEPTIONS: UNAVAILABILITY REQUIRED. [§25.0]

There are certain hearsay exceptions that apply only if the declarant is unavailable. The four hearsay exceptions that apply only if the declarant is unavailable are: **D**ying declarations; **A**gainst interest declarations; **F**amily and personal history statements; **T**estimony, former. Use the mnemonic **"DAFT"** to remember them.

1. UNAVAILABILITY DEFINED. [§25.1]

The federal rules and most states declare that a declarant is "unavailable" if she (a) is too **ill** to testify or is **dead**; (b) validly asserts a **privilege** not to testify; (c) **refuses to testify** despite being ordered by the court to do so; (d) testifies to a **lack of memory;** or (e) is **absent** and the proponent of the statement **cannot procure her attendance** (i.e., the declarant is outside the court's subpoena power) **or testimony** (i.e., the proponent can't take her deposition). [FRE 804(a)].

a. Mnemonic: "PRIMA". [§25.11]

You can remember the five grounds for unavailability by "PRIMA": **P**rivilege; **R**efusal to testify; **I**ll or dead; **M**emory; **A**bsent.

b. Common Law Compared [§25.12]

Common law states differ as to what constitutes unavailability for hearsay purposes; some jurisdictions even define unavailability differently for different hearsay exceptions. Nevertheless, **the federal rules go beyond many common law jurisdictions in allowing lack of memory and refusal to testify as grounds for unavailability.**

c. Absence as Ground For Unavailability. [§25.13]

If the proponent of a statement tries to show that the declarant is unavailable on the ground that she is absent, the proponent **must show that the declarant's attendance at trial cannot be procured.** In addition, **except** when the proponent is offering the statement under the **former testimony exception,** the proponent **must establish that he could not take the declarant's deposition.** [FRE 804(a)(5)].

d. Proponent Cannot Procure Unavailability. [§25.14]

If the proponent of the statement acts to prevent the declarant from testifying, the proponent cannot claim the declarant is unavailable. [FRE 804(a)].

2. DYING DECLARATIONS. [§26.0]

Statements made by a person who believes his death is imminent are said to be reliable because the person would not want to go to his maker "with a lie on his lips." This is, in large part, the basis for the dying declaration exception.

a. Common Law Version. [§26.1]

Skeptical of the reliability of dying declarations, the common law requires not only that (a) the declarant **believe his death is imminent,** but also (b) that the **statement concern the causes and circumstances of the impending death.** In addition, the common law allows dying declarations to be admitted (c) **only in the homicide prosecution of the declarant's killer.** This latter requirement makes clear that the common law (d) requires that the **declarant be dead.** It also shows that common law courts view the need for the evidence as a major justification for the exception.

b. Federal Rules. [§26.2]

Under FRE 804(b)(2), a statement qualifies as a dying declaration if (a) the declarant made the statement while **believing his death was imminent;** (b) the statement **concerns the causes or circumstances of what he believed to be his impending death;** (c) the declarant is **unavailable** and (d) the statement is offered in a **civil case or any homicide prosecution.**

(1) Federal Rule Compared With Common Law. [§26.21]

FRE 804(b)(2) broadens the dying declaration exception in two ways. First, although the **declarant** must be unavailable, he **need not be dead.** Second, dying declarations are **admissible in all civil cases and**

criminal homicide prosecutions. Several states have expanded the exception still further and allow dying declarations in all cases, civil and criminal.

> **(a) EXAMPLE. [§26.211]** Victim 1 and Victim 2 are shot by an assailant. Victim 1 tells Witness, "I'm a goner — Defendant shot us", and lapses into unconsciousness. Victim 1 does not die but remains in a coma. At Defendant's trial for the murder of Victim 2 (who did die), Witness's testimony as to Victim 1's statement would be admissible under the federal rules but not under the common law.

(2) Statement Must Concern Circumstances of Death. [§26.22]

The statement must relate to the causes or circumstances surrounding the declarant's death (or what he believed to be his imminent death). If the declarant is dying of cancer, his statement, "Defendant killed my friend Joe", will not qualify as a dying declaration.

(3) Declarant Must Be Ready to "Kick the Bucket". [§26.23]

All jurisdictions require that the statement be made with **a conscious, hopeless expectation of impending death.** In a law school exam, it must be made fairly clear that such an expectation exists. Remember that the court decides whether a statement qualifies under a hearsay exception, so the court must be satisfied that the declarant believed his death was imminent. If the facts are not clear, stress that (a) it is the court's decision and, (b) the court may consider hearsay in making its decision. Then discuss the facts that point toward and against the statement qualifying as a dying declaration.

3. DECLARATION AGAINST INTEREST. [§27.0]

Under common law, a statement qualifies for the declaration against interest exception if it was (a) against the declarant's **pecuniary** (financial) or **proprietary** (property) interest (b) **at the time the statement was made**; and (c) the declarant is **unavailable.** The federal rules and most states have broadened this exception slightly by including statements that are against a declarant's **penal interest** as well. [FRE 804(b)(2)].

a. Rationale. [§27.1]

This exception is premised on the notion that a person ordinarily doesn't say something adverse to her own interest unless it is true. The unavailability requirement assures that this hearsay exception will be used only when necessary.

b. Analysis of Elements. [§27.2]

(1) Unavailability. [§27.21]

Declarations against interest are admissible only when the declarant is unavailable.

(2) When Made. [§27.22]

The statement must have been against the declarant's interest **at the time the statement was made.** Look at the factual context of the statement to determine whether it is against interest and whether the declarant knew it. Statements that on their face appear to be against interest may not be so if other facts indicate that the declarant had not thought of possible adverse consequences or may have viewed the statement as self-serving.

(3) Pecuniary or Proprietary Interest. [§27.23]

A statement is against a person's pecuniary or proprietary interest when the person acknowledges facts that might adversely affect her financial well-being (e.g., "I owe X $100" or a receipt acknowledging payment) or limit her property rights (e.g., "I don't own Blackacre; X does").

(4) Civil Liability. [§27.24]

The federal rules and many states also include statements that would tend either to **subject the declarant to civil liability** (e.g., "the accident was my fault") or **render invalid a claim** by the declarant against another (e.g., "I knew the salesman was lying through his teeth when he told me the car had only 40,000 miles on it").

(5) Criminal Liability. [§27.25]

The federal rules and many states now allow the use of declarations against penal interest, i.e., **statements that tend to subject the declarant to criminal liability.** Traditionally, courts did not allow such statements because of the fear that criminal defendants could too easily establish reasonable doubt by getting a friend to testify, "I heard X say that he committed the crime." Consequently, the federal rules allow the use of **declarations against penal interest to exculpate (exonerate) an accused only when corroborating circumstances clearly indicate the trustworthiness of the statement.** Although the federal rule places no such limitation on the use of declarations against penal interest offered to **inculpate** an accused (e.g., "Accused and I committed the crime"), the Confrontation Clause may do so. (See §§38.2-38.232 below.)

(6) Social Interest. [§27.26]

A few states allow statements by a declarant that would tend to subject her to **hatred, ridicule, or disgrace.**

(7) Mixed Motives. [§27.27]

A statement against the declarant's interest may also contain collateral statements concerning other people's involvement or non-involvement in the occurrence. The collateral portions of the statement may themselves be (a) disserving as to the declarant's interest, (b) neutral as to the declarant's interest, or (c) self-serving as to the declarant. Whether the collateral portion of such a statement may be offered on behalf of or against a third party named in the statement will depend on how the collateral portion is viewed. (Remember, when the declarant's statement is offered as evidence against the declarant himsef it will be admissible as an admission by party opponent.)

(a) EXAMPLE — Disserving: [§27.271] Declarant, who is suspected of being only a small-time drug dealer, makes statements describing how a major drug-smuggling scheme works and naming some of the other key participants in the scheme. The mention of the other participants may be disserving to Declarant in that he thereby inculpates himself on conspiracy and possibly other charges.

(b) EXAMPLE — Neutral: [§27.272] Declarant makes a statement, "Joe and I robbed the Seven-Eleven last week. Defendant was not involved." Although the part of the statement in which Declarant acknowledges that he robbed the Seven-Eleven is clearly a declaration against his penal interest, the portion that absolves Defendant of any involvement is neutral as to Declarant's interest. The part that implicates Joe may also be neutral, except insofar as it might tend to subject Declarant to conspiracy charges in addition to the robbery charge.

(c) EXAMPLE — Self-Serving: [§27.273] Declarant makes a statement, "Joe and I robbed the Seven-Eleven last week. Joe shot the clerk. I was only standing watch; I didn't even know he had a gun." The first sentence is against Declarant's interest. The balance of the statement, however, tends to be self-serving.

Courts ordinarily will not admit self-serving collateral statements made during the course of a larger declaration against interest. They will admit collateral portions naming third parties if those portions are actually disserving to the declarant. Disagreement arises, however, over whether to admit neutral collateral statements. Traditionally, many courts have been willing to admit a declaration against interest not only to prove the facts related in the immediately disserving portion, but to prove the facts related in the collateral parts of the statement as well. (See Case Squibs section, *United States v. Barrett*.) The United States Supreme Court recently ruled, however, that the declaration against interest exception reaches only those parts of a statement that are disserving to the declarant. It does not sanction the admission of neutral or self-serving statements made in the course of a broader narrative that is generally disserving. (See Case Squibs section, *Williamson v. United States*.)

(8) Custodial Confessions. [§27.3]

The Supreme Court and many other courts have questioned whether a confession made by a suspect while under arrest which implicates others should qualify as a declaration against interest. Because a person in that circumstance has a strong motivation to curry favor with the prosecution, any collateral part that appears to cast blame on others is of dubious reliability and will ordinarily be excluded. In fact, the trial judge must question whether even the facially disserving part was truly disserving. (See Case Squibs section, *Williamson v. United States*.)

c. Declarations Against Interest vs. Admissions. [§27.4]

A declaration against interest must be disserving to the declarant at the time the statement is made. An admission by a party opponent need not be. A declaration against interest is admissible only when the declarant is unavailable. Admissions are admissible against a party opponent regardless of the availability of the declarant. (Remember the party opponent may be a corporation and its admission may be made by an employee). Finally, declarations against interest are admitted because they are reliable and so are admissible against all parties to a multi-party action. Admissions are admitted because of estoppel and are admissible only against the party opponent.

4. FORMER TESTIMONY. [§28.0]

The former testimony exception comes into play when the out-of-court statement that is now being offered was itself made as testimony in another hearing or deposition. If certain requirements are met, such statements are deemed sufficiently reliable to be admitted. [FRE 804(b)(1)].

a. Other Hearing or Deposition. [§28.1]

The former testimony may have been given at an earlier trial of the same case, the trial of another case, a deposition taken in connection with the same or another case, or at some other proceeding. It must have been given under oath.

b. Unavailability Required. [§28.2]

The declarant (i.e., the witness in the earlier hearing) must now be unavailable. The preference is still for live testimony.

c. Opportunity and Motive to Develop the Testimony. [§28.3]

Former testimony is admissible only if the party **against whom it is now being offered** had (a) the **opportunity** and (b) the **motive** to develop the testimony in the former hearing in much the same way that it would develop the testimony if the declarant were testifying in the current proceeding. This is what gives the former testimony its aura of reliability: the fact that the party against whom it is now being offered had the chance and the incentive to probe the witness's story at the earlier hearing. (See Case Squibs section, *United States v. Salerno.*)

(1) Predecessor in Interest Okay for Civil Cases. [§28.31]

In addition, the federal rules provide that in **civil cases,** even if the party against whom the testimony is now being offered did not have the opportunity and motive to develop the testimony at the earlier hearing, the former testimony is admissible if a **predecessor in interest of the party** had the opportunity and motive to do so. The meaning of predecessor in interest is somewhat cloudy. One reading is that the predecessor in interest must be someone in privity with the party against whom the testimony is now being offered. Federal courts have tended to interpret the requirement more loosely, requiring only that the predecessor in interest be someone who had a similar interest in developing the testimony. (See Case Squibs section, *Lloyd v. American Export Lines, Inc.*)

> **(a) EXAMPLE. [§28.311]** Arnold and Brenda are injured by Defendant's train at the same time. They bring separate actions against Defendant. In *Arnold v. Defendant,* Arnold testifies against Defendant. Arnold dies before Brenda's case goes to trial. In *Brenda v. Defendant,* Brenda offers Arnold's former testimony. It is admissible because Defendant, the party against whom it is now being offered, had the opportunity and motive to develop Arnold's testimony in *Arnold v. Defendant.*

> **(b) EXAMPLE. [§28.312]** Arnold and Brenda are injured by Defendant's train at the same time. They bring separate actions against Defendant. In *Arnold v. Defendant,* Witness testifies against Arnold. Witness dies before Brenda's case goes to trial. In *Brenda*

> *v. Defendant*, Defendant offers Witness's former testimony. It may be admissible. Although Brenda, the party against whom the testimony is now being offered, did not have the opportunity to develop Witness's testimony (since Brenda was not a party in *Arnold v. Defendant*), Arnold had the opportunity and the same motive to develop the testimony that Brenda would now have. If Arnold is considered Brenda's predecessor in interest (a matter of debate), Witness's former testimony would be admissible under the federal rules because this is a civil case.

(c) Former Testimony Need Not Have Been Developed. [§28.32]

The rule requires only that the party against whom the testimony is now offered (or, in a civil case, a predecessor in interest) have had **an opportunity** to develop the former testimony. The failure to take advantage of the opportunity does not render the exception inapplicable. Of course, the party may now argue that the failure to examine the declarant in the former proceeding is evidence of a lack of motive to develop the testimony in that proceeding.

d. Common Law Approach. [§28.4]

The majority common law rule is that former testimony is admissible only if the issues and parties in the former proceeding are identical to those at the trial in which the former testimony is now being offered. As indicated above, the federal rules depart from this approach, and so have many states.

e. Introduction of Former Testimony. [§28.5]

The normal mode of introducing former testimony is to have counsel or a witness **read from the transcript** of the earlier hearing. Beware that this involves double hearsay; the transcript is itself the court reporter's out-of-court statement, "This is what the witness said." Typically, the transcript will qualify as a business record.

5. STATEMENTS OF PERSONAL OR FAMILY HISTORY. [§29.0]

This is the last hearsay exception that requires unavailability of the declarant. It is not an important exception, however, and will be covered with other unimportant exceptions in §§32.0-32.13 below.

E. PRIOR STATEMENTS OF A WITNESS. [§30.0]

Recall that in the discussion of what is hearsay, we pointed out that **a witness can also be a hearsay declarant.** That is, a witness's own out-of-court statements can be hearsay even though the witness can be cross-examined about those statements. See §14.42 above. Because that does not make a lot of sense, the federal rules and many states now **exempt from the hearsay rule three kinds of statements previously made by a witness.** Technically, these are not hearsay exceptions. As is the case with admissions by a party opponent, they are simply defined as non-hearsay.

1. DECLARANT MUST TESTIFY AND BE SUBJECT TO CROSS-EXAMINATION. [§30.1]

These three hearsay exemptions cover only out-of-court statements made by someone who testifies at the current trial. In other words, they cover only statements by a declarant who is also a witness at the current trial. In addition, the declarant/witness must be subject, at the current trial, to cross-examination about the prior statement. A witness is "subject to cross-examination concerning the statement" even when the witness has suffered a memory loss and is unable to respond substantively to questions about the statement. (See Case Squibs section, *United States v. Owens*.)

a. Certain Prior Inconsistent Statements. [§30.2]

Recall that a witness may be impeached by showing that he has previously made statements inconsistent with his trial testimony. Under FRE 801(d)(1)(A), however, some prior inconsistent statements may be used not only for impeachment purposes, but as substantive evidence as well. If the **prior inconsistent statement** of the witness was made (a) **under oath,** (b) **subject to the penalty of perjury,** (c) **at an earlier trial, hearing, or other proceeding, or in a deposition,** it is defined as non-hearsay and may be used for its truth. For an example of this, see §52.121 below. Note that grand jury testimony meets these requirements. Thus, if a witness's trial testimony is inconsistent with his testimony before the grand jury, the grand jury testimony may be used not only to impeach him, but as substantive evidence as well.

b. Certain Prior Consistent Statements. [§30.3]

A witness may sometimes be rehabilitated by showing that he has previously made statements consistent with his trial testimony. Federal Rule 801(d)(1)(B) provides that certain **prior consistent statements** are non-hearsay and thus may be used as substantive evidence as well. The prior statement will qualify if it (a) is **consistent with the witness's trial testimony** and (b) is offered to **rebut a charge** (express or implied) that the witness either has **recently fabricated his testimony or is testifying from an improper motive or influence.** The prior consistent statement must have been made, however, before the motive to fabricate the story or the improper influence arose. See §55.22 below.

c. Prior Statements of Identification. [§30.4]

A witness's out-of-court **identification of a person** made after perceiving him is defined as non-hearsay in Federal Rule 801(d)(1)(C). Thus, the fact that a witness earlier picked the defendant out of a line-up is admissible not only to rehabilitate the witness (e.g., if the witness's ability to identify the defendant has been attacked) but also as substantive evidence (i.e., as evidence that the out-of-court identification of defendant is true). (See Case Squibs section, *United States v. Owens*.)

2. NOT REALLY HEARSAY EXCEPTIONS. [§30.5]

Remember, these three types of prior statements of witnesses are defined as non-hearsay and are technically not hearsay exceptions. This is of no practical importance (except perhaps on a law school exam).

F. MISCELLANEOUS EXCEPTIONS. [§31.0]

There are many relatively unimportant hearsay exceptions, most of which never see the light of day on a law school exam. Just in case, here they are.

1. PERSONAL OR FAMILY HISTORY. [§32.0]

A number of hearsay exceptions may be used to prove matters relating to someone's personal or family history.

a. Statements Regarding Personal or Family History. [§32.1]

Statements concerning either the declarant's own personal or family history or another person's personal or family history are admissible under FRE 804(b)(4).

(1) Declarant's Own History. [§32.11]

This exception covers statements concerning the declarant's own birth, adoption, marriage, divorce, legitimacy, relationship by blood, adoption or marriage, ancestry, or other similar fact. In contrast to the common law, the federal rule does not require the declarant to show that he had personal knowledge about the matter.

(2) Another's History. [§32.12]

The exception also covers statements concerning someone else's personal or family history (the above-stated matters plus the person's death) if the declarant was (a) **related to the other person** by blood, adoption or marriage or (b) was so **intimately associated** with the other's family as to be likely to have accurate information. Personal knowledge on the part of the declarant is required here.

(3) Declarant Must Be Unavailable. [§32.13]

This is one of the exceptions that apply only if the declarant is unavailable to testify.

b. Records of Vital Statistics. [§32.2]

Records of vital statistics — births, fetal deaths, deaths, marriages — are admissible if the report thereof was made to a public office pursuant to the requirements of law. [FRE 803(9)]. The person who reported the information need not herself have been a public official.

c. Records of Religious Organizations. [§32.3]

Statements contained in a **regularly kept record** of a religious organization **concerning personal or family history** such as births, deaths, marriages, divorces, deaths, legitimacy, ancestry, or relationship by blood or marriage are admissible under FRE 803(11).

d. Marriage, Baptismal, and Similar Certificates. [§32.4]

FRE 803(12) creates an exception for statements of fact contained in a certificate that the maker performed (a) a marriage or other ceremony or (b) administered a sacrament. The **maker** of the certificate must be a **clergyman, public official, or other person authorized** by the religious organization or law to perform the act certified. In addition, the certificate must have been made at the time of the act or within a reasonable time afterwards.

e. Family Records. [§32.5]

FRE 803(13) creates an exception for statements of fact concerning personal or family history found in family Bibles, genealogies, charts, inscriptions on family portraits, engravings on rings, urns, crypts, or tombstones, or the like.

f. Reputation. [§32.6]

FRE 803(19) creates an exception for a person's reputation concerning matters of his personal or family history. The reputation may exist among members of the person's family, among his associates, or in the community.

g. Judgments. [§32.7]

Under FRE 803(23), a prior judgment may be used as proof of matters of personal or family history if the particular matter was essential to the prior judgment.

2. ANCIENT DOCUMENTS. [§33.0]

If a document is old enough, statements in it are unlikely to have been made with a motive to falsify arising from impending litigation. Therefore, under FRE 803(16) a hearsay exception exists for statements contained in documents that are **at least 20 years old** and have been **authenticated.** This reduces the common law time period, which was 30 years.

3. PROPERTY INTERESTS. [§34.0]

Several exceptions may be used to prove facts relating to property or interests in property.

a. Records of Documents Affecting Property Interests. [§34.1]

If a record of a document that purports to establish or affect an interest in property is (a) the record of a public office and (b) local law authorizes the recording of such documents in that kind of office, the record may be used as proof of the **contents of the original** recorded document and of its **execution and delivery** by each person by whom it purports to have been executed. [FRE 803(14)].

b. Statements Contained in Documents Affecting Property Interests. [§34.2]

Under FRE 803(15), a hearsay exception is created for statements contained in documents that purport to establish or affect an interest in property **if the matter relates to the purpose of the document** (e.g., a deed recites that the grantors are all heirs of the last record owner). The exception cannot be used, however, if dealings by the property owners since the document was made have been inconsistent with the truth of the statement.

c. Reputation. [§34.3]

FRE 803(20) creates an exception for the reputation in the community as to boundaries of or customs affecting lands in the community.

d. Judgments. [§34.4]

Judgments may be used as proof of boundaries if such matters were essential to the judgment. [FRE 803(23)].

4. MARKET REPORTS AND COMMERCIAL PUBLICATIONS. [§35.0]

"Market quotations, tabulations, lists, directories, or other published compilations, generally used and relied upon by the public or by persons in particular occupations" are admissible. [FRE 803(17)].

5. REPUTATION. [§36.0]

Reputation evidence may be used for several different purposes. Some are discussed above: reputation for personal or family history and as to land boundaries and customs. Reputation evidence may also be used to prove **events of general history** important to the community, state or nation. [FRE 803(20)]. Finally, reputation evidence may be used to prove a **person's character.** [FRE 803(21)]. Recall, however, that evidence of a person's character is admissible only for certain purposes.

6. JUDGMENT OF PREVIOUS CONVICTION. [§37.0]

Evidence of a final judgment adjudging a person guilty of **a felony** is admissible to prove **any fact essential to sustain the judgment,** with certain limitations. First, this exception applies only if the judgment was entered after a trial or upon a guilty plea; it does not apply where the conviction was entered upon a plea of nolo contendere. Second, in criminal cases, the government may not use the fact that some person other than the accused has been convicted of a felony as proof of some fact that was essential to sustain that conviction. The government may, however, use another person's convictions for impeachment purposes.

> **a. EXAMPLE. [§37.1]** Defendant is being prosecuted as an accomplice to a robbery committed by Cohort. The prosecution may not offer evidence that Cohort was convicted of the robbery as proof that the robbery occurred and that Cohort was involved. The prosecution may, however, impeach defense witnesses with their prior convictions pursuant to Rule 609 (the rule governing impeachment with convictions).

G. CONFRONTATION CLAUSE. [§38.0]

The Sixth Amendment to the Constitution guarantees a criminal defendant the right "to be confronted with the witnesses against him." The Confrontation Clause limits the admissibility of hearsay **against a criminal defendant,** although it does not stand as an absolute bar to its admissibility. In recent years, the Supreme Court has issued a number of opinions that are beginning to clarify the extent to which the Confrontation Clause limits the prosecution's ability to introduce hearsay evidence. The simplest case is where the hearsay declarant testifies at trial and is subject to cross-examination.

1. NO CONFRONTATION CLAUSE PROBLEM IF HEARSAY DECLARANT TESTIFIES. [§38.1]

If the hearsay declarant testifies at the trial and can be cross-examined about his hearsay statements, there is no Confrontation Clause problem. This is true even if the declarant has no memory of the underlying event. (See Case Squibs section, *California v. Green, United States v. Owens.*)

2. IF DECLARANT DOES NOT TESTIFY: EARLY TWO-PART TEST. [§38.2]

In the early 1980's, the Supreme Court seemed to embark on a two-part test for Confrontation Clause analysis. In *Ohio v. Roberts,* 448 U.S. 56 (1980), the Court stated that the Confrontation Clause demanded first, that if the prosecution did not produce the declarant at trial it must demonstrate that the declarant was **unavailable** to testify at trial. Second, the hearsay must be **reliable**. (See Case Squibs section, *Ohio v. Roberts*.)

3. IF DECLARANT DOES NOT TESTIFY: MORE RECENT CASES. [§38.3]

More recently, the Court has indicated that the hearsay (other than that offered under the former testimony exception) may be admitted even if the prosecution does not produce the declarant and he is available to testify. In *United States v. Inadi*, 475 U.S. 387 (1986), the Court held that the hearsay statements of a co-conspirator of the defendant, offered as admissions by a party opponent, could be used against the defendant even though the prosecution chose not to call the declarant. Following that, in *White v. Illinois*, 502 U.S. 346 (1992), the Supreme Court stated that the *Ohio v. Roberts* unavailability requirement applies only when the hearsay statement was made in the course of a prior judicial proceeding. The court then held that the prosecution need not produce the declarant or demonstrate her unavailability before offering her hearsay statements under the exceptions for excited utterances and statements made for the purpose of receiving medical care. (See Case Squibs section, *Ohio v. Roberts, U.S. v. Inadi, White v. Illinois*.)

Note, of course, that the former testimony exception itself requires unavailability. Nothing would prevent a state, however, from creating a former testimony exception that did not itself require unavailability.

a. Hearsay Must Be Reliable. [§38.31]

If the declarant does not testify, the hearsay must be reliable to avoid a Confrontation Clause problem. Reliability may be established in either of two ways.

(1) Firmly Rooted Hearsay Exception. [§38.311]

If the hearsay falls within a firmly rooted hearsay exception, it is deemed reliable. The Court has sometimes looked to the length of time that a particular hearsay exception has been accepted. (See Case Squibs, *Bourjaily v. United States, White v. Illinois*.) But the Court has also held that, based on its widespread acceptance, the exception for statements for the purpose of medical diagnosis and treatment is firmly-rooted. (See Case Squibs section, *White v. Illinois*.)

(2) Particularized Guarantee of Trustworthiness. [§38.312]

If the hearsay does not fall within a firmly rooted hearsay exception, the prosecution must show that the statement possesses particularized guarantees of trustworthiness. That is, the circumstances surrounding the making of the statement must tend to show the statement's reliability. (See Case Squibs section, *Idaho v. Wright*.)

PROBLEM 1. Plaintiff sues Driver and Emmo Corp. (Driver's employer) for injuries to him and for the death of his wife Ruth resulting from a collision between Driver's truck and Plaintiff's car on December 3, 1989. Determine the admissibility of the following evidence.

(1) Plaintiff testifies that after the accident Driver said, "It wasn't my fault, the brakes failed."

Answer: Admissible against Driver as an admission by party opponent, even though at first glance it appears to an exculpatory statement. An admission need not be, or appear to be, against interest when made. Under the FRE, the statement is also admissible against Emmo Corp. as a vicarious admission. Driver was an employee of Emmo when he made the statement, and it concerns a matter within the scope of Driver's employment. At common law, the statement would not be admissible as a vicarious admission of Emmo without proof that Driver was authorized to speak on behalf of the company with regard to defects in his truck.

(2) Plaintiff calls Witness to testify that he was present at the scene of the accident. Although he was looking the other way, just after hearing the sound of the collision, he heard a voice scream, "That truck went barreling through the light."

Answer: Admissible as an excited utterance. There is no requirement that the declarant of the excited utterance be identified.

(3) Witness further testifies, "Just after the collision, Observer came up to me and said, 'I just heard Driver say that he dozed off at the wheel just before the accident.'"

Answer: This is double hearsay. The statement attributed to Driver is an admission by party opponent (Driver's own statement and a vicarious admission against Emmo). But the statement by Observer to Witness reporting what Driver said is also hearsay. Since there is no exception to cover this level of hearsay (there is no indication that this was an excited utterance), the testimony is inadmissible.

(4) Plaintiff testifies that just before Ruth died she said, "Get a priest; I'm going fast. Why did that truck driver have to be so careless? He went right through the red light and hit us."

Answer: Admissible as a dying declaration under the FRE, but not admissible at common law, which limits dying declarations to homicide actions.

(5) Plaintiff offers the accident report of Police Officer Smith which states, "I arrived at the scene of the accident two minutes after it was reported. I noticed five empty beer cans in the passenger compartment of Driver's truck and smelled alcohol on his breath."

Answer: Admissible as a business record if Plaintiff satisfies the court that it is the regular practice of the police department to keep such records; that it was made in the regular course of business; that Officer Smith made the report at or near the time of the accident; and that Officer Smith had personal knowledge of the events reported.

OUTLINE

(6) Police Officer Smith's report also states, "I interviewed Observer who told me that she saw Driver go through the red light."

> **Answer:** This is double hearsay and inadmissible. Officer Smith's report that Observer made such a statement is covered by the business record exception. However, the substance of what Observer said is hearsay for which there is no apparent exception.

(7) To prove the extent of his injuries and that his neck pains were caused solely by the accident, Plaintiff calls his physician, Dr. Fairby, to testify, "Over the course of several months of treatment, Plaintiff consistently complained to me of severe pain when he moved his neck. He told me that he had never experienced any such pain prior to the accident."

> **Answer:** Plaintiff's statements concerning the severe pain are admissible as statements of then existing physical condition. His statement that he had never before experienced such pain is admissible under the FRE as a statement of medical history made for purposes of diagnosis or treatment. This latter statement, however, is inadmissible under the common law.

PROBLEM 2. Defendant is charged with armed robbery. Determine the admissibility of each of the following statements.

(1) The prosecution offers evidence that after the robbery, Defendant bought a ticket to Argentina.

> **Answer:** This is admissible. It is not hearsay under the FRE because the act of purchasing a ticket to Argentina was not intended as an assertion of guilt and thus does not constitute a "statement" as that term is defined in FRE 801. Even if considered hearsay under common law (following the logic of *Wright v. Tatum*), it is admissible as an admission by party opponent.

(2) The prosecution calls Witness to testify. Witness testifies that he did not see Defendant the night of the robbery, and that Defendant never told him anything about it. The prosecution then offers a transcript of Witness's grand jury testimony in which he said, "Defendant came to my house the night of the robbery and told me he had stolen more than a thousand dollars from the Seven-Eleven."

> **Answer:** This is inadmissible hearsay at common law. In fact, as will be seen later (see §49.1 below), it is improper impeachment unless the prosecution shows it was surprised and injured by Witness's testimony. Under the FRE, however, this is admissible both to impeach Witness and to prove that Defendant stole more than a thousand dollars from the Seven Eleven. A witness's prior inconsistent statement is defined as non-hearsay if the witness is available to be cross-examined about the statement and the statement was (a) made under oath (b) subject to the penalty of perjury (c) at an earlier trial, hearing, or other proceeding, or in a deposition. Witness's grand jury testimony meets these requirements. Note that this question involves two other levels of hearsay. In his grand jury testimony Witness reports what Defendant told him. This is covered by the admission by party opponent exception. Further, the prosecution uses a transcript (i.e., the court reporter's statement, "This is what Witness said") to prove what the Witness told the grand jury. This is covered by the business record exception.

(3) Defendant calls Crony to testify, "My old friend Stark told me that he was the one who held up the Seven Eleven and that Defendant had nothing to do with it." Stark died two months prior to the trial.

Answer: Stark's declaration against penal interest is being offered to exculpate Defendant. Although the federal rules, unlike the common law, include declarations against penal interest in the declaration against interest exception, the statement would be inadmissible for two reasons. First, under the Supreme Court's decision in *Williamson,* the neutral, collateral part of the statement ("Defendant had nothing to do with it") does not qualify as a declaration against interest. Second, even if it did, declarations against penal interest must be corroborated if offered to exculpate the accused. Therefore, unless Defendant offers evidence to corroborate the trustworthiness of Stark's declaration against interest, it would be inadmissible for this second reason as well.

(4) Defendant had been tried earlier on this charge, but the first trial ended in a mistrial. Defendant now calls Cranston to testify that he heard Drake testify in the first trial that he (Drake) was with Defendant the entire night of the robbery.

Answer: Drake's former testimony will be admissible against the prosecution if (a) Drake is unavailable and (b) the prosecution had the opportunity and motive to develop Drake's testimony at the earlier hearing. Since the first hearing was an earlier trial of the exact same issues and Drake's testimony was adverse to the prosecution's case, it would seem that this latter requirement is met.

VIII. WITNESSES

A. COMPETENCY OF WITNESSES. [§39.0]

In the past, numerous categories of witnesses were deemed incompetent to testify because of concerns about their trustworthiness. At one time, parties were disqualified from testifying. Felons, atheists, children, and the insane have also been deemed incompetent. The federal rules have dropped almost all such restrictions; common law jurisdictions have dropped many.

1. NO MENTAL OR MORAL REQUIREMENTS UNDER FRE. [§39.1]

With the exception of judges and jurors, see §§39.4-39.5 below, the federal rules provide that **every person is competent to be a witness.** [FRE 601]. While a witness's youth, infirmity, mental illness, intoxicated state, prison record, etc. may be used to attack the strength of his testimony, these are not grounds for preventing the witness from testifying.

2. COMMON LAW: CAPACITY TO OBSERVE, RECALL, AND RELATE. [§39.2]

Many common law jurisdictions hold that a witness is incompetent to testify if she **lacks sufficient mental capacity** to accurately observe, recall or relate facts. Witnesses are, however, presumed to be competent. Their lack of capacity must be raised through an objection. The judge then has broad discretion in deciding the question of testimonial competence.

a. Age. [§39.21]

Although many jurisdictions used to have minimum age limits for witnesses, this is no longer the case. As long as a child possesses sufficient mental capacity to testify, she will be considered competent.

b. Insane Persons May Testify. [§39.22]

Insane persons may be competent to give meaningful testimony. An adjudication of incompetency to manage one's affairs or insanity is not conclusive of a person's competency to testify as a witness.

3. DEAD MAN'S STATUTE. [§39.3]

This is not likely to arise in an Evidence course that focuses on the federal rules. The only time the issue can arise in federal court is when a state law claim is being adjudicated, in which case the federal court uses the state law regarding competency of witnesses as well. Since there is little uniformity among the states on the Dead Man's Statute, it is very difficult to test it without reference to a particular state's rule.

a. Basics of the Dead Man's Statute. [§39.31]

Long ago, persons with a financial interest in the outcome of a case were deemed incompetent to testify. Although this rule has been abandoned in every state, a remnant of it still exists in many states. The essence of such "Dead Man's Statutes" (they vary in detail from state to state) is as follows: (1) In cases brought **by or against the personal representative of a deceased** (i.e., the executor or administrator of the deceased's estate) (2) a **party** (3) may not testify as to a **transaction** (4) with the **deceased**. The theory is that when one party to a transaction has died, it is unfair to allow the survivor to tell his side of the story because the deceased, of course, is unable to give his version.

4. COMPETENCY OF JUDGES AS WITNESSES. [§39.4]

A judge may not testify in a case over which the judge is presiding. The reason is obvious: imagine having to cross-examine the judge who is going to be ruling on your later objections. Having the judge testify is considered such bad practice that a party need not object to it in order to preserve the issue for appeal. [FRE 605].

5. COMPETENCY OF JURORS AS WITNESSES. [§39.5]

a. At the Trial. [§39.51]

A juror may not testify as a witness in the trial of a case in which the juror is sitting. The reasoning is much the same as it is for judges. To preserve error, however, objection must be made. The objecting party must be given an opportunity to object outside the presence of the jury. [FRE 606(a)].

b. At Hearing Challenging Validity of Verdict. [§39.52]

After a verdict is reached, lawyers often try to challenge the verdict on the ground that the jurors engaged in misconduct during jury deliberations. FRE 606(b) severely limits this practice by circumscribing the ability of jurors to testify about jury deliberations. The general rule is that a juror may not testify about (a) any **matter or statement** that occurred during the jury's deliberations or (b) **anything that influenced any juror's mental processes** in arriving at a verdict. This rule is based on a desire to protect jurors from harassment and promote the finality of their judgments.

c. Exceptions. [§39.521]

The only exceptions to this rule are that jurors may testify as to whether (a) **extraneous prejudicial information** was improperly brought to the jury's attention (e.g., a newspaper article) or (b) any **outside influence** was improperly brought to bear on a juror (e.g., threats to a juror's family). These exceptions, however, are narrow. For example, they do not allow a juror to testify that other jurors were using drugs or alcohol. *Tanner v. United States*, 483 U.S. 107 (1987).

6. COMPETENCY AND HYPNOSIS. [§39.6]

The law is in a state of flux regarding the competency of a witness who has previously been hypnotized. Due to skepticism about the reliability of hypnotic procedures, some courts do not allow such witnesses to testify at all. Others allow witnesses whose memory has been aided through hypnosis to testify if certain procedural safeguards are followed. Some states permit such testimony on an ad hoc basis. The Supreme Court has ruled that states may not invoke a per se rule of inadmissibility to prevent a criminal defendant who has been hypnotized from testifying in her own defense as to matters recalled after hypnosis. *Rock v. Arkansas*, 483 U.S. 44 (1987).

B. OATH OR AFFIRMATION. [§40.0]

Under FRE 603, witnesses are required to declare that they will testify truthfully, by an oath or affirmation "administered in a form calculated to awaken the witness' conscience and impress the witness' mind with the duty to do so." No finding is required that the witness understands the obligation to tell the truth. Many common law jurisdictions require such a finding, but the court has broad discretion. With young children, for example, it may be sufficient for the child to state that she understands "I will be punished if I tell a lie."

C. PERSONAL KNOWLEDGE. [§41.0]

With the exception of experts, see §56.23 below, witnesses may not testify unless they have personal knowledge of the matter about which they are testifying. [FRE 602]. Whether or not the witness possesses personal knowledge is a question to be determined by the jury. [FRE 104(b)]. A witness's testimony that she has personal knowledge is sufficient to establish this.

D. EXCLUSION OF WITNESSES: INVOKING "THE RULE." [§42.0]

In order to prevent a witness from tailoring his story to match (or contradict) the testimony of another witness, a party is entitled to invoke "The Rule." That is, the party may ask the court to **exclude all witnesses from the courtroom** so that they cannot hear what the other witnesses say. In addition, witnesses frequently will be instructed that they may not discuss their testimony with others. No one really knows why this rule is called "The Rule."

1. THREE EXCEPTIONS. [§42.1]

There are three types of witnesses who are exempt from being excluded from the trial:

(a) **"a party who is a natural person"** (i.e., a human being);

(b) an officer or employee of a non-natural party (e.g., a corporate party) who is designated as its **representative** by its lawyer; and

(c) a **person whose presence is shown to be essential** to the presentation of the party's cause (e.g., an expert whose testimony is going to be based on what other witnesses say).

E. EXAMINATION OF WITNESSES: INTRODUCTION. [§43.0]

Cross-examination, leading questions, and impeachment often go hand in hand. As a result, they are often spoken of interchangeably. They refer, however, to three different things. Therefore, it is important to keep the following distinctions in mind. **Cross-examination** refers to a stage of questioning; **leading questions,** to the form in which a question is asked; and **impeachment**, to the attempt to attack a witness's credibility. Although it does not happen that often, a witness may be impeached on direct examination through the use of non-leading questions.

1. STAGES OF EXAMINATION. [§44.0]

a. Direct Examination. [§44.1]

Direct examination refers to the initial round of questions put to a witness by the party that called the witness.

b. Cross-Examination. [§44.2]

After the calling party completes its direct examination, the opposing party conducts a cross-examination of the witness.

c. Redirect- and Recross-Examination. [§44.3]

After cross-examination, the calling party may conduct a redirect exam, followed by its opponent's recross-exam.

OUTLINE

d. Calling and Questioning Witnesses by the Court. [§44.4]

Under FRE 614, the trial court is authorized to call a witness on its own motion. If it does so, all parties are entitled to cross-examine the witness. In addition, the judge is permitted to interrogate any witness, whether called by the court or by a party.

2. OBJECTIONS AS TO FORM OF QUESTION. [§45.0]

The form in which a question is posed may be objectionable for many reasons.

a. Questions Calling for Narrative. [§45.1]

Open-ended questions that call for an undirected narrative by the witness may be objectionable. If, for example, counsel asks, "What happened that day?" there is a risk that the witness will relate irrelevant or otherwise inadmissible evidence. Opposing counsel is thus denied a fair opportunity to anticipate the answer and thereby make timely and effective objections. The judge has broad discretion to permit or prohibit such questions. [FRE 611(a)].

b. Leading Questions. [§45.2]

A leading question is **one that suggests the answer** the witness is to give. In other words, if an ordinary person would get the impression that the questioner desires one answer rather than another, it is a leading question. Questions that start "Isn't it true that . . ." or "Didn't you then . . ." are examples of leading questions.

(1) General Rule: Leading Questions Allowed on Cross, But Not on Direct. [§45.21]

Leading questions are generally **not allowed on direct examination** because it is assumed that a witness will be all too willing to follow the suggestion of the lawyer who called her to testify. Leading questions **may, however, be asked on cross-examination** since the witness is not likely to be receptive to opposing counsel's suggestions. [FRE 611(c)].

(2) Leading Questions Sometimes Allowed on Direct. [§45.22]

There are a few instances in which leading questions may be asked on direct examination:

(a) Preliminary Matters. [§45.221]

Leading questions may be asked if they relate to preliminary matters not in dispute, such as the name, address, and occupation of the witness. This saves time.

(b) Where Necessary. [§45.222]

Witnesses who are having **difficulty testifying in response to non-leading questions** may be asked leading questions. This includes witnesses with language problems, children, and mentally feeble witnesses. In addition, **if a witness is unable to remember** something, counsel may seek to jog her memory with a leading question (e.g., Q: "Did he say anything else?" A: "No." Q: "You don't remember him making any other statements?" A: "No." Q: "He didn't say anything about a gun?" A: "Oh, yes . . ."). The question should only ask what is necessary to refresh the witness's memory; it should not overly lead the witness.

(c) Witnesses Unlikely to Follow Lead. [§45.223]

Leading questions may be used on direct examination when the witness is (a) an **adverse party;** (b) a **witness identified with an adverse party** (e.g., the president of the defendant corporation); or (c) **hostile** (i.e., unresponsive to non-leading questions). [FRE 611(c)]

c. Argumentative Questions. [§45.3]

Questions that are used by counsel to make or emphasize some point or to argue to the jury rather than to elicit information (e.g., "Do you really expect the jury to believe that?") are objectionable.

d. Questions Assuming Facts Not in Evidence. [§45.4]

A question is improper if it assumes the existence of a fact or facts that have not been proved (e.g., "When did you stop beating your wife?" is improper if no evidence has been introduced that the witness ever beat his wife).

e. Compound Questions. [§45.5]

A question that contains two inquiries but calls for only one answer is improper if the answer would be misleading and unclear (e.g., "Did you see **and** hear X threaten his wife?"). If, however, the inquiries are so distinct and clearly call for separate answers, the question may be permitted (e.g., "Did you see D on that day and, if so, what time was it?").

f. Ambiguous or Unintelligible Questions. [§45.6]

A question must be clear and intelligible so that the witness and the jury can understand it. The court may, therefore, require counsel to restate, rephrase, or clarify an ambiguous or unintelligible question.

g. Questions Calling for Speculation [§45.7]

It is improper to ask a witness to speculate or to base an answer on pure conjecture.

h. Repetitive Questions: Asked and Answered. [§45.8]

Objection may be made if the witness already has been asked and answered a substantially identical question.

i. Non-Responsive Answers to Proper Questions. [§45.9]

A witness must respond only to the question asked and must not go off on tangents. The questioner may object to a non-responsive answer. In contrast, most jurisdictions do not allow opposing counsel to object on this ground. Opposing counsel may, however, object on other grounds if the testimony is otherwise inadmissible (e.g., contains hearsay) and request that the court instruct the witness to answer only the questions asked. The non-responsiveness of the answer may also excuse counsel's failure to object more quickly.

3. REFRESHING A WITNESS'S MEMORY. [§46.0]

Sometimes witnesses forget. When this happens, counsel may attempt to jog the witness's memory, to refresh his recollection. **Anything that will** help trigger the witness's memory may be used. It may be a writing (whether or not composed by the witness), a physical object, a leading question, or the rendition of a Willie Nelson song (by the lawyer, a videotape or by Willie Nelson himself). Typically, of course, a writing is used to refresh recollection.

a. If the Witness Remembers, No Hearsay Problem. [§46.1]

If the witness's memory is successfully refreshed, he can testify from memory and no hearsay problem is presented.

b. Refreshing Item is Not Evidence. [§46.2]

The item used to refresh memory is not evidence; **it is only a device that was used to jog the witness's memory and is not itself being offered as proof.** Therefore, it need not be authenticated, comply with the Best Evidence Rule, fall within a hearsay exception, or meet any other requirement of admissibility.

c. But Procedural Safeguards Exist. [§46.3]

When a **document** is used to refresh a witness's memory, courts fear that the witness who says his memory is refreshed is really remembering only what he just read in the refreshing document. Therefore, when a document is used to refresh a witness's recollection, some procedural safeguards apply.

(1) Memory Refreshed While Witness is Testifying. [§46.31]

If a witness's memory is refreshed with a document while he is on the stand, opposing counsel is entitled to **inspect** the document, **cross-examine** the witness about it, and **introduce** into evidence relevant portions of the document. [FRE 612].

(2) Memory Refreshed Before Trial. [§46.32]

If the witness reviews a document to refresh his memory **before he testifies**, FRE 612 gives the court **discretion** to order counsel to turn over the document to his opponent for inspection, cross-examination, and introduction of relevant portions. The common law, however, does not authorize the judge to do this when memory is refreshed prior to trial.

4. NATURE AND SCOPE OF CROSS-EXAMINATION. [§47.0]

a. Form of Questioning. [§47.1]

A cross-examiner ordinarily has broad leeway in using leading questions and in repeating the same question. However, the trial court is given a great deal of control over such matters and its rulings are rarely upset on appeal.

b. Scope of Cross-Examination. [§47.2]

FRE 611(b) adopts the majority rule that cross-examination is **limited to the subject matter of the direct examination and matters affecting the witness's credibility.** Ordinarily, if information unrelated to the direct testimony is sought from a particular witness, he must be recalled later by the party seeking the additional information. The federal rule does, however, give the trial court discretion to permit inquiry during cross-examination into "additional matters as if on direct examination."

NOTE: Minority Rule. [§47.21] A substantial minority of states allow **"wide-open"** cross-examination (i.e., questioning as to any relevant issue in the case).

c. Redirect- and Recross-Examination. [§47.3]

Redirect examination is ordinarily limited to **matters brought out in the preceding cross-examination.** Similarly, recross-examination is ordinarily limited to matters explored in the preceding redirect exam. The court, however, has discretion to allow a party to raise issues on redirect that were omitted from the direct examination due to oversight.

5. RIGHT TO CONFRONTATION. [§48.0]

Questions under the Confrontation Clause of the Sixth Amendment arise in two settings relevant to the discussion here.

a. Right to Cross-Examine Adverse Witnesses. [§48.1]

The right to cross-examine a witness is considered so important that direct testimony will be stricken if a witness cannot be subjected to full cross-examination due to sickness, death, or a refusal to answer. But reasonable limits may be placed on the method and extent of cross-examination. It is the **opportunity** for effective cross-examination, not effective cross-examination, that is protected. *Delaware v. Fensterer*, 474 U.S. 15 (1985).

b. Right to Face Accuser. [§48.2]

The Confrontation Clause limits the ability of the state to have its witnesses testify outside the presence of the accused. The Supreme Court has sanctioned a state procedure by which a child abuse victim may testify via closed-circuit television, but only if the trial judge first finds that the child would be traumatized by testifying in the presence of the defendant. (See Case Squibs Section, *Coy v. Iowa; Maryland v. Craig.*)

F. IMPEACHMENT IN GENERAL. [§49.0]

Impeaching a witness involves an attack on the witness's credibility, that is, an attempt to show that the witness is lying, mistaken, or both.

1. IMPEACHING ONE'S OWN WITNESS. [§49.1]

Ordinarily, a party is going to try to impeach the witnesses called by its opponent. Occasionally, however, a party may want to impeach one of its own witnesses. The common law and FRE disagree as to when a party may impeach its own witness.

a. Common Law Voucher Rule. [§49.11]

At common law, one who calls a witness is said to vouch for his truthfulness. Therefore, the common law ordinarily forbids a party from impeaching its own witness. An exception is made, however, when the witness unexpectedly testifies in a manner injurious to the calling party. This is known as the **surprise and injury** requirement.

b. Federal Rules: No Voucher Rule. [§49.12]

FRE 607 and many state codes **abandon the voucher rule,** thereby allowing a party to impeach its own witness.

2. FIVE TECHNIQUES OF IMPEACHMENT: "BICCC". [§49.2]

There are five basic ways of attacking a witness's credibility, each of which has its own set of rules. If you can remember the brand name of a cheap pen or razor, you can remember these five techniques: **"BICCC."** Bias, Inconsistent Statements, Capacity, Character, Contradiction.

a. Capacity. [§50.0]

Perhaps the most obvious means of impeaching a witness is by showing defects in the witness's ability to see, hear, recall, or recount the facts.

(1) Physical or Mental Disabilities. [§50.1]

Insanity or other relevant psychological abnormalities may be used to impeach a witness (e.g., "Don't you frequently have hallucinations?" "Don't you sometimes have trouble distinguishing fact from fantasy?"). A witness may be questioned about her **drug or alcohol use at the time** she perceived the event (e.g., "Isn't it true that you had consumed three double scotches shortly before the events you just described?").

(2) Memory. [§50.2]

A cross-examiner may test the memory of a witness by questions concerning the details of events about which the witness has testified (e.g., "What time was that?" "How many people were there?").

(3) No Foundation Requirement. [§50.3]

No foundation need be laid before asking a witness questions that reveal a lack of capacity. Nor is any foundation required before introducing extrinsic evidence of lack of capacity.

(4) Extrinsic Evidence Allowed. [§50.4]

Extrinsic evidence (i.e., evidence other than testimony from the witness) may be offered to prove lack of capacity.

(a) Psychiatric Opinion. [§50.41]

In a small number of cases, courts have admitted expert testimony regarding a witness's ability to tell the truth (e.g., "In my opinion, Witness is a sociopathic liar."). But courts are generally reluctant to permit so-called experts to give their opinion as to whether a particular witness is telling the truth. Despite many efforts to present such testimony in child abuse cases, courts rarely allow it. In any event, if expert opinion is called for, a good poker player is probably a lot better at telling whether a witness is lying than is a psychiatrist.

b. Bias. [§51.0]

A witness may be impeached by showing that he has some reason, independent of the merits of the case, to give testimony favoring one side or the other. Bias may arise from a variety of sources: a **personal relationship** with a party (e.g., a relative), **animosity** (e.g., a desire for revenge), a **financial interest** in the outcome (e.g., the witness is the creditor of a party), **intimidation**, the **desire to curry favor** with the prosecution (e.g., the witness has criminal charges pending against him), or the witness is being **paid** by a party to testify.

(1) Ability to Show Bias Important. [§51.1]

The Supreme Court has held that undue limits on an accused's ability to show the bias of a prosecution witness is unconstitutional. *Davis v. Alaska*, 415 U.S. 308 (1974).

(2) Foundation Requirement. [§51.2]

Some jurisdictions require that the **witness must be asked about his alleged bias before extrinsic evidence** of acts or statements evidencing the bias may be offered. The **federal rules contain no such foundation requirement.**

(3) Extrinsic Evidence. [§51.3]

Extrinsic evidence may be offered to prove bias. The court must determine the admissibility of such evidence under **general relevancy principles,** balancing the probative value of the evidence against the danger of unfair prejudice, confusion, waste of time, etc. For example, where the witness has admitted to the acts or statements showing bias, the court may exclude the extrinsic evidence on the ground that it is cumulative. (See Case Squibs Section, *United States v. Abel*)

c. Prior Inconsistent Statements "PINS". [§52.0]

The fact that a witness has previously made statements that are inconsistent with his trial testimony may be used to impeach him.

(1) Theory: Why Prior Inconsistent Statements are Not Hearsay When Offered to Impeach. [§52.1]

Suppose Defendant is on trial for murder. The prosecution's key witness is Witness, who told the police on the day after the murder that he saw Defendant shoot Victim. However, when the prosecutor calls Witness to testify, Witness states that he did not see the shooting. The prosecutor then tries to offer Witness's earlier statement to the police to prove that Witness saw the shooting and that Defendant was the gunman. The evidence is inadmissible. Recall from the discussion of hearsay that a witness's own out-of-court statements are hearsay if offered for the truth of the matter asserted. **Witness's statement to the police is hearsay if offered as substantive evidence** (i.e, to prove that Defendant shot Victim). **But the prosecutor may be able to offer Witness's statement to the police to impeach Witness without running afoul of the hearsay rule.** Why? Because the fact that Witness previously made a statement that is inconsistent with his testimony at trial tends to detract from his credibility. It demonstrates that he "blows hot and cold," telling one story one time and another story another time. In theory, **the prosecutor is not asking the jury to believe that Witness's statement to the police is true.** All the prosecutor wants to show (in theory) is that Witness is not a credible witness.

(2) Limiting Instruction. [§52.11]

When a party impeaches a witness with his prior inconsistent statement ("PINS"), its opponent is entitled to a limiting instruction. In the above example, the judge will instruct the jury that Witness's statement to the police may be considered by them only as evidence of Witness's credibility and not as evidence that Defendant shot Witness. Quite understandably, the jury will be totally perplexed by this.

(3) Some Prior Inconsistent Statements are Better Than Others. [§52.12]

Recall again from the discussion of hearsay that the federal rules declare that some prior statements of a witness are not hearsay. (See §30.0.) If the witness's **PINS** was made (a) under **oath**, (b) subject to the **penalty of perjury**, (c) **at an earlier trial, hearing, or other proceeding, or in a deposition,** FRE 801(d)(1)(a) states that it is not hearsay. This means it can be used for its truth as well as to impeach.

(a) EXAMPLE. [§52.121] Suppose that Witness told the grand jury that he saw Defendant shoot Victim. Since that PINS meets the requirements of FRE 801(d)(1)(a), the prosecutor may use it both to impeach Witness and as evidence that Defendant shot Victim.

---

(4) Foundation Requirement. [§52.2]

The federal rules abandon the traditional foundation requirement of the common law, a requirement that is still followed in many jurisdictions.

(a) Common Law. [§52.21]

The common law requires that a foundation be laid in order to impeach a witness with his PINS. First, the **witness must be asked about the PINS before extrinsic evidence** of the statement may be offered. Second, the **witness must be asked about the PINS in a certain way.** The question must include (a) the identity of the **person** to whom the statement purportedly was made, (b) the **time** and **place** it was made, and (c) the **substance** of the statement.

(i) EXAMPLE. [§52.211] "Isn't it true that the day after Victim was shot you spoke to Officer Smith at the station house? And didn't you tell her that you saw Defendant shoot Victim?"

(ii) Written Statements: The Queen is Dead. [§52.212]

In an old English case, *Queen Caroline's Case* (often referred to simply as The Queen's Case), the court held that before a witness could even be asked about a written PINS, the witness had to be shown and given the opportunity to read the writing in which the PINS appeared. Few jurisdictions still adhere to this rule.

(b) Federal Rule. [§52.22]

FRE 613 **abandons the common law foundation requirement,** as have many states. Under FRE 613, a witness may be asked about a PINS without first informing the witness as to identity, time, place, or the contents of the statement.

(i) EXAMPLE. [§52.221] "Isn't it true that you have previously stated that you did see Defendant shoot Victim?"

---

(5) Extrinsic Evidence of Prior Inconsistent Statements ("PINS"). [§52.3]

Two factors affect whether extrinsic evidence may be presented to prove that the witness made a PINS: (a) procedures (foundation requirement) and (b) whether the PINS relates to a collateral matter.

(a) Procedure. [§52.31]

The **common law** allows extrinsic evidence of a PINS **only if the witness first refuses to admit** having made the statement. In contrast, **FRE 613(b)** provides that **extrinsic evidence of a PINS is admissible** so long as (a) the witness is given an opportunity to explain or deny the statement and (b) opposing counsel is given the chance to question the witness about the statement. This opportunity may come, however, after the PINS has been proved. Therefore, extrinsic evidence of a witness's PINS will be permitted if the witness is available to be recalled to the stand. Even this minimal requirement may be waived under FRE 613(b) "in the interests of justice."

(b) Collateral Matter. [§52.32]

If the PINS relates to a collateral matter, extrinsic evidence is not permitted. (For an explanation of what is and is not collateral, see §54.1 below.)

d. Character for Truthfulness. [§53.0]

A witness may be impeached by showing his poor character for truthfulness. Such evidence is offered for the inference that the witness is now acting in accordance with his character trait, i.e., that he is testifying untruthfully. This is the third exception to the general rule prohibiting the use of character evidence to show conduct. (See §11.22.)

e. Three Ways to Prove Untruthful Character. [§53.1]

There are three ways to prove a witness's untruthful character: (a) opinion or reputation testimony; (b) specific acts that did not result in a conviction; and (c) convictions. Each method of proof has its own rules.

(1) Opinion or Reputation. [§53.2]

To impeach Witness 1, the attacking party may call Witness 2 to testify to her opinion of Witness 1's honesty (e.g., "In my opinion, Witness 1 is an untruthful individual.") or to Witness 1's reputation in the community (e.g., "I am familiar with Witness 1's reputation in the community for truthfulness and it is terrible."). Witness 2, however, is limited to stating her opinion or relating the reputation. She may not cite specific instances of dishonest conduct by Witness 1 to support the opinion or reputation. [FRE 608(a)].

(a) Evidence of Good Character Allowed After Attack. [§53.21]

The proponent of Witness 1 may not offer evidence of Witness 1's good character for truthfulness until his character has come under attack. At that point, the proponent of Witness 1 may call its own reputation or opinion witnesses to testify to Witness 1's good character for truthfulness. [FRE 608(a)].

(b) But at a Price. [§53.211]

Witness 1's opinion or reputation witnesses are **subject to cross-examination** with "Did you know" and "Have you heard" questions (e.g., "Did you know [Have you heard] that Witness 1 embezzled $1,000 from his daughter's Brownie troop last year?"). The rules here are the same as for other opinion and reputation witnesses: the questions may be asked, but the questioner is bound by the answer. Even if the witness answers in the negative, no extrinsic evidence will be permitted to show that Witness 1 actually embezzled the money. [FRE 608(b)]. (See §11.4132 above).

(2) Specific Acts Not Resulting in Conviction. [§53.3]

In the discretion of the court, Witness 1 may himself be asked on cross-examination about **specific things he has done that bear on his truthful disposition.** [FRE 608(b)]. Thus, on cross-examination Witness 1 may be asked, "Isn't it true that you embezzled $1,000 from your daughter's Brownie troop last year?"

(a) Act Must Relate to Truthfulness. [§53.31]

The cited conduct must be probative of untruthful character. Thus, questions relating to acts of dishonesty — acts of deceit, fraud, lying, etc. — are likely to be allowed. Questions about violent conduct are not.

(b) Bound By Answer. [§53.32]

The questioner is bound by the witness's answer. Extrinsic evidence may not be offered to prove that the witness actually engaged in the specific conduct.

(c) Minority Rule. [§53.33]

Some jurisdictions do not permit a witness to be impeached this way.

(3) Convictions. [§53.4]

The fact that a witness has been convicted of certain crimes may be used to prove the witness's untruthful character. States differ as to the details of the rules governing this method of impeachment (e.g., as to the type of crimes that may be used and the type of balancing test employed).

(a) FRE: Crimes Involving Dishonesty or False Statement. [§53.41]

FRE 609 allows a witness to be impeached by showing that he has been convicted of a crime involving dishonesty or false statement. **It does not matter whether the crime was a misdemeanor or felony.** The court **may not balance** the probative value of the conviction against the danger of unfair prejudice. The impeachment must be allowed. [FRE 609(a)(2)].

(i) Dishonesty or False Statement Defined. [§53.411]

Crimes involving dishonesty or false statement include: perjury, false statement, criminal fraud, embezzlement, false pretenses, and other crimes involving some element of deceit, untruthfulness or falsity.

(b) FRE: Felonies Not Involving Dishonesty or False Statement. [§53.42]

If a witness has been convicted of a crime that did not involve dishonesty or false statement, he may still be impeached with the crime if it was a felony. (A felony is a crime punishable — not punished — by death or imprisonment for more than a year.) However, under FRE 609(a)(1), the court **must balance the probative value of the conviction as bearing on credibility against the danger of unfair prejudice.** One balancing test is prescribed for criminal defendants, and another for all other witnesses.

(i) Witness is Criminal Defendant. [§53.421]

If the witness being impeached is the accused, a felony not involving dishonesty or false statement may be used to impeach him only if the court determines that its **probative value outweighs its prejudicial effect.**

> **(ii) EXAMPLE. [§53.4211]** Defendant, on trial for murder, testifies in his own defense. The prosecution seeks to impeach him by proving that he had previously been convicted of a felony assault. The court should allow this only if it determines that the probative value of the assault **as evidence of Defendant's untruthfulness** outweighs the danger of unfair prejudice (i.e., that the jury will use it as evidence of Defendant's violent nature).

(iii) Witness is Anyone Else. [§53.422]

If the witness being impeached is anyone other than the accused, a felony not involving dishonesty or false statement ordinarily may be used to impeach him. The court may, however, exclude the evidence if it determines that its **probative value is substantially outweighed by the danger of unfair prejudice.**

(c) Special Balancing Test For Remote Convictions. [§53.43]

If a conviction is very old ("remote"), it may be used to impeach a witness only if the court specifically finds that its **probative value substantially outweighs its prejudicial effect.** A conviction is remote if **ten years** have elapsed since the witness was released from confinement for that conviction. If the witness never served any time, the ten years runs from the date of conviction. The special balancing test applies even if the remote conviction was for a crime involving dishonesty or false statement. [FRE 609(b)].

(d) Rehabilitation or Pardon. [§53.44]

A conviction may not be used for impeachment if it has been the subject of (a) a pardon, annulment, or certificate of rehabilitation, based on a finding of rehabilitation, and the witness has not subsequently been convicted of a felony, or (b) a pardon or annulment based on a finding of innocence.

(e) Proof of Convictions. [§53.45]

A witness may be asked about an impeaching conviction or the conviction may be proved by means of a public record. It is improper to refer to any aggravating facts or details of the crime (e.g., "Isn't it true you were convicted of beating your wife and son with a baseball bat?").

(4) WARNING: These Rules Apply Only to Attacks on the Witness's Character for Truthfulness. [§53.5]

Look out for situations where evidence of a specific act that did not result in a conviction (or a conviction that would not qualify under the above rules) is used to impeach **by a theory other than showing the witness's poor character** for truthfulness.

(a) EXAMPLE. [§53.51] Suppose Defendant Company seeks to impeach one of Plaintiff's witnesses by asking him, "Isn't it true you threatened to kill the president of Defendant Company last year?" Although such a question could not be asked to prove the witness's untruthful character (threats of violence don't go to truthfulness), it may be used to demonstrate that the witness is **biased** against Defendant Company. Since the theory of impeachment is bias, the question may be asked and, if the witness denies that he made the threat, extrinsic evidence may be offered to prove that he did. Moral: Always ask: What is the Evidence Being Offered to Prove.

---

f. Contradiction. [§54.0]

A routine method of attacking a witness's credibility is to try to get the witness to retract or contradict something to which she had earlier testified. There is no problem in doing that. The only issue that arises in connection with this last technique of impeachment is: when will the impeaching party be allowed to offer **extrinsic evidence** for the purpose of contradicting some aspect of the witness's testimony.

(1) The Collateral Matter Rule [§54.1]

The collateral matter rule is easily stated (but less easily understood). If the extrinsic evidence is relevant solely because it tends to discredit the witness, it is said to relate to a collateral matter and is therefore inadmissible. If, however, the evidence is also relevant to prove or disprove a substantive fact in dispute, it is not collateral, and extrinsic evidence may be offered.

(a) EXAMPLE: Collateral Matter. [§54.11] Defendant is on trial for committing a bank robbery in Boston on October 1. To support his alibi defense, he calls Alex, the owner of a sporting goods store in New Haven. Alex testifies that Defendant worked in his sporting goods store all day long on October 1. On cross-examination, Prosecutor asks Alex, "Would you say that Defendant had worked in your store every day for the preceding month?" Alex answers, "Yes." During its rebuttal case, Prosecutor then calls Fred to testify that he was with Defendant on a camping trip on September 4 through 6. This would contradict Alex's testimony that Defendant had worked in the store every day for the preceding month. Fred's testimony, however, goes to a collateral issue and is inadmissible. It is not relevant to any substantive fact: no one cares where Defendant was in early September. The only point in eliciting Fred's testimony would be to discredit Alex by showing that one of his answers (albeit to an inconsequential question) is wrong.

> **(b) EXAMPLE: Not Collateral. [§54.12]** Same case. During its
> rebuttal case, Prosecutor calls Jerry to testify that he works in Alex's
> sporting goods store, and that Defendant did not work there on
> October 1, the day of the bank robbery. This testimony is admissible.
> It contradicts Alex's testimony and discredits him, but it is also directly
> relevant to a substantive issue in the case: Where was Defendant
> the day of the crime?

(2) Really a Matter of Balancing. [§54.2]

The federal rules and most state rules say nothing about the collateral
matter test. In fact, the reason for excluding extrinsic evidence on
collateral matters is that the probative value of such evidence is rarely
worth the time and the danger of diverting the jury's attention from the
real issues in the case. Therefore, courts exclude this evidence on the
basis of a FRE 403 balancing.

(3) Apply This Rule With Prior Inconsistent Statements ("PINS") Also. [§54.3]

Even if the procedural prerequisites have been met, extrinsic evidence
of a PINS may be offered only if the statement is relevant to a
substantive issue in the case. If a witness gives testimony that is
inconsistent with a previous statement only as to an inconsequential
detail (e.g., the witness testifies at trial that he was wearing a blue
sweater that day and had earlier said he was wearing a green sweater),
extrinsic evidence of that PINS will not be allowed.

3. SUPPORTING A WITNESS'S CREDIBILITY. [§55.0]

The process of impeachment is aimed at destroying a witness's credibility.
Bolstering and rehabilitation seek to build up the credibility of a witness.

a. Bolstering. [§55.1]

Bolstering refers to efforts to build up the credibility of a witness before
it is attacked. Many courts and texts state that, as a general matter,
bolstering is not permitted because witnesses are presumed to be credible
until they are attacked. This is not quite accurate. The FRE (and most
state rules) contain no general rule prohibiting bolstering. In fact, courts
routinely allow some degree of bolstering. For example, **background
facts** about a witness (e.g., family, employment, address, how long she
has lived in the community) may be elicited from the witness in an effort
to allow the jury to gauge her standing and assess her credibility. An
eyewitness will be allowed to testify to her powers of **perception** (e.g.,
that she has 20/20 vision) or her **lack of bias** (e.g., she does not know
the defendant and has no reason to accuse him). The rules against
bolstering really are directed toward preventing evidence of (a) a
witness's good character for truthfulness and (b) a witness's prior
consistent statements.

(1) Witness's Truthful Character. [§55.11]

As discussed above (§53.21), evidence of a witness's truthful character
may be offered **only after an attack** has been leveled at the witness's
character for truthfulness. This traditional common-law rule was
codified in FRE 608(a).

(2) Witness's Prior Consistent Statements. [§55.12]

The rule limiting the use of a witness's prior consistent statements to enhance the witness's credibility in the absence of an attack on the witness's credibility flows from the view that a witness's own out-of-court statements are hearsay if offered for their truth. Allowing a party to elicit a witness's out-of-court statements on direct examination in the guise of enhancing the witness's credibility would allow the party effectively to circumvent the hearsay rule. A witness's prior consistent statements may, however, be used if (a) they are **independently admissible** under a hearsay exception or exemption (e.g., the witness's statement qualifies as an excited utterance or is a prior statement of identification); or (b) to **rehabilitate** the witness **in certain circumstances** (see §55.22 below).

b. Rehabilitation. [§55.2]

Once a witness's credibility has been attacked, her proponent may, like "all the king's horses and all the king's men," try to put her back together again. This is the process of rehabilitation. The general rule here is simple. **The rehabilitation technique must match the impeachment technique.** If the witness has been attacked by showing bias, try to show lack of bias (e.g., "Yeah, I was mad at Plaintiff for a long time, but I forgave him years ago"); if the attack is lack of capacity, show capacity (e.g., "No, I wasn't wearing my glasses, [pause] but I was wearing my contact lenses.").

(1) Truthful Character. [§55.21]

A witness whose character for truthfulness has been attacked may be rehabilitated with reputation or opinion evidence of her truthful character, in accordance with the rules stated above.

(2) Prior Consistent Statements: Recent Fabrication, Yes; "PINS," No. [§55.22]

Although it may not seem logical, the fact that a witness who has been impeached with her PINS **may not** be rehabilitated by showing that she previously made statements consistent with her trial testimony. The justification for this rule is that a witness whose credibility has been attacked by showing that she tells Story A one time and Story B another time is not made more credible by a showing that she told Story A twice and Story B only once. Prior consistent statements may, however, be used to rebut a charge that the witness **changed her story or recently fabricated her testimony** if the prior statements were made before the motive to change the story or fabricate the testimony arose. (See Case Squibs section, *United States v. Tome*.) Recall that such prior consistent statements are admissible not only to rehabilitate, but as substantive evidence as well. (See §30.3).

PROBLEM 1. Plaintiff sues Defendant for deceptive trade practices, alleging that Defendant misrepresented the condition of the used Buick Plaintiff purchased from Defendant.

(1) Plaintiff calls Willard to testify that he heard Defendant tell Plaintiff that the engine was in mint condition. On cross-examination, Defendant seeks to ask Willard, "Isn't it true that you were convicted of felony assault three years ago?"

Answer: Since this is a felony that did not involve dishonesty or false statement, it may be used to impeach Willard unless the court determines that its probative value as impeachment evidence is substantially outweighed by the danger of unfair prejudice.

(2) Defendant also seeks to ask Willard, "Isn't it true that when my investigator spoke to you in your office last week, you told her that Defendant never said the engine was in mint condition?"

Answer: This is proper. The question reveals the person to whom the prior statement was made, the time and place it was made, and the substance of the statement. The federal rules and some states do not require that such a foundation be laid.

(3) Suppose Willard denies having made such a statement to the investigator. During Defendant's case-in-chief, he calls the investigator to testify, "Willard told me last week that Defendant never said the engine was in mint condition."

Answer: This is admissible to impeach Willard. Extrinsic evidence of a witness's prior inconsistent statement may be offered if the witness has been asked about, and denies having made, the statement. Under the federal rules, the witness does not even have to first be asked about the prior inconsistent statement. As long as the witness has the opportunity to deny or explain the statement, and opposing counsel has the opportunity to question him about the statement, extrinsic evidence of the statement will be admitted. Of course, if the inconsistency goes to a collateral matter, extrinsic evidence will not be permitted. That is not a problem here, as the inconsistency goes to the heart of the case.

(4) Defendant calls Mechanic to testify that he inspected the car before Plaintiff picked it up, and that it was in good working order and had no defects. Mechanic is a recent immigrant to the United States, speaks minimal English, is illiterate, and was recently discharged after a lengthy hospitalization for mental illness. Plaintiff claims that Mechanic is incompetent to testify.

Answer: Objection overruled under the federal rules. Except as expressly provided in the rules, all persons are competent to testify. If necessary, Mechanic may testify through an interpreter. Even in those jurisdictions which retain rules of witness competency, Plaintiff would have to show that Mechanic lacks sufficient intellectual capacity to relate the events.

(5) Mechanic testifies. On cross-examination, Plaintiff seeks to ask, "Isn't it true that both you and your wife work for Defendant?"

> **Answer:** Admissible as tending to show Mechanic may be biased.

(6) The jury returns a verdict for Plaintiff. In support of his motion for a new trial, Defendant calls Juror to testify, "No one on the jury thought that Defendant had misrepresented the condition of the car. We just felt sorry for Plaintiff and wanted to give him something. We figured Defendant's insurer would pick up the tab."

> **Answer:** Inadmissible. Jurors ordinarily are not allowed to testify as to what happened during jury deliberations. An exception is made only to allow testimony regarding any extraneous prejudicial information that was brought to the jury's attention or outside influence that was improperly brought to bear on a juror.

PROBLEM 2. Defendant is on trial for stealing various items from Victim's house.

(1) Prosecution calls Victim to testify. When Prosecution asks Victim to list all the items that were stolen from her house, Victim says, "It was such a long time ago, I can't really remember." However, after Prosecutor shows her a written list, she states, "I remember now", and tells the jury what was stolen. Defendant objects on hearsay grounds.

> **Answer:** Objection overruled. Prosecution has refreshed Victim's recollection. Victim then testified from memory. No hearsay was introduced. Defendant is entitled to inspect the writing that was used to refresh Victim's recollection, to cross-examine her about it, and to introduce relevant portions into evidence.

(2) Defendant testifies and denies having committed the crime. On cross-examination, Prosecution asks, "Isn't it true that you were convicted two years ago for theft by false pretenses?"

> **Answer:** Since the prior conviction is for a crime involving dishonesty or false statement, the impeachment is proper. No balancing test applies.

(3) Defendant later calls Wendy to testify, "I have known Defendant for ten years, and in my opinion he is a very honest person."

> **Answer:** Admissible. Once a witness's character for truthfulness has been attacked, he may rehabilitate it with evidence of his truthful character, either in the form of reputation or opinion evidence.

IX. OPINIONS AND EXPERT TESTIMONY

A. OPINION TESTIMONY IN GENERAL. [§56.0] The law of evidence has developed a body of law that governs when a witness may give testimony in the form of an opinion, draw an inference from the facts, or state a conclusion. There is one set of rules for "expert" witnesses and another for non-expert ("lay") witnesses.

OUTLINE

1. LAY WITNESS OPINIONS. [§56.1]

A **lay witness** is a witness who is not testifying as an expert. An "expert" may testify as a lay witness when she testifies about something outside the field of her expertise. For example, a doctor who witnessed a car collision would be testifying as a lay witness when she relates that she saw the defendant go through the red light.

a. Common Law Rule. [§56.11]

The oft-stated common law rule was that **lay witnesses were not allowed to testify in the form of an opinion.** Because lay witnesses were no more skilled than jurors at drawing inferences or conclusions from the facts, they were limited to relating the facts and leaving it to the jury to draw its own conclusions.

(1) Illusory Distinction Between Fact and Opinion. [§56.111]

The common law rule was based on the notion that facts could be distinguished from opinions. But such a **distinction is virtually impossible to draw.** For example, if a witness testified that it was windy or that two people were married, objection could be made that the witness was giving an opinion and should be forced to relate the facts which led the witness to reach such a conclusion.

(2) Numerous Exceptions. [§56.112]

As a result, numerous exceptions were made to the common law rule. Courts allowed witnesses to testify as to what were referred as **"short-hand renditions of fact"** or **"collective facts."** Witnesses thus were allowed to testify that someone was **drunk** (or not), to matters of **identification** (handwriting, voice, visual), **mental competency, vehicular speed, colors, smells, intoxication, or emotions,** and **to opinions about themselves** (e.g., value of own property or services, physical condition, personal history), to give but a few examples.

b. Modern Approach. [§56.12]

The federal rules and many states have abandoned the common law prohibition on lay witness opinions. Now, **lay witnesses may testify in the form of an opinion or inference if two requirements are met. First,** the opinion must be **rationally based on the witness's perception. Second,** it must be **helpful** to a clear understanding of the witness's testimony or the determination of a fact in issue. [FRE 701]. This approach eliminates the need to draw meaningless distinctions between fact and opinion and allows witnesses who would be tongue-tied by a rigid application of the no-opinion rule to testify in a manner that will be helpful to the factfinder.

(1) Perception of the Witness. [§56.121]

The witness must have **personal knowledge** of the events from which he is drawing his opinion. For example, a witness may not testify that the defendant was "speeding" without having actually seen the defendant driving. In contrast, experts may testify as to opinions without having personal knowledge of the underlying facts.

(2) Rationally Derived. [§56.1211]

In addition, a lay witness's opinion must be **rationally derived from his personal knowledge.** This requirement prevents a lay witness from testifying to an opinion that is irrational or requires specialized knowledge, such as that someone appeared to have a ruptured spleen.

(3) Helpfulness. [§56.122]

Lay opinion testimony must also be **helpful to a clear understanding** of the witness's testimony **or to a determination of a fact in issue.** Witnesses, especially inarticulate ones, may find themselves unable to communicate effectively if they are allowed to relate only the most concrete of facts.

(4) Comparison With Common Law. [§56.123]

Since the common law rule was riddled with exceptions, the more liberal sounding modern approach does not change the law that much. Nevertheless, courts are somewhat more receptive to lay opinions now than under the common law. For example, courts are more likely to allow a witness to testify to her opinion concerning the meaning of another's conduct, such as that someone "nodded yes," "indicated agreement," or "started" or "provoked" a fight.

(5) Foundation. [§56.124]

A question may sometimes arise as to whether a lay witness has personal knowledge of the facts upon which he is basing his opinion. The burden is on the witness's proponent to make this showing. For example, a lay witness who testifies that smoke smelled like marijuana may first be required to establish her familiarity with the smell of marijuana.

(6) Preference for Facts. [§56.125]

The more central the matter is to the issue in dispute, the more likely a court will require a witness to relate the facts within her knowledge rather than to merely state her opinion. For example, although courts routinely allow witnesses to state that someone was "married," if the marital status of a party is at the center of a dispute (e.g., a bigamy prosecution) the court is more likely to require the witness to give specifics.

B. EXPERT TESTIMONY. [§56.2]

Unlike lay opinion testimony, courts have long valued and admitted the opinions of experts. Courts have recognized that experts are able to draw inferences which jurors are not competent to draw. In fact, in some cases, a party cannot prevail as a matter of law without presenting expert testimony. **Two requirements** must be met before expert testimony will be admitted. The **first** has to do with the **subject matter** of the testimony; the **second**, with the **qualifications of the witness.**

1. SUBJECT MATTER. [§56.21]

The federal rules and many modern codes allow expert testimony regarding **scientific, technical, or other specialized knowledge** if it will **assist** the factfinder to understand the evidence or to determine a fact in issue. [FRE 702]. This is a broad standard. So long as the testimony concerns some type of "specialized knowledge" and will be helpful to the jury, it is admissible.

a. Common Law Rule. [§56.211]

At common law, some courts allowed expert testimony only if it related to a matter **beyond the common knowledge and experience** of the factfinder. The modern, more expansive approach permits expert testimony concerning a matter within a jury's competence so long as the expert's specialized knowledge might help the jury.

b. Types of Expert Testimony. [§56.212]

It would be both impossible and pointless to compile an exhaustive list of the various fields in which experts have been permitted to testify. The topics include medical practice, earning capacity, peanut farming, accident reconstruction, meaning of slang terms in the drug trade, engineering, design, handwriting, etc. Expert opinion is usually rejected, however, when offered as to whether a witness has testified truthfully. Courts have split on whether (or when) an expert should be permitted to testify as to the reliability of eyewitness testimony.

2. QUALIFICATIONS. [§56.22]

Before an expert may give an opinion, she must be shown to possess the requisite specialized knowledge. No magic formula exists for how that knowledge must be obtained. It may come through **formal education, as** evidenced by degrees and certificates, or it may come through **informal study, self-study, or experience.** The only question is whether the witness possesses the specialized knowledge.

a. Voir Dire. [§56.221]

The proponent of the witness must prove her qualifications. Usually this is done by offering testimony as to the witness's education, experience, etc. Before the court accepts her as an expert, the opposing party ordinarily has the right to "take the witness on voir dire" to cross-examine her about her qualifications.

b. Preliminary Question. [§56.222]

The admissibility of expert testimony is a preliminary question for the judge to decide. The judge's ruling will be reversed only for an abuse of discretion.

3. BASIS OF EXPERT OPINIONS. [§56.23]

Unlike lay witnesses, **experts need not base their opinions on personal knowledge.**

a. Common Law. [§56.231]

Under common law rules, an expert may base an opinion on (1) **personal knowledge,** (2) **facts in the record,** or (3) a **combination** of the two.

(1) Hypothetical Question. [§56.2311]

When an expert bases an opinion (in whole or in part) on facts not within his personal knowledge, the facts are typically provided to him through a hypothetical question. Under this procedure, the lawyer recites a series of facts, asks the expert to assume the truth of these facts, and then asks the expert to give his opinion. All facts contained in the hypothetical question must be in evidence by the close of the case.

> **(a) EXAMPLE. [§56.23111]** "Dr. Nostrum, assuming Casey had a high fever, was allergic to sulfa drugs, and had a history of rheumatic fever, what, if anything, would a reasonable doctor in Mudville prescribe if Casey complained of violent chest pains?"

(b) Expert Observes Testimony. [§56.23112]

A variant of the hypothetical question may be used when the expert observes the testimony of other witnesses. The lawyer may then ask the expert to assume the truth of the other witnesses' testimony (or some parts of it) and render an opinion.

b. Modern Approach. [§56.232]

The federal rules and the rules of many jurisdictions liberalize somewhat the proper basis for expert testimony. Under Federal Rule 703, **an expert may base his opinion on facts "perceived by or made known to the expert at or before the hearing."**

(1) Includes Common Law Methods. [§56.2321]

This includes all the methods permitted at common law.

(2) Goes Beyond Common Law. [§56.2322]

This liberalizes the common law by allowing an expert to base an opinion **solely** on facts outside his personal knowledge and not in the record. However, an expert may base an opinion on facts that are not admitted in evidence (or that would even be admissible in evidence) only if those facts are of a **type reasonably relied upon** by experts in the same field. [FRE 703].

> **(a) EXAMPLE. [§56.23221]** A doctor may base an opinion on medical records he has reviewed, conversations with other medical personnel about the patient, and interviews with the patient's family, even if none of these has been introduced into evidence, so long as the court decides that these are the types of things that other doctors in the field reasonably rely upon in making diagnoses.

(3) Hypothetical Question Not Required. [§56.2323]

Experts who lack personal knowledge about the underlying facts may give their opinions without being asked a hypothetical question. Federal Rule 705 authorizes an expert to state his opinion **without prior disclosure of the underlying facts,** leaving it to the cross-examiner to probe the basis of the opinion. The rule, however, empowers the court to require the expert to first disclose the underlying facts. Note that **Rule 705 does not abolish use of the hypothetical question.** It merely makes its use **optional.**

4. EXAMINATION OF EXPERT WITNESSES. [§56.24]

In addition to being subject on cross-examination to the kinds of questions asked of other witnesses, an expert may be questioned as to: (a) his **qualifications**; (b) the **bases** of his opinions; (c) the **compensation** he is receiving for testifying; and (d) discrepancies between opinions expressed by the expert and statements contained in treatises and articles.

a. Treatises and Articles: Common Law. [§56.241]

Under the common law rule, a cross-examiner is permitted to **impeach** an expert by pointing out discrepancies between the expert's testimony and statements made in a treatise or article if the witness has acknowledged the **authoritative** nature of the treatise or article or that he **relied upon it** in forming his opinion.

b. Treatises and Articles: Federal Rule. [§56.242]

An expert may be impeached as under the common law. In addition, the federal rules create a **hearsay exception** for statements in treatises, periodicals, or pamphlets that have been established as reliable authority by expert testimony or judicial notice. [FRE 803(18)]. See §22.0 above. Statements in such works may be read to the jury to the extent that they are **called to the attention of an expert on cross-examination** or **relied upon** by an expert witness **on direct examination.**

c. Court Appointed Experts. [§56.25]

The court may, on its own motion, appoint and call an expert witness. [FRE 706].

5. OPINIONS ON ULTIMATE ISSUES [§56.3]

Common law courts frequently exclude opinions that embrace the ultimate issue in the case on the ground that such opinions "invade the province of the jury." **The federal rules and most states reject this as a valid objection.** [FRE 704(a)]. Nevertheless, an opinion — lay or expert — is admissible only if it meets the helpfulness test. Therefore, courts still frequently exclude opinions as to **mixed questions of law and fact,** especially when the danger exists that the witness is not familiar with the proper legal standard.

> ### a. EXAMPLE. [§56.31]
> Testimony that a testator "lacked testamentary capacity" is likely to be excluded, whereas testimony that the testator "had the capacity to know the nature and extent of his property and the natural objects of his bounty and to formulate a rational scheme of distribution" is likely to be admitted.

b. Hinckley Rule. [§56.32]

After John Hinckley was acquitted by reason of insanity in the shooting of President Reagan, Congress amended Rule 704 to prohibit experts from testifying as to whether a criminal defendant "did or did not have the **mental state or condition** constituting an **element of the crime charged** or of a **defense** thereto." This means that psychiatrists may not state "In my opinion, Defendant was insane [lacked the intent to kill] at the time of shooting." But they may still testify as to the nature and ramifications of any mental illness afflicting a defendant.

6. NOVEL SCIENTIFIC EVIDENCE. [§56.4]

When expert testimony is offered concerning some new scientific test, theory, or principle, courts differ on the proper standard for admissibility. For many years, courts employed a special threshold test (the *Frye* test) which limited the admissibility of novel scientific evidence. The use of a special threshold test has been justified partly on the ground that jurors tend to overvalue scientific evidence and partly on the ground that trial judges are ill-equipped to evaluate the validity of new scientific techniques. The *Frye* test has been greatly criticized, however, and has been abandoned in the federal courts and in many states.

a. The *Frye* Test. [§56.41]

Derived from a 1923 Court of Appeals case (*Frye v. U.S., 293 F. 1013 (D.C. Cir. 1923)*), the *Frye* test states that the proponent of novel scientific evidence must first demonstrate that the proffered test, theory, or principle has gained **general acceptance in the scientific community.**

b. Federal Rules. [§56.42]

The federal rules and most state codes make no mention of the *Frye* standard , and in *Daubert v. Merrell Dow Pharmaceuticals, Inc.*, 509 U.S. 579, 113 S.Ct. 2786 (1993), the Supreme Court held that the *Frye*-general acceptance test had not been incorporated in the federal rules. Instead, the admissibility of novel scientific evidence (in fact, of all scientific evidence) is governed by the standards set forth in Rule 702, which addresses the admissibility of expert testimony. Now, to qualify for admission, the evidence must be (a) **scientifically valid** and (b) must have a **valid scientific connection** to the pertinent inquiry (i.e., it must be relevant to the issue to which it is directed). (See Case Squibs section, *Daubert v. Merrell Dow Pharmaceuticals, Inc.*)

(1) Factors in Deciding Admissibility. [§56.421]

The *Daubert* opinion stressed that the trial judge must make these threshold determinations before admitting the evidence. It then set forth four factors that a trial judge might consider in determining whether the proffered evidence is scientifically valid: (1) whether the theory or technique in question has been or can be **tested**; (2) whether the theory or technique has been subjected to **peer review and publication**; (3) the known or potential **rate of error** of the particular theory or technique and whether means exist for controlling its operation; and (4) the **extent** to which the theory or technique has been **accepted**. Then, even if the court determines that the demands of Rule 702 have been satisfied, Rule 403 may still provide grounds for exclusion.

c. Establishing Validity. [§56.43]

Obviously, both the *Frye* and *Daubert* tests require the proponent of the evidence to establish the validity of the underlying scientific test, theory, or principle. For example, suppose the prosecution calls an expert to testify that, through voiceprint comparison, he can identify the defendant as the person who made a particular recorded phone call. At the least, the prosecution must establish that individuals have unique voiceprints that can be accurately charted and successfully identified. The *Frye* test would also require that the theory and techniques underlying voiceprint analysis must be generally accepted in the scientific community.

(1) Testimony. [§56.431]

The validity of the relevant scientific test, theory, or principle (and its general acceptance, if necessary) may be proved through expert testimony.

(2) Judicial Notice. [§56.432]

Once a test, theory or principle has become sufficiently well established, a court may take judicial notice of its validity. For example, courts no longer require proof of the principles underlying the use of radar, fingerprints, or ballistics tests.

(3) Proper Application. [§56.433]

Even where the underlying principles have been widely accepted and there is no need to present evidence as to their validity, proof must still be presented to show that they were **properly applied in this particular instance.** For example, although no proof is required regarding the general theory underlying the use of radar guns, the prosecution will still have to establish that the radar gun used to clock the defendant at 77 mph was in good working order and was used by someone who knew how to operate it properly.

d. Lie Detectors. [§56.44]

Results of lie detector (i.e., polygraph) tests are **normally inadmissible.** However, a growing number of courts admit lie detector evidence if the parties **stipulate** to its admissibility in advance of the test. Recently the Eleventh Circuit held that under certain conditions, polygraph evidence may be used to **impeach or corroborate** the testimony of a witness. (*U.S. v. Piccinonna,* 885 F.2d 1529 (11th Cir. 1989)).

e. DNA. [§56.45]

Courts thus far have **generally admitted** evidence by which an individual is identified by comparing the DNA patterns obtained from a sample taken from the individual with those obtained from a sample of fluid, hair, or other substance found, say, at the scene of the crime. The underlying scientific principles are fairly well accepted. Opponents of the evidence argue, however, that the lab techniques used are not nearly as accurate as the proponents claim.

f. Other Scientific Tests. [§56.46]

Numerous other scientific tests, theories, and principles are the subject of **controversy,** either on the ground of the lack of validity of the underlying theory or the inability to apply the theory in a way that produces accurate results. Thus, courts disagree as to the admissibility of **voiceprint** evidence, **hypnotically-induced recollection, bite-mark** evidence, testimony concerning **rape trauma syndrome or psycholinguistics,** as well as many other tests or theories.

PROBLEM. Defendant is charged with the robbery of Victim. Victim reports that although he did not see the robber's face, he did tear off a piece of the robber's shirt as the robber escaped.

(1) State offers Victim who testifies that: "The robber was about five feet tall and weighed about 200 pounds. He had a very high voice, and was wearing an Army fatigue cap, combat boots, and tie-dyed jeans."

> **Answer:** Admissible under both the common law and federal rules, even though the testimony is full of opinions, conclusions and characterizations. They are rationally based on the witness's own perception of the robber and it will be helpful for the jury to hear this testimony.

(2) State offers the testimony of Dr. Amino, a professor of chemistry, who states that he has developed a means of identifying persons from body chemicals that adhere to clothing. He testifies that he analyzed the piece of shirt torn from the robber and compared it to a piece of Defendant's clothing and that, in his opinion, Defendant was wearing the shirt from which the sample was taken.

> **Answer:** Certainly inadmissible under the *Frye* standard. No evidence has been presented that there is general acceptance of this test in the scientific community. Probably inadmissible even in a court that rejects the *Frye* standard. The lack of general acceptance is certainly a factor the court may take into account in deciding whether the evidence is scientifically valid. Since general acceptance is not the sole criterion, however, the admissibility of this testimony will depend on whether the state is able to convince the judge that Dr. Amino's test is scientifically valid.

(3) Dr. Mason testifies in support of Defendant's claim of insanity. On cross-examination, Dr. Mason is asked whether she read and considered Dr. Hooke's essays on "Simulating Insanity." Dr. Mason admits having read one of the essays but says she does not remember it. Dr. Mason is then asked: "How do you reconcile your opinion of Defendant with Dr. Hooke's conclusion that, 'It is virtually impossible to conclude whether or not a person is insane if that person consciously seeks to mislead you?'"

> **Answer:** Under the common law rule, this question is improper because Dr. Mason did not rely on Dr. Hooke's essay in reaching her opinion or acknowledge that Dr. Hooke's essay was authoritative. Under the federal rules, this question would be proper if the cross-examiner has established (through Dr. Mason, some other expert, or by judicial notice) that the quoted essay is reliable authority.

X. AUTHENTICATION

A. AUTHENTICATION. [§57.0]

Before a writing can be introduced into evidence, it must be "authenticated;" that is, **its proponent must establish that it is what it purports to be.** Under the federal rules, the authentication requirement applies not only to writings, but to other forms of physical evidence (e.g., the murder weapon) and to less tangible things, such as voices. [FRE 901].

1. CONDITIONAL RELEVANCE STANDARD. [§57.1]

The authentication requirement is really a means of establishing the relevance of the proffered item. **The standard** for authentication, however, is the low one associated with **conditional relevance.** See §5.5 above. The proponent of the evidence need only introduce **enough evidence for a reasonable juror to find that the item is what it purports to be.** [FRE 901(a)]. Even if the court does not believe that an item is what it purports to be, it is still authenticated if a reasonable juror could find that it is.

> **a. EXAMPLE. [§57.11]** Plaintiff wants to introduce a letter allegedly written by Defendant that contains admissions damaging to Defendant's case. Plaintiff must first authenticate the letter by showing that the letter is what it purports to be. As long as Plaintiff introduces sufficient evidence for a reasonable juror to find that it is a letter written by Defendant, Plaintiff has authenticated it. This holds true even if the court does not itself believe that Defendant wrote the letter. Ultimately, the jury will decide whether it is or is not Defendant's letter.

2. REAL AND DEMONSTRATIVE EVIDENCE. [§57.2]

The term **real evidence** refers to tangible items that actually played a role in the matter in dispute (e.g., the murder weapon, the contract in issue). **Demonstrative evidence** refers to tangible items that did not actually play a role in the matter in dispute, but are used for illustrative purposes (e.g., a map, photograph, skeleton). The proponent of a piece of demonstrative evidence must establish that the evidence is a **fair and accurate representation of what it purports to depict.**

B. AUTHENTICATION OF WRITINGS. [§58.0]

There are several ways in which a writing may be authenticated.

1. PERSONAL KNOWLEDGE. [§58.1]

A writing may be authenticated by a person who has personal knowledge that the writing is what it is claimed to be. [FRE 901(b)(1)]. For example, a witness may testify that she authored the document or saw the purported author execute the document.

2. AUTHENTICATION BY CIRCUMSTANTIAL EVIDENCE. [§58.2]

A writing may be authenticated by circumstantial evidence. There are innumerable ways in which this might be done. Some standard techniques of authentication by circumstantial evidence have evolved over the years.

a. Handwriting. [§58.21]

A document may be authenticated through the author's handwriting.

(1) Lay Witness. [§58.211]

A lay witness who has personal knowledge of a person's handwriting may give an opinion that a specific writing was or was not made by that person. Under the federal rules, however, a lay witness's familiarity with the handwriting must not have been acquired for purposes of the litigation. [FRE 901(b)(2)].

(2) Expert Witness. [§58.212]

An expert witness may compare a genuine sample of the purported author's handwriting (i.e., an "exemplar") with the writing in question, and give an opinion as to authorship. On the same basis, an expert may also identify typewriting as coming from a particular typewriter. [FRE 901(b)(3)].

(3) Comparison by the Trier of Fact. [§58.213]

A genuine exemplar of the purported author's handwriting and the contested writing may be submitted directly to the factfinder for comparison. [FRE 901(b)(3)].

(a) Genuineness of Exemplar. [§58.2131]

The exemplar itself must be established as genuine before it can be used for comparison purposes. At common law, the court had to be satisfied that it was genuine. Under FRE 901(b)(3), an exemplar may be used if its proponent introduces sufficient evidence to support a finding that it is genuine.

b. Reply-Message Doctrine. [§58.22]

If (a) the contents of a writing indicate that it is in reply to a previous communication addressed to the purported author (e.g., "referring to your letter of March 8 . . . "), and (b) it is unlikely that anyone other than the purported author would have sent the response, the writing will be authenticated. [FRE 901(b)(4)].

c. Ancient Documents. [§58.23]

A writing may be authenticated under this doctrine if it (a) is in such a **condition** as to create **no suspicion** as to its authenticity; (b) was **found where it would have likely been kept;** and (c) is at least **20 years old.** [FRE 901(b)(8)]. At **common law,** a document had to be at least **30 years old** to invoke the ancient documents doctrine.

d. Public Records or Reports. [§58.24]

Evidence that a public record or report has been recorded or filed in a public office (e.g., a deed) suffices for authentication. [FRE 901(b)(7).].

e. Content. [§58.25]

A writing may be authenticated if its contents include information known only by purported author. [FRE 901(b)(4)].

C. AUTHENTICATION OF OBJECTS. [§59.0]

All tangible objects must be authenticated before being admitted into evidence. As was the case with writings, authentication may be done in innumerable ways. The objective is to show that the item is what it purports to be.

1. PERSONAL KNOWLEDGE. [§59.1]

A witness may testify that he recognizes the object based on its unique markings, properly affixed labels, or any other reasonable basis. [FRE 901(b)(1)].

2. AUTHENTICATION BY CIRCUMSTANTIAL EVIDENCE [§59.2]

An object may be authenticated by circumstantial evidence. There are many ways this may be done.

a. Distinctive Characteristics. [§59.21]

An object's distinctive characteristics, appearance, contents, or internal patterns may be used to show that it is what it purports to be. [FRE 901(b)(4)].

> **(1) EXAMPLE. [§59.211]** Fingerprints found at the scene of the burglary can be shown to be defendant's by their distinctive characteristics.

b. Chain of Custody. [§59.22]

An object may be authenticated by proving an unbroken chain of custody from the time it came into its proponent's possession until its submission into evidence. The proponent should be able to account for its whereabouts at all times in order to negate the possibility of tampering with the object. However, courts will often admit objects even when the proponent is unable to establish absolutely each link in the custody or chain.

3. PHOTOS, MAPS, MODELS. [§59.3]

Photographs, maps, and models are often used as demonstrative evidence and thus admissible so long as the witness testifies from personal knowledge that the exhibit is a **fair representation** of what it purports to be. **The photographer or person who prepared the exhibit need not testify.**

4. X-RAYS. [§59.4]

With the exception of Superman (with his "x-ray vision"), no one can testify from personal knowledge that an x-ray is a fair and accurate representation of the object depicted. Instead, authentication here requires testimony that the **process used is accurate** (the court may take judicial notice of this) and that the **machine used was in good working order.**

5. COMPUTER SIMULATIONS. [§59.5]

A computer simulation demonstrating how an event occurred may be used if a proper foundation is laid. This typically will entail a showing that (a) the data used as a basis for the recreation is accurate (e.g., using data obtained from the "black box" in the recreation of an airplane crash), (b) the data was correctly entered, and (c) the software used to produce the simulation can accurately produce the relevant images. This may require testimony from several witnesses. The qualifications of the person or persons who produced the simulation will also have to be established.

D. AUTHENTICATION OF VOICES. [§60.0]

With the advent of the telephone and audio recordings came the need to develop ways of establishing in court that a voice heard or recorded belonged to a particular person.

1. PERSONAL KNOWLEDGE. [§60.1]

A voice may be identified (whether heard firsthand or on an audio recording) by any person who testifies that he recognizes the voice based upon having heard it under circumstances connecting it with the alleged speaker. [FRE 901(b)(5)].

2. AUTHENTICATION BY CIRCUMSTANTIAL EVIDENCE. [§60.2]

Voices may be authenticated through any one of a number of techniques involving circumstantial evidence.

a. Contents. [§60.21]

As is the case with writings, the identity of a speaker may be shown if the contents of the statement include information known only by the purported speaker. The reply-message doctrine (see §58.22) also applies to spoken communications. [FRE 901(b)(4)].

b. Distinctive Characteristics. [§60.22]

The identity of a speaker may also be shown by the distinctive characteristics of the speaker, such as a strange accent or idiosyncratic use of language. [FRE 901(b)(4)].

c. Voice Prints. [§60.23]

The courts are split as to whether voice prints may be used to identify a speaker.

d. Special Rules for Telephone Communications. [§60.24]

Merely producing evidence that a speaker identified herself as "Sue Snow" is not sufficient to establish that the speaker was in fact Sue Snow. In addition to the methods of authentication listed above, there are special rules that have been developed for telephone communications.

(1) Personal Identity. [§60.241]

An individual may be identified as the speaker if a witness testifies that (a) he properly dialed the **number** (b) **listed** in the telephone directory and (c) circumstances, **including self-identification,** show the person answering to be the one listed and called. [FRE 901(b)(6)].

> **(a) EXAMPLE. [§60.2411]** W testifies that she looked up Sue Snow's number in the phone book, dialed it, and that the person who answered said, "This is Sue Snow." This is sufficient to identify the speaker as Sue Snow.

(2) Business. [§60.242]

A witness may establish that he spoke to a representative of a business if she testifies that she (a) **properly dialed** the **number** (b) **listed** in the telephone directory and (c) the **conversation related to the type of business** commonly transacted over the telephone. [FRE 901(b)(6)].

E. SELF-AUTHENTICATION. [§61.0]

With some items, the likelihood of forgery or tampering is deemed to be so small that they are "self-authenticating." That is, **the proponent of such an item is not required to present any evidence to establish that the item is what it purports to be.** All the proponent needs to do is present the item at trial. To remember which items are self-authenticating, use the mnemonic **"CONTAC":** Commercial paper; Official publications; Trade inscriptions; Newspapers and periodicals; Acknowledged documents; Certain public records. [FRE 902].

1. COMMERCIAL PAPER. [§61.1]

To the extent provided by general commercial law, commercial paper, signatures on commercial paper, and related documents are self-authenticating. [FRE 902(9)].

2. OFFICIAL PUBLICATIONS. [§61.2]

Publications purporting to be issued by public authority, such as the reports of a government agency, are self-authenticating. [FRE 902(5)].

3. NEWSPAPERS AND PERIODICALS. [§61.3]

Newspapers and periodicals are self-authenticating. In a libel action against the Kalamazoo News, for example, the plaintiff has only to bring in a copy of the offending paper. He need not present further evidence that it really is a copy of the Kalamazoo News. [FRE 902(6)].

4. TRADE INSCRIPTIONS AND THE LIKE. [§61.4]

Under the federal rules, ownership, control, or origin may be established by an inscription, sign, tag, or label that (a) purports to have been affixed in the course of the business and (b) indicates ownership, control, or origin. [FRE 902(7)].

> **a. EXAMPLE [§61.41]** Plaintiff offers into evidence a can bearing the label "Red Tomato Co., Inc." in which she claims to have found a dead mouse. This is sufficient to authenticate the can as a product of the defendant Red Tomato Company.

5. ACKNOWLEDGED DOCUMENTS. [§61.5]

A document that has already been acknowledged before a notary public or other officer authorized by law to take acknowledgements is self-authenticating. [FRE 902(8)].

6. CERTAIN PUBLIC RECORDS. [§61.6]

Public records may be self-authenticating. The **requirements vary,** depending on whether the document is foreign or domestic, under seal or not, and whether it is certified as correct or not. It is not worth memorizing the particulars unless your teacher indicates that he or she thinks it is important. [FRE 902(1)-(4)].

PROBLEM 1. Defendant is charged with the criminal extortion of Victim.

(1) The prosecutor calls Victim to testify that someone called him at his dry cleaner shop, identified himself as Defendant, and threatened to burn the shop down.

> **Answer:** Inadmissible. Mere self-identification is not enough to establish that it was Defendant who called Victim.

(2) Victim testifies that he received an unsigned, handwritten note threatening him. Defendant objects that it has not been authenticated. The prosecutor responds by promising to offer evidence that the note was written on very unusual paper of the type that Defendant regularly used and with the kind of ink that Defendant regularly used.

> **Answer:** Since the distinctive type of paper and ink tend to show that Defendant wrote the note, the court may conditionally admit the evidence, subject to the prosecutor producing the promised evidence.

(3) The prosecutor seeks to submit the note to the jury along with a sample of Defendant's handwriting made in court at the judge's direction.

> **Answer:** This is permissible. The trier of fact may make its own comparison of the proffered writing with a genuine exemplar of the purported author's handwriting.

PROBLEM 2. Denise, a Navy pilot, is killed when her plane crashes. Her husband Hubert brings a wrongful death action against Aircraft Co., the manufacturer of the plane. Hubert claims that the plane's defective design caused the accident.

(1) Hubert seeks to authenticate a photograph of the crash site through the testimony of one of the people who investigated the crash. Aircraft Co. objects, claiming that Hubert has not produced the person who took the photograph, and thus has failed to authenticate the photo.

> **Answer:** As long as the investigator testifies that the photo fairly and accurately depicts the crash scene, the photo has been properly authenticated. Objection overruled.

(2) Aircraft Co. seeks to introduce a pamphlet published by the Federal Aviation Administration that reports the safety record of various types of aircraft. Aircraft Co. fails to call any witness to establish that the pamphlet really was published by the FAA. Hubert objects, contending that the pamphlet was not properly authenticated.

> **Answer:** Objection overruled. Books, pamphlets and other publications purporting to be issued by a public authority are self-authenticating and require no sponsoring witness.

XI. BEST EVIDENCE RULE

A. BEST EVIDENCE RULE ("BER"). [§62.0]

The Best Evidence Rule is one of the most confusing rules in the law of evidence. **Despite its name, the Best Evidence Rule does not require a party to offer the best evidence available. Instead, it requires only that when a party seeks to prove the contents of a writing, recording, or photograph, the party must use the original writing, recording, or photograph.** In fact, the phrase "Best Evidence Rule" is so misleading that the federal rules have dropped it. The section of the FRE dealing with the BER is called "Contents of Writings, Recordings, and Photographs."

1. RATIONALE. [§62.1]

The BER is a product of the days when documents were hand-copied by monks and the Bob Crachits of the world. The risk of error in transcription was significant and so the law developed a preference for the original of a writing. With technological advances such as the Xerox machine, this danger has been reduced and the law of evidence has, therefore, created exceptions to the BER. Today, the BER can best be justified on efficiency grounds. By preferring production of a writing over testimony about the writing, it eliminates disputes about what the writing says.

B. ANALYSIS OF A BER PROBLEM. [§62.2]

Because the BER provides that when a party seeks to prove the contents of a writing, recording, or photograph, the party must use the original writing, recording, or photograph unless an exception applies, **four questions** arise. **First,** what do we mean by **"proving the contents"** of a writing, etc.? **Second,** what qualifies as a **"writing, recording, or photograph"**? **Third,** what qualifies as an **"original"**? **Fourth,** what are the **exceptions** to the BER?

1. PROVING THE CONTENTS OF A WRITING. [§62.21]

The most difficult part of BER analysis relates to the threshold question of whether the offered evidence is used to prove the contents of a writing, recording, or photograph. This element of the rule is satisfied if the evidence falls into one of the following three categories. If it does not, the BER does not apply.

a. Category 1: Writings with Independent Legal Significance. [§62.211]

Where the fundamental issue in a case relates to rights or obligations arising **directly** from a writing, etc., the precise words (i.e., the contents) of the writing possess **independent legal significance.** In such cases, even slight variations of the words can significantly and directly affect the legal relationships, and because of the fear of fraud or mistake, the original writing is required.

(1) Types of Actions. [§62.2111]

This category applies whenever the litigation directly involves a writing such as a **contract, lease, will, written libel, photograph,** or **book** (e.g., a copyright action). It does not apply where the writing is only "evidence" of a fact (e.g., receipts, minutes, transcripts). The writing itself must have a direct legal impact.

> **(a) EXAMPLE. [§62.2112]** Plaintiff sues Defendant for breach of a written contract. In his testimony, Plaintiff states what he believes to be an essential provision of the agreement. Defendant's BER objection would be sustained as the terms (contents) of the writing are themselves in issue.

(b) No Hearsay Problems. [§62.2113]

Although writings are out-of-court statements, the types of writings that fall under Category 1 BER analysis are not hearsay because they are operative facts (i.e., words of independent legal significance).

b. Category 2: Writing Offered in Evidence. [§62.212]

If a party physically offers a writing in evidence, she thereby puts the terms of the writing in issue (by asking the trier of fact to rely on it). Thus, if Defendant seeks to prove that she paid Plaintiff $100 by offering a receipt from the transaction, she must offer the original unless one of the exceptions to the BER applies. But Defendant may also prove payment by testifying, "I remember paying Plaintiff $100." In the latter instance, she is not proving the fact through a writing and so the BER does not apply.

c. Category 3: Testimony Relying Upon a Writing. [§62.213]

The most elusive context in which the BER applies involves testimony in which the **witness relies totally upon a writing.** If the witness is telling the trier of fact what the writing says, the writing, not the witness, is the basis of the information. Consequently, the witness has put the writing into issue and must produce the original unless one of the exceptions to the BER applies.

> **(1) EXAMPLES. [§62.2131]** Defendant seeks to prove that she paid Plaintiff $500 on March 1 by using a business record that contains that information. This implicates the BER. She must introduce the original of the record unless one of the exceptions to the BER applies. Similarly, if Defendant testifies, "my records show that I paid Plaintiff $500 on March 1," she is seeking to prove the contents of those records and the BER applies. In contrast, if Defendant testifies "I remember paying Plaintiff $500 on March 1," there is no BER problem because she is testifying as to her independent knowledge of an event. The fact that the event has been memorialized in a business record does not matter. (See Case Squibs section, *Meyers v. United States*.)

(2) Hearsay Problems. [§62.2132]

Both **Category 2** and **Category 3** of the BER analysis may raise **hearsay problems** as well. For example, when Defendant attempts to use her business records to prove that she paid Plaintiff, Plaintiff can raise both hearsay and BER objections. Defendant can meet the hearsay objection by showing that the record qualifies under the business record exception and the BER objection by producing the original.

2. WRITING, RECORDING, PHOTOGRAPH DEFINED. [§62.22]

These terms are **defined broadly so as to include every tangible process of recording words, pictures or sounds.** Thus a **"writing"** includes not only printed material but material recorded on a computer tape or disk. [FRE 1001(1)]. **"Photographs"** include movies, video tapes and X-rays. [FRE 1001(2)]. Although photographs are usually used in trial for illustrative purposes, occasionally a party tries to prove the contents of a photograph.

> **a. EXAMPLE. [§62.221]** If Defendant is prosecuted for selling obscene photographs, an officer may not testify as to the content of the photos. The pictures themselves are in issue and must be produced.

OUTLINE

3. ORIGINAL DEFINED. [§62.23]

The original typically is the writing or recording itself. [FRE 1001(3)]. But other things count as "originals" for BER purposes.

a. Counterparts. [§62.231]

If the person executing or issuing the writing **intends a counterpart to have the same effect,** the counterpart will be considered an original. [FRE 1001(3)]. For example, if parties to a contract make and sign two copies of the contract, each will be considered an "original." These are sometimes referred to as "duplicate originals."

b. Photographs. [§62.232]

An original of a photograph includes the **negative** or **any print** made from the negative. [FRE 1001(2)].

c. Computer Printouts. [§62.233]

Any printout or other output readable by sight, shown to reflect the data accurately, is an original. [FRE 1001(3)].

4. EXCEPTIONS. [§62.24]

There are several exceptions to the BER. Some of the exceptions **allow a particular kind of evidence to be used in lieu of the original.** Some of the exceptions **dispense with the BER entirely,** and allow any kind of proof (oral or written) of the contents of the writing.

a. Duplicate. [§62.241]

Unless a genuine question is raised about the authenticity of the original, a duplicate may be used in lieu of the original. [FRE 1003].

(1) Duplicate Defined. [§62.2411]

A duplicate is a counterpart produced by the **same impression** as the original (e.g., a carbon copy), from the **same matrix** (e.g., from the same printing plate), **by means of photography** (e.g., a picture of a document such as a microfilm), or **by mechanical or electronic re-recording** or **by chemical reproduction** or **other equivalent techniques.** [FRE 1001(4)]. In other words, a duplicate is a copy that is produced by a **technique that accurately reproduces the original.**

b. Public Records. [§62.242]

A **certified copy** of a public record may be used in lieu of the original. Alternatively, a copy that is **testified to be correct** by a witness who has compared it with the original may be used. [FRE 1005].

c. Summaries. [§62.243]

If the original is **voluminous**, its contents may be presented in the form of a **chart, summary, or calculation.** Opposing parties, however, must have been afforded reasonable opportunity to inspect and copy the original. [FRE 1006].

d. Unavailability of Original. [§62.244]

If the original is unavailable **through no fault of the proponent, any evidence** (oral or written) may be used.

(1) Lost or Destroyed. [§62.2441]

If the original is lost or destroyed, the BER is inapplicable, unless the proponent lost or destroyed the original in bad faith. [FRE 1004(1)].

(2) Original Not Obtainable. [§62.2442]

If the original cannot be obtained by judicial process or procedure (e.g., because it is outside the court's subpoena jurisdiction), the BER is inapplicable. [FRE 1004(2)].

(3) Original in Opponent's Possession. [§62.2443]

If the opponent has control of the original, has been put on notice that its contents would be the subject of proof at trial, and does not produce it, the BER is inapplicable. [FRE 1004(3)].

e. Collateral Matters. [§62.245]

If the contents of the writing, recording, or photograph do not closely relate to a controlling issue in the case, the BER is inapplicable. [FRE 1004(4)].

f. Chattels. [§62.246]

If the writing appears on something that is impracticable to produce in court (e.g., a tombstone), the court will find that the object is a chattel rather than a writing and declare the BER inapplicable. (See Case Squibs section, *United States v. Duffy*.)

5. EXPERT TESTIMONY. [§62.25]

Where an expert testifies and bases an opinion on a writing, recording, or photograph, there is no BER problem. An expert may base an opinion on facts that are not admissible in evidence if they are the kinds of facts that such experts reasonably rely upon. [FRE 703]. Therefore, if a doctor bases an opinion on an X-ray she has reviewed, she may give her opinion as to what the X-ray revealed without running afoul of the BER.

REVIEW PROBLEMS — BEST EVIDENCE RULE ("BER")

PROBLEM. Tenant sues Landlord for breaching the terms of their lease.

(1) Tenant testifies that the lease requires Landlord to pay for all appliance repairs costing more than $50.

Answer: Inadmissible. Because Tenant's claim arises directly from the lease, the lease has independent legal significance. Thus, Tenant is testifying as to the contents of the lease (Category 1) and the BER applies.

(2) Tenant testifies that he had to have his refrigerator repaired at a cost of $100 and that Landlord failed to reimburse him.

Answer: Admissible. Even though there may be a dispute about the cost of the repair and the bill may be the most accurate evidence of this, the BER does not apply. Tenant is testifying as to something about which he has knowledge independent of the writing.

(3) Landlord testifies that Tenant sent him the bill for the refrigerator repair and that the charge was only $40.

Answer: Inadmissible. Landlord is testifying as to what the bill stated. Therefore, he is testifying as to the contents of this writing (Category 3) and the BER applies.

XII. PRIVILEGES

A. PRIVILEGES IN GENERAL. [§63.0]

The existence of privileges demonstrates that the law of evidence is not solely concerned with achieving accurate factfinding. Privileges result in the exclusion from evidence of information that may be quite probative. The law recognizes privileges because it has determined that the cost incurred by the loss of reliable evidence is outweighed by the social benefits that accrue from having privileges. Because the cost is high, however, courts often state that privileges are to be construed narrowly.

1. TWO KINDS OF PRIVILEGES. [§63.1]

Privileges may be divided into (a) a group that protects **confidential communications** and (b) a group of **miscellaneous** privileges.

2. FEDERAL RULES: [§63.2]

The proposed federal rules contained privilege rules that proved to be quite controversial. Many critics thought the proposed privilege for state secrets was too broad. Others complained the proposed privileges were not broad enough; they lacked, for example, a doctor-patient privilege. Rather than resolving the controversy itself, Congress left the issue to the courts. Thus, FRE 501, the only privilege rule in the FRE, provides that privileges are to be "governed by the **principles of the common law**" as interpreted by the courts **"in light of reason and experience."** However, in diversity cases and other cases in which state substantive law governs, the federal courts must apply state privilege law.

3. VARIATION AMONG STATES. [§63.3]

Less uniformity exists among jurisdictions regarding privileges than as to any other area of the law of evidence. Therefore, if you are being tested about a particular jurisdiction's privilege rules, it is important to learn that jurisdiction's rules. Nevertheless, there are certain basics that are common to most jurisdictions.

B. CONFIDENTIAL COMMUNICATION PRIVILEGES: OVERVIEW. [§64.0]

The generally accepted confidential communication privileges are: the **attorney-client** privilege; the **physician-patient** privilege; the **psychotherapist-patient** privilege; the **husband-wife** privilege; and the privilege for communications to a **clergyman**. In addition, scattered states recognize a privilege for communications between: accountant and client; parent and child; and social worker and client.

1. RATIONALE. [§64.1]

Each of the confidential communication privileges is based on the view that **guaranteeing confidentiality is necessary to foster what society deems to be an important relationship.** The benefits gained from fostering the relationship outweigh the harm caused by shielding the communication from disclosure.

2. SCOPE OF PRIVILEGE. [§64.2]

A confidential communication privilege allows the holder of the privilege (a) to refuse to disclose and (b) to prevent others from disclosing the protected communication.

3. IMPORTANT: COMMUNICATIONS ARE PRIVILEGED; INFORMATION IS NOT. [§64.3]

It is crucial to understand that **communication privileges protect communications, but not the underlying information.** Thus, when Plaintiff deposes Defendant, Plaintiff will not be able to ask Defendant, **"Did you tell your lawyer** that you ran the stop sign?" But Plaintiff will be allowed to ask Defendant, "Did you run the stop sign?" A party is not allowed to insulate relevant information from disclosure simply by relating it to his lawyer.

4. ATTACK PLAN. [§64.4]

You can easily detect and answer most privilege questions if you ask yourself the following six questions whenever you suspect a confidential communication privilege may be lurking.

1. **Relationship.** Is there a privileged relationship? 2. **Communication.** Was there a germane communication? 3. **Confidentiality.** Was the communication confidential? 4. **Holder.** Is the holder asserting the privilege? 5. **Waiver.** Did the holder waive the privilege? 6. **Exceptions.** Is there an exception to the privilege?

C. ATTORNEY-CLIENT PRIVILEGE. [§65.0]

Every state recognizes the attorney-client privilege, either by statute or common law. The privilege allows (a) a client (b) to refuse to disclose and to prevent others from disclosing (c) confidential (d) communications (e) made between the attorney and client or their representatives (f) for the purpose of facilitating the rendition of legal services.

1. ATTORNEY-CLIENT RELATIONSHIP. [§65.1]

There must be an attorney-client relationship for the privilege to apply.

a. Lawyer. [§65.11]

A lawyer is someone who is licensed to practice law. If someone mistakenly believes the person in whom he is confiding is a lawyer, the common law states there is no privileged relationship. Most jurisdictions, however, now recognize the relationship if the client's mistake was a reasonable one.

b. Client. [§65.12]

A client may be an individual or an entity such as a corporation. **One who consults a lawyer with the idea of obtaining legal services** is considered a client. Thus, an attorney-client relationship will be recognized even if the client and lawyer had no prior relationship, the lawyer is not formally retained by the client, the lawyer is not paid, or the lawyer eventually declines to represent the client.

c. Representatives of Lawyers and Clients. [§65.13]

Confidential communications may pass through representatives of lawyers and clients.

(1) Representative of Lawyer. [§65.131]

Someone employed by the lawyer to assist in the rendition of legal services (such as a clerk, paralegal, or even an expert whom the lawyer consults) is a representative of the lawyer. Thus, confidential statements made by a client to an accountant whom the lawyer has employed to assist in rendering legal advice will be protected.

(2) Representative of Client. [§65.132]

When a client is a corporation, the question arises: "Who speaks for the corporation?" For example, suppose an explosion occurs at a company plant. In preparing for litigation, the company's lawyer interviews corporate officials and employees. Which if any of these conversations will be protected by the attorney-client privilege? Several tests have been advanced.

(a) Control Group Test. [§65.1321]

Only members of the control group of a corporation (e.g., officers and directors) are representatives of the client whose communications to the corporation's lawyer are privileged.

(b) Diversified Industries Test. [§65.1322]

In *Diversified Industries, Inc. v. Meredith,* 572 F.2d 596 (8th Cir. 1978), the Eighth Circuit held that the attorney-client privilege protects a communication made by an employee who is outside the control group if (a) the employee made the communication **at the behest of his superior** (b) the superior made the request **so the corporation could secure legal advice;** and the communication (c) was made **for the purpose of securing legal advice,** (d) concerned a matter **within the scope of the employee's duties,** and (e) was **not disseminated** beyond those persons who needed to know its contents.

(c) Supreme Court Rejects Control Group Test. [§65.1323]

(See Case Squibs section, *Upjohn Co. v. United States.*) In *Upjohn Co. v. United States,* the Court rejected the control group test but declined to set forth a test for courts to follow. However, in upholding the privilege claim, the Court seemed to cite factors consistent with the criteria set forth in the *Diversified Industries* case.

2. COMMUNICATION. [§65.2]

The privilege applies only to **communications that are germane** to the attorney-client relationship.

a. Must be Germane. [§65.21]

A communication is privileged only if it was **made for the purpose of facilitating the rendition of legal services.**

(1) Lawyer in Non-Lawyer Capacity. [§65.211]

Communications are not privileged when they are made to a lawyer acting in a capacity other than as an attorney (e.g., as a business partner, tax preparer, witness to a will).

b. Communication. [§65.22]

Communications generally are verbal, either oral or written. Non-verbal statements intended to communicate information (such as nodding or pointing) are also communications.

(1) Observations. [§65.221]

Observations made by the lawyer during the relationship are generally not considered communications. For example, a lawyer may be required to tell that her client was bleeding or screaming inappropriately during a consultation.

(2) Writings. [§65.222]

A writing by a client that did not originate as a communication to her lawyer is not privileged, even if she subsequently turns it over to the lawyer. For example, the privilege does not cover pre-existing business files or personal letters that a client hands over to her lawyer. In contrast, if a client writes down **for her lawyer** the history of a dispute, the privilege will apply.

3. CONFIDENTIALITY. [§65.3]

To be privileged, a communication must have been made in confidence.

a. Presence of Third Persons. [§65.31]

If someone other than the lawyer, client, their representatives, or a person reasonably necessary for the transmission of information (e.g., an interpreter) is made privy to the communication, confidentiality is not present. Thus, the presence of a secretary, clerk, interpreter, or consultant does not destroy confidentiality; the presence of a friend whose attendance is unnecessary does.

b. Intent to Maintain Confidentiality Decisive. [§65.32]

Most courts now hold that a communication is confidential **if the client intended** that it would be disclosed only to (a) the lawyer and (b) anyone else to whom disclosure was necessary to help provide legal services or communicate the information.

(1) Eavesdroppers. [§65.321]

Under this standard, a lawyer-client conversation that is overheard by an eavesdropper **retains its confidentiality so long as it was the client's intent that it remain confidential.** Some jurisdictions, however, still adhere to the common law view that an eavesdropper (or someone who uncovers a written communication) is permitted to testify as to the communication. (See Case Squibs section, *Clark v. State*.)

(2) Communication Made With Intent to Disclose. [§65.322]

A communication is not privileged if the client tells the lawyer something with the intent that the lawyer disclose it to a third person.

4. CLIENT IS HOLDER. [§65.4]

The client is the holder of the privilege and is thus entitled to assert it or waive it. The lawyer may assert it **on the client's behalf,** as may the trial judge, if the client is not present or represented at the proceeding. **The privilege survives the client's death** and may be asserted by the client's successor or personal representative.

5. PRIVILEGE MAY BE WAIVED. [§65.5]

A communication loses its privileged status if the client (a) **fails to assert** the privilege in a timely fashion or (b) **voluntarily reveals a significant part** of the communication. If someone other than the client makes an unauthorized disclosure, the privilege is not lost.

a. Privileged Disclosure. [§65.51]

If a client discloses a privileged communication to someone else with whom the client has privileged relationship, no waiver occurs. For example, if a client tells his wife what his lawyer told him, the privilege still applies, as client's confidential communications with his wife are themselves privileged.

6. EXCEPTIONS. [§65.6]

There are several exceptions to the attorney-client privilege.

a. Crime or Fraud. [§65.61]

The privilege does not attach to any communications made by a client who is seeking the lawyer's advice **to enable the client to commit what he knew or should have known was a crime or fraud.** (See Case Squibs section, *Clark v. State.*)

b. Breach of Duty. [§65.62]

Communications relevant to an issue of breach of duty between the lawyer and client (e.g., failure to pay fees, malpractice) are not privileged.

c. Joint Clients. [§65.63]

Where two or more clients consult a lawyer upon a matter of common interest (e.g., Abercrombie and Fitch, partners, consult Lawyer), their communications are not privileged if one of them seeks to offer the evidence **against the other.**

d. Document Attested By Lawyer. [§65.64]

Communications relevant to an issue concerning a document to which the lawyer was an attesting witness are not privileged.

e. Claimants Through Deceased Client. [§65.65]

If two or more parties are claiming through the same deceased client, communications relevant to their dispute are not privileged. Thus, if a will is ambiguous as to which of the client's two nieces was supposed to take under her will, relevant communications to the lawyer who drafted the will may be revealed.

7. PRIVILEGE v. WORK PRODUCT v. OBLIGATION TO MAINTAIN CONFIDENTIALITY. [§65.7]

These three doctrines are related, but distinct. The **attorney-client privilege** empowers the client to refuse to reveal, and to prevent someone else from revealing, attorney-client communications. The **work product** doctrine shields from discovery certain information created or obtained by the lawyer in anticipation of litigation or preparation for trial. This **includes information obtained from third parties** and therefore not covered by the attorney-client privilege. The professional **obligation to maintain confidentiality is imposed by professional rules of ethics** (e.g., the Code of Professional Responsibility or Rules of Professional Conduct). This obligation **forbids lawyers from voluntarily disclosing information** about their clients, including information not protected by the privilege.

D. PHYSICIAN-PATIENT PRIVILEGE. [§66.0]

Although **many states recognize** a physician-patient privilege, the **federal courts of appeals** have thus far unanimously **rejected** this privilege. Even where the privilege is recognized, however, it is **riddled with exceptions** and is virtually useless as a means of encouraging patients to confide in their physicians. Consequently, proponents of the physician-patient privilege often emphasize its role in protecting patients' **privacy** interests, even if it has little or no effect on an individual's decision to seek medical advice or to confide in the physician.

1. PHYSICIAN-PATIENT RELATIONSHIP. [§66.1]

The patient must consult the doctor for purposes of diagnosis or treatment. The physician must be licensed to practice medicine. If the patient consults someone whom she mistakenly but reasonably believes to be a doctor, the privilege applies.

2. COMMUNICATIONS. [§66.2]

The concept of germane communications is broader than in the lawyer-client arena. Protected communications include a patient's medical and hospital records, direct communications between the doctor and patient, and information observed by the doctor through physical examinations and tests. For example, the results of a blood-alcohol test performed on a patient are privileged.

3. CONFIDENTIALITY. [§66.3]

The privilege protects only confidential communications. The presence of necessary third parties (nurses, attendants, consultants, and the like) does not destroy confidentiality. In addition, the privilege applies when a patient communicates with her physician through an intermediary (e.g., a family member).

4. PATIENT IS HOLDER. [§66.4]

The patient is the holder of the privilege. The physician may assert the privilege on behalf of the patient. If the patient is incompetent, her guardian may assert it on her behalf. **The privilege does not die with the patient;** it may be asserted by her personal representative, and in some states, by her successor.

5. WAIVER. [§66.5]

Waiver is accomplished in the same way as the attorney-client privilege: by the holder's **failure to assert** it or by **voluntary disclosure of a significant part** of the privileged communication.

6. EXCEPTIONS. [§66.6]

Different states have different exceptions. The following are the most common and most important.

a. Criminal Proceedings. [§66.61]

In many states the privilege does not apply in criminal proceedings.

b. Patient-Litigant. [§66.62]

If the patient (or the patient's representative if the patient is dead) puts her physical or mental condition into issue, the privilege may not be asserted to prevent the disclosure and introduction of relevant medical evidence. Thus, if a plaintiff claims that her ailment resulted from using the defendant's product, she would not be able to assert the privilege to prevent the defendant from discovering and introducing her medical records to rebut her claim.

c. Breach of Duty. [§66.63]

The privilege is not available in fee disputes or malpractice actions between the physician and patient.

d. Court-Appointed Physician. [§66.64]

No privilege attaches when a patient is examined by a court-appointed physician.

E. PSYCHOTHERAPIST-PATIENT PRIVILEGE. [§67.0]

Every state has a psychotherapist-patient privilege of some kind, and in 1996, the **Supreme Court recognized** a psychotherapist-patient privilege under FRE 501. *Jaffee v. Redmond*, U.S. (1996).

1. PSYCHOTHERAPIST-PATIENT RELATIONSHIP. [§67.1]

States vary as to how they define psychotherapist (e.g., whether therapists other than psychiatrists and psychologists are included). The Supreme Court has extended the privilege to communications made licensed social workers in the course of psychotherapy.

2. EXCEPTIONS. [§67.2]

As is the case with the physician-patient privilege, the exceptions vary from state to state. Those applicable to the physician-patient privilege are often applicable to the psychotherapist-patient privilege as well. In *Jaffee*, the Supreme Court noted that exceptions to the priviledge wil undoubtedly have to be created. The Court declined, however, to enumerate what those exceptions might be.

F. COMMUNICATIONS TO CLERGYMEN. [§68.0]

Most states recognize a privilege for communications made to a member of the clergy. Some are narrow in scope and apply only to confessions made to a priest. Others are much broader and apply to any confidential communication made to a minister, priest, rabbi, or other similar functionary of a religious organization in his or her capacity as a spiritual adviser. This may include, for example, communications made to a minister by someone seeking marriage counseling. There are no generally accepted exceptions to this privilege.

G. ACCOUNTANT-CLIENT PRIVILEGE. [§69.0]

Most states do not recognize an accountant-client privilege.

H. MARITAL COMMUNICATION PRIVILEGE. [§70.0]

There are **two privileges involving spouses**. One is for **confidential communications made during the marriage;** the other privilege (the testimonial privilege) permits a person to **refuse to testify against her spouse in a criminal case.** We deal here with the communication privilege, which is founded on the rather dubious notion that spouses will be deterred from confiding in one another unless the law gives them the right to prevent the disclosure of their confidences during the course of a trial.

1. MARITAL RELATIONSHIP. [§70.1]

The parties to the communication must be legally married **at the time the communication is made.**

a. Effect of Divorce. [§70.11]

The privilege survives divorce but relates only to communications made during the marriage. Remember, this privilege is designed to protect communications made in the bosom of the marital relationship.

b. Married But Separated. [§70.12]

Federal courts are increasingly willing to hold that a communication made between a husband and wife whose marriage is no longer viable (although it is technically still legally intact) is not protected by the privilege.

2. COMMUNICATION. [§70.2]

Courts are split over what is a "communication." Some courts hold that only verbal statements and non-verbal acts intended to be communicative (e.g., nodding, pointing) are protected. Others favor a broader interpretation, embracing private observations made during the marriage if it appears that one spouse, relying upon the confidential nature of the marital relationship, allowed the other spouse to observe.

> **a. EXAMPLE. [§70.21]** Husband comes home one night with a sack full of money. He makes no attempt to hide it from his wife. When she asks him what it is, he tells her it is money he has just stolen from a convenience store. While his comment to her clearly qualifies as a communication, courts disagree as to whether her observation of the sack of money is a protected communication. Most would hold that it is not privileged.

3. CONFIDENTIALITY. [§70.3]

The communication must be made privately. The presence of even the couple's child is enough to destroy confidentiality.

4. BOTH SPOUSES ARE HOLDERS. [§70.4]

Most courts hold that both spouses are holders of the privilege and either one may assert it. Thus, if Husband wants to testify as to a communication and Wife invokes the privilege, Husband will not be permitted to testify. Some states, however, vest the privilege only in the communicating spouse.

5. WAIVER. [§70.5]

The privilege is waived the same way as other communication privileges.

6. EXCEPTIONS. [§70.6]

Recognized exceptions to the marital communications privilege vary from jurisdiction to jurisdiction. The following are the most common.

a. Actions Between Spouses. [§70.61]

The privilege may not be asserted in an action between the spouses, such as a divorce proceeding.

b. Crime or Fraud. [§70.62]

Communications made by a spouse in furtherance of a crime or fraud are not protected.

c. Crime Against Family Member. [§70.63]

An exception is made in many jurisdictions when the spouse is charged with a crime against a family member (e.g., wife beating, child abuse).

I. PARENT-CHILD. [§71.0]

By analogy to the marital communication privilege, numerous commentators and litigants have argued for recognition of a privilege for parent-child communications. Both the federal courts and the overwhelming majority of state courts have **rejected** such a privilege.

J. MISCELLANEOUS PRIVILEGES. [§72.0]

A number of privileges have been created for matters other than confidential communications. These include the **spousal testimonial** privilege; the **voter's** privilege; the **trade secrets** privilege; the **informer's identity** privilege; the **state secrets** privilege; and the **journalist's** privilege. In addition, the constitution provides a basis for the **executive** privilege as well as the **privilege against self-incrimination.**

K. SPOUSAL TESTIMONIAL PRIVILEGE. [§73.0]

This is the second of the two husband-wife privileges. Unlike the privilege for marital communications, the testimonial privilege applies in **criminal cases only.**

1. COMMON LAW RULE. [§73.1]

The common law rule gives a criminal defendant the **right to prevent his spouse from testifying** against him (or to prevent him from testifying against her). That is, the privilege is held by the accused, not the testifying spouse. This rule is still followed in many states.

2. MODERN TREND. [§73.2]

The modern trend is to give a spouse the **right to refuse to testify against a criminal defendant** spouse. This vests the privilege in the witness spouse, not the defendant spouse. If the witness spouse chooses to testify, she may do so. The Supreme Court has followed the modern trend. (See Case Squibs section, *Trammel v. United States.*)

3. RATIONALE. [§73.3]

The spousal testimonial privilege is usually justified on the ground that forcing a spouse to give testimony that could result in her spouse's conviction places the testifying spouse in an untenable position. She must either testify adversely to her spouse, commit perjury, or face contempt for refusing to testify. This is deemed too destructive of the marital relationship. In short, the theory is: It's not nice to force a wife to testify against her husband (or vice-versa) in a criminal case.

4. END OF MARRIAGE, END OF PRIVILEGE. [§73.4]

Although it may not be nice to force a wife to testify against her criminal defendant husband, the law has no qualms about compelling an ex-wife to testify against her ex-husband. **The right of a spouse to refuse to testify against a spouse terminates with the end of the marriage.**

5. EVEN IF SPOUSE TESTIFIES, COMMUNICATION PRIVILEGE STILL EXISTS. [§73.5]

The marital communication and spousal testimonial privileges are **two independent privileges.** Therefore, even in a jurisdiction that allows the wife to choose to testify against her husband, the husband may prevent her from revealing confidential communications made to her during the marriage.

> **a. EXAMPLE. [§73.51]** Husband is on trial in federal court for bank robbery. The prosecutor calls Wife to testify that (a) the night of the robbery she saw Husband come into the house carrying a satchel marked "First State Bank" and (b) Husband told her that night that he had committed the bank robbery. Wife may assert her spousal testimonial privilege and refuse to testify. Even if she chooses to testify, however, Husband may prevent her from relating what he told her. That is a confidential communication. But in most jurisdictions, her observation of Husband carrying the satchel is not considered a confidential communication, and Husband cannot prevent Wife from testifying about it.

> **b. EXAMPLE. [§73.52]** Husband is on trial in federal court for bank robbery. The prosecutor calls Ex-Wife to testify that (a) the night of the robbery (at which time they were still married) she saw Husband come into the house carrying a satchel marked "First State Bank" and (b) Husband told her that night that he had committed the bank robbery. Ex-Wife asserts her testimonial privilege and refuses to testify against him. She cannot do this. Since she is an ex-wife, she may be forced to testify against her former spouse. Husband may, however, prevent her from testifying as to what he told her. That is a confidential communication.

6. EXCEPTIONS. [§73.6]

Certain exceptions have been recognized to the testimonial privilege.

a. Crime Against Family Member. [§73.61]

An exception is made in many jurisdictions when the spouse is charged with a crime against a family member (e.g., wife beating, child abuse). In such cases, therefore, the spouse can be compelled to testify.

b. Marrying the Eyewitness. [§73.62]

In some jurisdictions, the testimonial privilege does not apply to events that occurred before the marriage. This is to prevent an accused from marrying an important witness against him and keeping her off the stand.

7. MARITAL COMMUNICATION DISTINGUISHED FROM SPOUSAL TESTIMONIAL PRIVILEGE. [§73.7]

The marital **communication privilege** protects (a) confidential communications (b) made during the marriage. If a communication was made during marriage, it remains privileged even if the marriage subsequently ends. The communication privilege applies in both civil and criminal cases. The **spousal testimonial privilege** (a) applies only in criminal cases and (b) allows a spouse to refuse to testify against her criminal defendant spouse about anything. The right to refuse to testify disappears with the end of the marriage.

L. POLITICAL VOTE. [§74.0]

A person may refuse to reveal how he voted in a secret ballot unless he voted illegally.

M. TRADE SECRETS. [§75.0]

The trade secrets privilege allows a person to refuse to disclose (and prevent others from disclosing) a trade secret owned by him. This is a qualified privilege, however, and the court may order disclosure pursuant to a protective order.

N. IDENTITY OF INFORMER. [§76.0]

The government may refuse to disclose the identity of a person who has furnished information to law enforcement officials regarding illegal conduct. However, if the court finds it is probable that the informer can give testimony necessary to a fair trial and the government still refuses to disclose the informer's identity, the court must dismiss the relevant charges against the defendant. (See Case Squibs section, *McCray v. Illinois.*)

O. STATE SECRETS. [§77.0]

A privilege for matters such as military secrets and other classified information has traditionally been recognized. *United States v. Reynolds,* 345 U.S. 1 (1953). Case law is limited, however, and Congress has enacted special legislation to deal with this problem.

P. EXECUTIVE PRIVILEGE. [§78.0]

The executive privilege protects the confidential communications between the president and his immediate advisers. The privilege is only a qualified one, however, and does not protect communications if there exists a demonstrated, specific need for the information in a criminal trial. (See Case Squibs section, *United States v. Nixon.*)

Q. JOURNALIST'S PRIVILEGE. [§79.0]

The Supreme Court has held that the First Amendment does not create a privilege that allows journalists to refuse to divulge information about the sources of their stories. *Branzburg v. Hayes,* 408 U.S. 665 (1972). Many states have enacted statutory privileges with varying coverage and exceptions. Even in states with broad statutory privileges, however, the privilege may have to yield to a defendant's right to compulsory process. (See Case Squibs section, *Matter of Farber.*)

R. PRIVILEGE AGAINST SELF-INCRIMINATION. [§80.0]

The Fifth Amendment privilege against self-incrimination has two components. First, it protects an individual from being (a) compelled to engage (b) in testimonial conduct (c) that would tend to incriminate himself. Second, it gives a criminal defendant the right not to take the stand, thereby forbidding the prosecution from calling the accused as a witness.

1. ACTIVITY MUST BE COMPELLED. [§80.1]

The privilege against self-incrimination only protects an individual from being **compelled** from engaging in testimonial activity. Thus the contents of **voluntarily created** written materials (e.g., a diary) are not privileged. In addition, **the privilege is personal**: a defendant may not prevent someone else (e.g., a co-defendant) from testifying in an incriminating manner.

2. ACTIVITY MUST BE TESTIMONIAL. [§80.2]

The privilege protects against compelled **testimonial** activity. If the compelled activity is non-testimonial in nature, the privilege is inapplicable.

a. Testimonial Activity Defined. [§80.21]

Compelled activity is testimonial in nature if the individual is **being forced to reveal, directly or indirectly, his knowledge of facts or his belief about a matter.**

b. Examples of Non-Testimonial Activity. [§80.22]

An individual may be compelled to provide a blood sample, participate in a line-up, read a transcript, give a handwriting exemplar, submit to a breathalyzer test, and sign a consent directive authorizing a bank to disclose records of any account over which the individual may happen to have a right of withdrawal.

c. Implicit Testimonial Activity. [§80.23]

An individual may refuse to comply with a subpoena directing him to produce enumerated documents. **Although the contents of the documents are not themselves protected** (because they were voluntarily created), **the act of production may involve implicit testimonial activity.** That is, when an individual hands over the requested materials, he is implicitly admitting that the materials exist, that they are in his possession, and that these are the requested materials. (See Case Squibs section, *United States v. Doe*.)

3. MUST TEND TO INCRIMINATE. [§80.3]

The privilege protects against compelled testimonial activity only if it would tend to incriminate the individual. Information tends to incriminate an individual **if it would constitute a link in a chain of evidence that might lead to his conviction.**

a. Civil Liability Not Incriminatory. [§80.31]

The fact that an answer might result in civil, rather than criminal, liability is not sufficient to invoke the privilege. However, if a penalty that is nominally civil is really criminal in nature (e.g., the consequences of being adjudged a juvenile delinquent), the privilege may be invoked. **In re Gault**, 387 U.S. 1 (1967).

b. Privilege May Be Invoked in Civil Proceedings. [§80.32]

Whether an answer tends to incriminate is determined **by the consequences that may befall the witness, not the type of proceeding** in which the answer is compelled. For example, a witness in a civil fraud action may invoke the privilege and refuse to discuss his role in the fraud

— not because the answers might result in civil liability, but because the answers might be used to convict him of criminal fraud.

c. Immunity. [§80.33]

The danger of incrimination may be removed by granting the witness immunity. State or federal prosecutors may grant a person immunity which, at the least, guarantees that the testimony the person gives (and the fruits of such testimony) cannot be used against him in subsequent criminal proceedings. Having been given such **use immunity,** the witness can no longer contend that his answers would tend to incriminate him and thus can be compelled to testify. A broader form of immunity is **transactional immunity,** under which the witness may not be prosecuted at all for the criminal transactions discussed in his testimony.

4. RIGHT NOT TO TESTIFY. [§80.4]

A criminal defendant has a right not to testify. The prosecution may not call the defendant and force him to assert this privilege. Further, the prosecutor may not comment upon the defendant's failure to take the stand and argue that the jury should draw a negative inference therefrom. (See Case Squibs section, *Griffin v. California*.)

a. Comment in Civil Cases. [§80.41]

In contrast to criminal cases, some courts allow civil litigants to comment upon their opponent's invocation of the privilege against self-incrimination and permit the court to instruct the jury that it may draw a negative inference therefrom.

5. WAIVER. [§80.5]

If a party, including the defendant in a criminal case, voluntarily testifies, he waives the right to refuse to answer questions on cross-examination that are related to the testimony. However, a party who has testified in one proceeding may change his mind and invoke the privilege against self-incrimination in a later proceeding and refuse to testify.

PROBLEM 1. Defendant is on trial for murder.

(1) The prosecution calls Lockhart to testify. Lockhart, who was an eyewitness to the crime, recognized Defendant because she had represented him in an earlier criminal case. Lockhart seeks to testify that she saw Defendant kill Victim. Defendant objects, citing the attorney-client privilege.

> **Answer:** Objection overruled. The attorney-client privilege protects only confidential communications between lawyer and client made for the purpose of furthering the rendition of legal services. Lockhart is testifying as to what she observed as an eyewitness, not as to a confidential communication made to her by Defendant.

(2) The prosecution seeks to call Defendant to the stand and force him to claim the privilege against self-incrimination in response to its questions.

> **Answer:** The prosecution may not do this. The privilege against self-incrimination gives the defendant in a criminal case the right not to be called as a witness.

(3) The prosecution makes a closing argument to the jury which includes the following statement, "One person in this courtroom knows for sure what happened that night. But did Defendant take the stand and tell you what happened? Did he tell you, 'I didn't do it?, No.' "

> **Answer:** This is improper. The prosecution may not comment on a defendant's failure to testify in his own behalf.

PROBLEM 2. Plano brings a wrongful death action against Drone. He alleges that Drone, while driving under the influence of alcohol and drugs, veered into the car driven by Plano's wife and killed her.

(1) Plano calls Drone's wife and seeks to ask her, "How many drinks did Drone have before he left the house that night?" Drone's wife asserts her privilege not to testify against her husband.

> **Answer:** Drone's wife must testify. The privilege not to testify against one's spouse applies only in criminal cases.

(2) Plano seeks to ask Drone's wife whether Drone said anything to her about the accident. Drone objects, asserting the privilege for marital communications.

> **Answer:** As long as the communications between Drone and his wife were made confidentially, they are privileged. The communication privilege applies in civil cases as well as criminal.

XIII. JUDICIAL NOTICE

A. JUDICIAL NOTICE. [§81.0]

Judicial notice is an **evidentiary shortcut.** It allows trial and appellate courts to accept certain facts or propositions of law as true without requiring formal proof.

1. RATIONALE. [§81.1]

Judicial notice is designed to (1) **save time and expense** in proving facts that are not subject to reasonable dispute and (2) **avoid the disrespect** for the court system that would result if trials resulted in factual findings that everyone knows to be false.

B. THREE TYPES OF JUDICIAL NOTICE: "L.A. LAW". [§81.2]

Courts may take judicial notice of (1) **legislative facts,** (2) **adjudicative facts,** and (3) **law.** (**Mnemonic** device: L.A. Law). The Federal Rules of Evidence contain provisions governing only judicial notice of **adjudicative facts.** [FRE 201].

1. ADJUDICATIVE FACTS. [§81.3]

Adjudicative facts are **facts that relate to the immediate parties or event.** For example, was the defendant intoxicated? Had the sun set by the time of the accident? Judicial notice may be taken of an adjudicative fact if it is **indisputable.** There are **two situations** in which this occurs.

a. Facts in Common Knowledge. [§81.31]

Courts may take judicial notice of facts that **well-informed persons** in the community **generally know and accept.**

(1) Well-Informed Persons. [§81.311]

Not everyone in the community must know the fact for it to be judicially noticed. The standard is whether well-informed persons in the community in which the court is sitting know it. [FRE 201(b)(1)].

> **(a) EXAMPLE. [§81.3111]** A court sitting in Chicago may judicially notice that the Chicago Cubs play in Wrigley Field and that until recently the Cubs played home games only during the daytime.

(2) Judge's Own Knowledge. [§81.312]

Private knowledge of certain facts by the judge is not sufficient for judicial notice. Thus, a judge familiar with a particular intersection cannot take judicial notice of its unique characteristics unless the party seeking judicial notice can show that those facts are generally known in the community.

b. Readily Verifiable Facts. [§81.32]

Certain facts are not generally known, but can be **easily verified by resort to sources whose accuracy cannot reasonably be questioned.** [FRE 201(b)(2)].

(1) Sources of Verification. [§81.321]

The verification must come from a reputable and reasonably accessible source that establishes the truth of the fact beyond reasonable dispute.

> **(2) EXAMPLES. [§81.322]** Courts may take judicial notice of **natural phenomena** (e.g., time of sunrise or sunset), **chronology** (e.g., December 30, 1988 was a Friday), **history** (e.g., President Kennedy was assassinated on November 22, 1963), **geography** (e.g., the tallest mountain in the U.S. is in Alaska), **demography** (e.g., the population of a city), and **scientific theories, facts, and conclusions** (e.g., that heated oxygen will combine with lead to form lead oxide). This last category includes the **scientific basis** for various tests (e.g., radar, ballistic, breathalyzer, DNA).

c. Effect of Judicial Notice. [§81.33]

The effect of judicially noticing a fact depends on whether it is a civil or criminal case.

(1) Civil. [§81.331]

If a court takes judicial notice of a fact in a civil case, it will instruct the jury to **accept the truth of that fact.** Once the fact is noticed, **evidence to disprove its truth is inadmissible.** [FRE 201(g)].

(2) Criminal. [§81.332]

Under the federal rules and in many jurisdictions, the court in a criminal case is permitted only to instruct the jury that it **may, but is not required to, accept the truth** of a judicially noticed fact. [FRE 201(g)].

2. LEGISLATIVE FACTS. [§81.4]

Legislative facts are those facts that a court considers in making **policy decisions** in the course of **interpreting various common-law doctrines, statutes, and the constitution.** In this context, the court is operating as a quasi **law-making body** and its determinations are based on certain social, political, and economic assumptions which are not amenable to indisputable proof. For example, in determining whether the witness spouse or defendant spouse should be the holder of the spousal testimonial privilege, the court's decision is informed by certain assumptions about marital relationships.

a. Not Codified. [§81.41]

Neither the federal rules nor most state evidence rules contain provisions governing judicial notice of legislative facts. Courts may notice legislative facts without regard to whether they are indisputable and may consider reports, books, articles, studies, etc., without following any particular procedure. (See Case Squibs section, *United States v. Gould.*)

3. JUDICIAL NOTICE OF LAW. [§81.5]

With a few exceptions, judges may take judicial notice of the law. That is, judges may do their own research to determine what the relevant law is; they are not restricted to considering only the evidence that the parties present. The **two exceptions** to this general rule are **foreign law** and **municipal ordinances.** Jurisdictions vary as to whether foreign law and municipal ordinances must be proved or whether courts may take notice of them. For example, the Federal Rules of Civil Procedure provide for judicial notice of foreign law. [§F.R.C.P. 44.1]. Municipal ordinances are usually singled out for special treatment (and must be proved) because they are less accessible than state laws or regulations.

4. PROCEDURES. [§81.6]

A court may take judicial notice of adjudicative facts **on its own motion. Upon request** by a party, a court **must** take judicial notice if supplied with the necessary information by the party.

a. Hearing. [§81.61]

A party may request a hearing regarding the **propriety** of taking judicial notice (i.e., whether this is a fact that is generally known) and the **tenor** of the matter noticed (i.e., although the fact is generally known, whether the court got it right).

5. WHEN NOTICE MAY BE TAKEN. [§81.7]

Judicial notice may be taken **at any time.** Even an appellate court may take judicial notice of facts not presented to the trial court.

Problem 1. Plaintiff sues Defendant for injuries suffered when their cars collided.

(1) As part of her proof that Defendant would have been able to stop at the intersection had he been driving at a reasonable speed, Plaintiff asks the court to take judicial notice that a car traveling at 60 miles per hour is traveling 88 feet per second.

> **Answer:** The court should take judicial notice of this. Although this may not be a commonly known fact, it is easily verified by multiplying the number of feet in a mile (a fact that can be easily verified by reference to unimpeachable sources) by 60 (miles per hour) and dividing the product by the number of seconds in an hour (a generally known fact).

(2) Defendant asks the court to take judicial notice that the light at the intersection was not working on the day of the collision.

> **Answer:** This is not the proper subject of judicial notice. It is an adjudicative fact that is neither generally known nor easily verifiable by resort to unimpeachable sources. Defendant must offer proof that the light was malfunctioning on the day in question.

(3) In response to Defendant's request that the court take judicial notice that the light at the intersection was not working on the day of the collision, the judge states that although she would not ordinarily take judicial notice of such a fact, it happens that she drove by the intersection that day and observed that the light was not working and so will take judicial notice of the fact.

> **Answer:** The judge has acted improperly. A judge may not take judicial notice of an adjudicative fact based on her own knowledge of such a fact.

Problem 2. Defendant is convicted for possession of an unregistered handgun. Prosecution seeks to enhance Defendant's sentence by proving that Defendant had a prior felony conviction. Although Defendant concedes that he had been previously convicted in the State of Hypothet for marijuana possession, he asks the court to take notice that marijuana possession is only a misdemeanor in Hypothet.

> **Answer:** The court make take judicial notice of the laws of a sister state.

XIV. BURDENS OF PROOF AND PRESUMPTIONS

A. BURDENS OF PROOF. [§82.0]

There are two senses in which the term "burden of proof" is typically employed. It is sometimes used to refer to the **burden of production** (also known as the burden of going forward with the evidence). At other times it is used to refer to the **burden of persuasion** (also known as the risk of non-persuasion). The party that bears the burden of production and fails to meet it loses without getting to the jury. The party that bears the burden of persuasion may get to the jury but will lose if it fails to meet this burden.

OUTLINE

1. WHO BEARS THE BURDEN OF PERSUASION. [§82.1]

The substantive law determines which party bears the burden of persuasion as to an issue.

a. Civil Cases. [§82.11]

Generally, the plaintiff has the burden of persuasion as to the elements of its claim, while the defendant bears the burden of persuasion as to any defenses raised. For example, if Plaintiff sues Defendant for defamation, Plaintiff has the burden of proving that a defamatory statement was made by Defendant. On the other hand, if Defendant seeks to assert truth as a defense, Defendant has the burden of establishing the truth of the statement.

b. Criminal Cases. [§82.12]

The prosecution has the burden of persuasion as to every element of the crime charged. This is mandated by the Due Process Clause. *In re Winship*, 397 U.S. 358 (1970). The burden of persuasion as to an affirmative defense (such as self-defense or insanity), however, may constitutionally be placed on the defendant. *Leland v. Oregon*, 343 U.S. 790 (1952) (insanity); *Martin v. Ohio*, 107 U.S. 1098 (1987) (self-defense).

2. HOW HEAVY IS THE BURDEN OF PERSUASION. [§82.2]

The weight of the burden of persuasion varies with the type of case.

a. Preponderance of the Evidence. [§82.21]

Ordinarily, the party with the burden of persuasion in a civil case must prove its case by a preponderance of the evidence. This means that it must satisfy the factfinder that it is **more likely than not** that the facts that establish its claim exist. This is the 50-50 standard. In a typical civil case, the plaintiff must convince the jury that the odds are better than 50-50 that its version of the facts is true.

b. Clear and Convincing Evidence. [§82.22]

In some instances (e.g., some kinds of fraud) the jury must be convinced of the relevant facts by "clear and convincing evidence." This is a higher standard of proof, although courts make no effort to quantify it.

c. Beyond a Reasonable Doubt. [§82.23]

This is the familiar standard of proof for criminal cases. The prosecution must meet its burden of persuasion as to each element of the crime by presenting proof that satisfies the jury "beyond a reasonable doubt." *In re Winship*, 397 U.S. 358 (1970).

3. BURDEN OF PRODUCTION. [§82.3]

The burden of production (the burden of going forward with the evidence) is a means of allocating decision-making between the judge and jury. **A party that fails to meet its burden of production will lose without getting to the jury;** that is, the judge will grant a directed verdict against the party.

a. Meeting the Burden of Production. [§82.31]

A party meets its burden of production if it produces **enough evidence so that a reasonable juror could find for the party.** A party with the burden of production as to a particular fact need not persuade the judge that the fact exists; it is sufficient that the judge believes that a reasonable juror could believe that it exists.

4. TRAFFIC LIGHT EXPLANATION OF BURDENS. [§82.4]

Imagine that Plaintiff sues Defendant for damages arising out of an auto accident. The only issue is whether Defendant drove negligently. The amount of damages is stipulated. This is a typical civil case: Plaintiff has the burden of persuasion.

a. Red Light. [§82.41]

Suppose the only evidence Plaintiff introduces is that Plaintiff's and Defendant's cars collided. No evidence indicating Defendant was at fault is introduced. Defendant would be entitled to a directed verdict because no reasonable juror could find that Defendant was negligent. Thus, the judge would (figuratively) hold up a red light, stopping Plaintiff from getting his case to the jury. Plaintiff has not only failed to meet his burden of persuasion, he has failed to meet his burden of production.

b. Yellow Light. [§82.42]

Suppose Plaintiff introduces some evidence (not particularly strong, however) indicating that Defendant was at fault. Defendant's motion for a directed verdict would now fail. A reasonable juror could find for Plaintiff; but he could also reasonably find for Defendant. Thus, the judge would hold up a yellow light, allowing the case to go to the jury. Plaintiff has met his burden of production. Whether he has met his burden of persuasion is up to the jury.

c. Green Light. [§82.43]

Suppose Plaintiff introduces a great deal of unchallenged evidence establishing Defendant's negligence. At this point, if Defendant fails to produce some counter-evidence, the judge would have to grant Plaintiff's motion for a directed verdict. In other words, absent some evidence from Defendant, the judge would have to conclude that no reasonable juror could rule for Defendant. At this point, the judge would hold up a red light **to Defendant**, preventing Defendant from getting to the jury (hence the green light for Plaintiff). **The burden of production has, therefore, shifted from Plaintiff to Defendant**.

d. Yellow Light Again. [§82.44]

Suppose Defendant now introduces some counter-evidence. At this point, the judge would conclude that a reasonable juror could find either for Plaintiff or Defendant and let the case go to the jury. Defendant would have met her burden of production.

e. Although Burden of Production May Shift, Burden of Persuasion Does Not. [§82.45]

Note that in the above example, the burden of production shifted to Defendant when the evidence was overwhelmingly against her. However, the burden of persuasion never shifted; it remained with Plaintiff throughout.

B. PRESUMPTIONS IN CIVIL CASES. [§83.0]

Normally, the jury has discretion in deciding what inferences should be drawn from the evidence. A presumption, however, is **a procedural device which requires the jury to draw a particular conclusion from certain proved facts**.

1. BASIC AND PRESUMED FACTS. [§83.1]

The proved fact from which the prescribed conclusion must be drawn is called the **basic** fact. The prescribed conclusion is called the **presumed** fact, which must be inferred if the basic fact is proved.

> **a. EXAMPLE. [§83.11]** The law presumes that a letter that was properly addressed and mailed will be received in due course by the addressee. Note that even without this presumption, the jury could permissibly infer receipt of a letter from evidence of proper mailing. The presumption, however, **requires** the jury to find that the letter was received if they believe the letter was properly addressed and mailed. (This presumption may be rebutted. More on that later.) The facts of "proper addressing" and "proper mailing" are the basic facts which must be proved; "receipt of the letter" is the presumed fact which must be inferred if the basic facts are proved.

2. HOW PRESUMPTIONS WORK IN GENERAL. [§83.2]

In dealing with presumptions, it is important to distinguish between the treatment of basic facts and presumed facts.

a. Basic Facts. [§83.21]

Presumptions come into play only if the proponent proves the basic facts. If there is no dispute about the basic facts, the presumption is triggered. If there is a dispute about the basic facts, the presumption comes into play only if the jury finds that the basic facts exist. **The opponent of a presumption may always try to show that the basic facts don't exist.**

b. Effect of Triggering the Presumption. [§83.22]

If the basic facts are found to exist, the presumption is triggered. **The effect of the presumption differs, however, depending on whether it is an irrebuttable (or conclusive) presumption or a rebuttable**

OUTLINE

presumption. If a conclusive presumption is triggered, its opponent may not attempt to disprove the **presumed** fact. With a rebuttable presumption, the opponent may try to disprove the presumed fact as well as the basic facts.

3. IRREBUTTABLE (CONCLUSIVE) PRESUMPTIONS. [§83.3]

With an irrebuttable presumption, if the basic facts are shown to exist, the presumed fact is **conclusively established.** No evidence contrary to the presumed fact will be received.

---

a. EXAMPLE. [§83.31] Suppose a jurisdiction has a conclusive presumption that a child born to a married woman is presumed to be legitimate if the woman was cohabiting with her husband at the time of conception. If the basic facts required to trigger the presumption are established (i.e., that the mother was married and cohabiting with her husband at the time of conception), the presumed fact (i.e., that the child is legitimate) is conclusively established. Evidence that might prove the husband is not the biological father (e.g., blood tests) will not be received.

---

b. Really a Substantive Rule of Law In Disguise. [§83.32]

A conclusive presumption is really a substantive rule of law masquerading as a rule of evidence. In the above example, the presumption effectively states that, under certain circumstances, biological and legal paternity are two different things.

c. Basic Facts May Be Challenged. [§83.33]

Remember, even a conclusive presumption operates only if the factfinder is convinced of the existence of the basic facts. Therefore, **the party opposing an irrebuttable presumption may always challenge the existence of the basic facts.** In the above example, for instance, evidence might be offered that husband and wife were not cohabiting at the time of conception.

4. REBUTTABLE PRESUMPTIONS. [§83.4]

Most presumptions are rebuttable. If the basic facts of a rebuttable presumption are proved, the jury is required to find the presumed fact unless the opponent of the presumption rebuts it. How much evidence the opponent must produce to negate the effect of the presumption depends on the jurisdiction's approach to rebuttable presumptions. There are **two basic approaches** to rebuttable presumptions.

a. Presumption Shifts Burden of Persuasion. [§83.41]

One view of rebuttable presumptions (often referred to as the **Morgan-McCormick** approach, in honor of two famous Evidence scholars) is that they **shift the burden of persuasion.** If the proponent triggers the presumption by establishing the basic facts, **the jury must find that the presumed fact exists unless the opponent persuades it that the presumed fact does not exist.** That is, the effect of this type of presumption is to place on the opponent the burden of persuading the jury that the presumed fact does not exist.

> **(1) EXAMPLE. [§83.411]** Plaintiff is trying to prove that Defendant received a particular letter. Plaintiff testifies that she properly addressed and mailed the letter to Defendant. Defendant cross-examines plaintiff about her testimony. Later, Defendant testifies that he never received the letter. The judge should instruct the jury that if they find that Plaintiff addressed and mailed the letter to Defendant, they **must** find that Defendant received it **unless** Defendant convinces them by a preponderance of the evidence that he did not receive it.

(2) Designed to Further Public Policy. [§83.412]

By shifting the burden of persuasion to the opponent of the presumed fact, the Morgan-McCormick presumption makes it more likely that the presumed fact will be found. This reflects a view that presumptions should be used to promote public policy by increasing the likelihood that juries will reach certain outcomes.

b. Presumption Shifts Production Burden: The Bursting Bubble Approach. [§83.42]

Under this approach (sometimes referred to as the Thayer-Wigmore approach, also in honor of two famous Evidence scholars), the presumption acts merely to **shift the burden of production** to the opponent. In other words, the opponent of the presumption may negate its effect merely by producing **evidence that would allow a juror to find that the presumed fact does not exist. If the opponent does this, the presumption disappears** from the case (the bubble bursts). Thus, this type of presumption has a practical effect only if the opponent of the presumption fails to produce evidence to rebut the presumed fact.

> **(1) EXAMPLE. [§83.421]** Plaintiff is trying to prove that Defendant received a particular letter. Plaintiff testifies that she properly addressed and mailed the letter to Defendant. Defendant cross-examines Plaintiff about her testimony. Later, Defendant testifies that he never received the letter. **Under the bursting bubble approach, the judge should not give the jury an instruction.** By testifying that he did not receive the letter, Defendant has produced sufficient evidence for the jury to find that the presumed fact (receipt of the letter) does not exist. Thus he has met his production burden and eliminated the presumption from the case. Remember, Defendant does not have to persuade the judge or jury that he did not receive the letter in order to negate the presumption; he need only produce evidence of non-receipt.

(2) Presumption is Gone, But Logical Inference Remains. [§83.422]

Although the procedural effect of the presumption may be overcome, any logical inference that flows from the basic facts remains. Thus, if the jury believes that the letter was properly addressed and mailed, it may still infer that Defendant received it.

(3) Presumption Only a Procedural Convenience. [§83.423]

The bursting bubble approach to presumptions reflects a view that presumptions are merely **procedural conveniences designed to**

expedite litigation and (sometimes) to force the party with greater access to the evidence to come forward with it. Under this view, therefore, they should be given little weight.

c. Determining Which View to Apply. [§83.43]

FRE 301 adopts the weaker form of presumption, **shifting only the burden of production and not the burden of persuasion** to the opponent of the presumption. (In diversity and other cases in which state law governs, the federal rules defer to the state law of presumptions.) If an exam question is not based on the federal rules, it will probably indicate how the relevant jurisdiction treats presumptions. If it does not, and it is an essay question, discuss both views. Keep in mind that the bursting bubble (FRE) approach views presumptions merely as a procedural convenience, whereas the Morgan-McCormick approach views presumptions as a means of advancing public policy.

d. Jury Not Told Directly About "Presumption." [§83.44]

A jury is not told directly about the existence of a presumption. The judge simply instructs the jury as to the consequence of finding the basic facts. That is, without ever mentioning the word "presumption," the judge will instruct the jury, "If you find [the basic facts], then . . ." Of course, what the consequence will be of finding the basic facts depends on the type of presumption.

5. SUMMARY OF PRESUMPTIONS IN CIVIL CASES. [§83.5]

In dealing with presumptions, it is important to **focus on three things:** (a) the **type** of presumption involved; (b) whether the **basic facts** have been contested; and (c) whether evidence has been introduced that disputes the existence of the **presumed facts**. The following are examples of instructions that would be given the jury depending on these three factors. In each example, the basic facts are abbreviated as "BF" and the presumed fact as "PF".

a. Instructions for Conclusive Presumptions. [§83.51]

Remember, if the basic facts are established, the opponent will not be allowed to disprove the presumed fact.

(1) Basic Facts Uncontroverted. [§83.511]
"You must find PF."

(2) Basic Facts Disputed. [§83.512]
"If you find BF, you must find PF."

b. Instructions for Morgan-McCormick Presumptions. [§83.52]

Remember, this type of presumption shifts the burden of persuasion to the opponent of the presumption.

(1) BF Uncontroverted, No Evidence on PF. [§83.521]
"You must find PF."

(2) BF Disputed, No Evidence on PF. [§83.522]
"If you find BF, you must find PF."

(3) BF Uncontroverted, Evidence Disputing PF. [§83.523]

"You must find PF unless Opponent persuades you by a preponderance of the evidence that PF does not exist."

(4) BF Disputed, Evidence Disputing PF. [§83.524]

"If you find BF, you must find PF unless Opponent persuades you by a preponderance of the evidence that PF does not exist."

c. Instructions For Bursting Bubble Presumptions. [§83.53]

Recall again that this type of presumption merely shifts the production burden to the opponent of the presumption.

(1) BF Uncontroverted, No Evidence on PF. [§83.531]

"You must find PF."

(2) BF Disputed, No Evidence on PF. [§83.532]

"If you find BF, you must find PF."

(3) BF Uncontroverted, Evidence Disputing PF. [§83.533]

No instruction. Remember: once the opponent introduces evidence from which a juror could find that the presumed fact does not exist, **the presumption disappears** from the case. The jury may still infer the presumed fact from the basic fact, but this is as a matter of logic and not because of the presumption.

(4) BF Disputed, Evidence Disputing PF. [§83.534]

No instruction.

Summary of Presumptions in Civil Cases

IRREBUTTABLE PRESUMPTIONS

	PF Not Controverted	PF Controverted
BF Not Controverted	You must find PF (or dircted verdict on issue)	You must find PF (or directed verdict on issue) [Opponent may not contovert PF]
BF Controverted	If you find BF, you must find PF	If you find BF, you must find PF [Opponent may not controvert PF]

REBUTTABLE PRESUMPTIONS — MORGAN – MCCORMICK (Shifting burden of persuasion)

	PF Not Controverted	PF Controverted
BF Not Controverted	You must find PF (or directed verdict on issue)	You must find PF unless opponent persuades you that PF does not exist
BF Controverted	If you find BF, you must find PF	If you find BF, you must find PF unless opponent persuades you that PF does not exist

	PF Not Controverted	PF Controverted
BF Not Controverted	You must find PF (or directed verdict on issue)	Presumption gone (though inference may be drawn)
BF Controverted	If you find BF, you must find PF	Presumption gone (though inference may be drawn)

6. BATTLE OF THE PRESUMPTIONS: CONFLICTING PRESUMPTIONS. [§83.6]

Suppose two presumptions are relevant to the same case and the basic facts of Presumption 1 create a presumption that Presumed Fact A exists, while the basic facts of Presumption 2 create a presumption that Presumed Fact A does **not** exist. If both are bursting bubble presumptions, this presents no problem. When the basic facts of Presumption 1 are established, there is sufficient evidence of Presumed Fact A to knock Presumption 2 out of the case, and vice versa. If they are not both bursting bubble presumptions, courts tend to apply the presumption that is based on stronger considerations of logic and policy.

7. PRESUMPTIONS IN CRIMINAL CASES. [§84.0]

Recall that the constitution requires the state to prove each element of the crime beyond a reasonable doubt. This limits the ability of the state to use a presumption to prove an element of a crime. (See Case Squibs section, *Sandstrom v. Montana*.)

a. Permissive Inferences. [§84.1]

A "permissive" inference is one in which the court tells the jury that it **may infer** the "presumed" fact from proof of the basic fact. The jury is free to accept or reject the inference and is still told that it must find that the prosecution has proved all elements of the crime beyond a reasonable doubt. A permissive inference is constitutional if (a) under the facts of the case, the connection between the basic fact and the presumed fact is rational and (b) the presumed fact more likely than not flows from the basic fact.

b. Mandatory Inferences. [§84.2]

A "mandatory" inference is one in which the court tells the jury that if it finds the basic fact, it **must find** the presumed fact **unless the defendant comes forward with evidence to rebut the presumed fact.** The jury is not free to disregard the presumption unless the defendant comes forward with counter-evidence. The Supreme Court has stated that a mandatory inference is permissible only if the court finds, independent of the facts of the particular case, that the proof of the basic facts establishes the existence of the presumed fact beyond a reasonable doubt. (See Case Squibs section, *County Court of Ulster County v. Allen*.) The Court has yet to uphold the constitutionality of a given mandatory presumption.

(1) Plaintiff brings a paternity action against Defendant. She alleges that the child was conceived while she and Defendant were married. The relevant jurisdiction recognizes common law marriages and has a statute that provides, "The husband of a woman who conceives a child while the woman and husband were married is irrebuttably presumed to be the father of the child." Plaintiff objects when Defendant attempts to introduce evidence to prove that they were not married at the time the child was conceived.

> **Answer:** Objection overruled. The opponent of a presumption may always try to show the non-existence of the presumed facts; in this case, that he and Plaintiff were not married at the time of conception.

(2) Pedestrian sues Carson for injuries suffered when Carson's car, driven by Algernon, hit Pedestrian. The jurisdiction has a statute that provides, "The driver of a car involved in an accident shall be presumed to be the agent of the owner of the car. This presumption shall have the effect of shifting the burden of persuasion." Prior to trial, Carson stipulates that the car is his. At trial, Pedestrian introduces evidence linking Algernon to Carson. In his defense, Carson testifies that he had never heard of Algernon prior to the accident and that Algernon had taken the car without permission. How should the judge charge the jury?

> **Answer:** Because the presumed facts are undisputed, the presumption is triggered and shifts the burden of persuasion on the agency issue to Carson. Therefore, the judge should instruct the jury that they are to find that Algernon was Carson's agent unless Carson persuades them by a preponderance of the evidence that Algernon was not his agent.

XV. PRACTICE MULTIPLE CHOICE QUESTIONS

Questions 1-3 are based on the following fact situation.

Phillips purchased a suit of thermal underwear manufactured by Makorp from synthetic materials. While he was attempting to stamp out a fire, Phillips' thermal underwear caught fire and burned in a melting fashion up to his waist. He suffered a heart attack a half hour later. In a suit against Makorp, Phillips alleged that negligence and breach of warranty caused both the burn and the heart attack. Phillips testified to the foregoing.

1.   Dr. Jones, a physician, having listened to Phillips' testimony, is called by Phillips and asked whether, assuming the truth of such testimony, Phillips' subsequent heart attack could have resulted from the burns. His opinion is:

(A)   Admissible as a response to a hypothetical question.

(B)   Admissible, because the physician's expertise enables him to judge the credibility of Phillips' testimony.

(C)   Inadmissible, because a hypothetical question may not be based on prior testimony.

(D)   Inadmissible, because an expert's opinion may not be based solely on information provided by a lay person.

2.   Dr. Black, a physician, is called by Phillips to testify that, on the basis of her examination of Phillips and the blood study reports by an independent laboratory, reports which were not introduced in evidence, she believes that Phillips has a permanent disability. This testimony is:

(A)   Admissible, because such laboratory reports are business records.

(B)   Admissible if such reports are reasonably relied upon in medical practice.

(C)   Inadmissible unless Dr. Black has been shown to be qualified to conduct laboratory blood analyses.

(D)   Inadmissible, because Dr. Black's testimony cannot be based on tests performed by persons not under her supervision.

3.   Phillips testified that his purchase of the underwear occurred on April 17th, a fact of minor importance in the case. He stated that he could identify the date because his secretary had taken the day off to attend the first game of the baseball season and he had checked his com-

pany's payroll records to verify the date. Makorp moves to strike the testimony as to the date. The motion should be:

(A)   Sustained, because the best evidence of the information contained in the payroll records is the records themselves.

(B)   Sustained, because Phillips' testimony is based upon hearsay declarations contained in the payroll records.

(C)   Overruled if the judge has personal knowledge of the date on which the baseball seasoned opened.

(D)   Overruled, because the payroll records relate to a collateral matter.

Question 4

In an action to recover for personal injuries arising out of an automobile accident, Plaintiff calls Bystander to testify. Claiming the privilege against self-incrimination, Bystander refuses to answer a question as to whether she was at the scene of the accident. Plaintiff moves that Bystander be ordered to answer the question. The judge should allow Bystander to remain silent only if:

(A)   The judge is convinced that she will incriminate herself.

(B)   There is clear and convincing evidence that she will incriminate herself.

(C)   There is a preponderance of evidence that she will incriminate herself.

(D)   The judge believes that there is some reasonable possibility that she will incriminate herself.

Question 5

Potts sued Dobbs on a product liability claim. Louis testified for Potts. On cross-examination, which of the following questions is the trial judge most likely to rule improper?

(A)   "Isn't it a fact that you are Potts' close friend?"

(B)   "Isn't it true that you are known in the community as "Louie the Lush" because of your addiction to alcohol?"

(C)   "Didn't you fail to report some income on your tax return last year?"

(D) "Weren't you convicted, seven years ago in this court, of obtaining money under false pretenses?"

Questions 6-8 are based on the following fact situation.

Drew was tried for the July 21 murder of Victor.

6. In his case in chief, Drew called as his first witness, Wilma, to testify to Drew's reputation in his community as a "peaceable man." The testimony is:

(A) Admissible as tending to prove Drew is believable.

(B) Admissible as tending to prove Drew is innocent.

(C) Inadmissible, because Drew has not testified.

(D) Inadmissible, because reputation is not a proper way to prove character.

7. Drew called William to testify that on July 20 Drew said that he was about to leave that day to visit relatives in a distant state. The testimony is:

(A) Admissible, because it is a declaration of present mental state.

(B) Admissible, because it is not hearsay.

(C) Inadmissible, because it is irrelevant.

(D) Inadmissible, because it is hearsay not within any exception.

8. Drew called Wilson to testify to alibi. On cross-examination of Wilson, the prosecutor asked, "Isn't it a fact that you are Drew's first cousin?" The question is:

(A) Proper, because it goes to bias.

(B) Proper, because a relative is not competent to give reputation testimony.

(C) Improper, because the question goes beyond the scope of direct examination.

(D) Improper, because the evidence being sought is irrelevant.

Question 9

Alice was held up at the point of a gun, an unusual revolver with a red-painted barrel, while she was clerking in a neighborhood grocery store. Dennis is charged with armed robbery of Alice.

The prosecutor calls Winthrop to testify that, a week after the robbery of Alice, he was robbed by Dennis with a pistol that had red paint on the barrel. Winthrop's testimony is:

(A) Admissible as establishing an identifying circumstance.

(B) Admissible as showing that Dennis was willing to commit robbery.

(C) Inadmissible, because it is improper character evidence.

(D) Inadmissible, because its probative value is substantially outweighed by the danger of unfair prejudice.

Question 10

Dunn is charged with committing perjury before a legislative committee. The prosecution may prove what Dunn said to the committee through:

(A) The stenographer who recorded Dunn's testimony.

(B) The transcript of the testimony.

(C) The testimony of a spectator who was present when Dunn testified before the committee.

(D) All of the above.

Question 11

Donat is charged with a theft that occurred on June 15. Prosecution seeks to call Donat's ex-wife, Wendy, to testify that on June 16 she found a watch in Donat's nightstand, which the prosecution had already proved was among the items taken in the June 15 theft. Donat and Wendy were divorced three months after the theft.

This testimony is:

(A) Inadmissible because the state may not force Wendy to testify against Donat, her former spouse.

(B) Inadmissible because it is hearsay.

(C) Inadmissible because it violates Donat's privilege against self-incrimination.

(D) Admissible because she is not testifying as to a confidential communication made during the marriage.

Question 12

Deffen consults with Lawyer regarding Deffen's indictment for securities fraud. Deffen admits to having engaged in some of the charged conduct. Lawyer declines to represent her and accepts no payment. Deffen subsequently hires a different lawyer.

At Deffen's trial, which of the following is true?

(A) Lawyer's secretary, who was present during the consultation, may testify as to Deffen's statements.

(B) An FBI agent, who had bugged Lawyer's office, may testify to what he heard when he eavesdropped on Deffen and Lawyer's conversation.

(C) Lawyer may testify as to Deffen's statements because he did not take the case.

(D) Deffen may prevent any of the above from testifying as to the contents of his communications with Lawyer.

Questions 13-15 are based on the following fact situation.

Pablo brings an action for damage to his automobile, allegedly caused by the negligence of Dana. Upon direct examination, Pablo is asked to describe in detail the damage to his vehicle. He states that he cannot remember the details, as the collision in question occurred four years prior to the trial.

13. His attorney then hands him a written estimate of repairs prepared a few days after the collision by a mechanic at the Acme Garage. This is:

(A) Permissible to refresh Pablo's present memory.

(B) Never permitted unless the judge first examines the item and gives his discretionary permission.

(C) Improper because the item has not been authenticated.

(D) Proper because the estimate is reliable past recollection recorded.

14. Pablo testifies that he recognizes the estimate, which includes a list of all the damaged parts of his vehicle, and that he was present when it was prepared. Pablo then requests permission to read the estimate aloud.

The request should be:

(A) Granted.

(B) Granted only if the judge gives a limiting instruction restricting its use for non-substantive purposes.

(C) Granted only if there is no jury.

(D) Denied.

15. Pablo then calls Jones, the owner of Acme Garage, who testifies that he recognizes the estimate as being on a printed form used in the regular course of his business, that such forms were filled out only by qualified estimators immediately after viewing the car in question, and

that although he did not prepare the estimate, the figures "look right" to him.

The testimony:

(A) Must be stricken because Jones does not have personal knowledge of the estimate.

(B) Sufficiently qualifies the estimate to allow the judge to admit it as a business record.

(C) Is admissible as an admission.

(D) Is admissible as a declaration against interest.

Question 16

Paul sues Dean for injuries suffered in an automobile accident. To prove that Dean did not have a driver's license, Paul calls Wanda to testify that Dean told her a week before the accident that he had failed his road test.

This testimony is:

(A) Inadmissible because Wanda may be lying.

(B) Admissible as an admission by a party opponent.

(C) Admissible only if Dean is unavailable.

(D) Inadmissible hearsay.

Question 17

Doppler is being tried for bank robbery and conspiracy to commit robbery. To prove that his participation in the robbery was coerced, Doppler testifies that his fellow robbers told him that if he did not participate in the robbery he would be shot.

This testimony is:

(A) Not hearsay.

(B) Not hearsay only if Doppler reasonably believed the statements of his fellow robbers.

(C) Hearsay, but admissible as declaration against interest.

(D) Hearsay, but admissible as an excited utterance.

Question 18

Portia was injured in an automobile collision at the intersection of Main and South. She sued the city, claiming that the city negligently failed to trim trees and shrubs around the stop sign at the intersection, thereby allowing the stop sign to be obscured. Portia offers into evidence five letters that the city admits having received prior to accident, all of which complain that the stop sign is not visible from the road.

This evidence is:

(A)   Admissible to prove only that the stop sign was not visible.

(B)   Admissible to prove only that the city knew or should have known that the stop sign was not visible.

(C)   Admissible to prove both that the stop sign was not visible and that the city knew or should have known that.

(D)   Inadmissible to prove either that the stop sign was not visible or that the city knew or should have known that.

Question 19

Pratt sues George for slander. At trial, Pratt seeks to testify that George said to him a few weeks before trial, "Maybe I shouldn't have said those things I said about you. But your claim for $50,000 is ridiculous. I'll give you $10,000 if you'll drop your claim."

This testimony is:

(A)   Admissible because George's statement is an admission.

(B)   Inadmissible because George's statement is hearsay not within any exception.

(C)   Inadmissible because George's statement was an attempt to settle Pratt's claim.

(D)   Inadmissible because admission of George's statement would violate his privilege against self-incrimination.

Questions 20-21 are based on the following facts.

Dent is being tried for the June 21 murder of victim.

20.   Prosecution calls Winn to testify that he saw Dent shoot the victim. Winn has recently immigrated to this country, and does not speak English. In addition, Winn was released from a mental institution, following a four-month stay at the institution.

Which of the following statements is true?

(A)   Winn is incompetent to testify because he cannot speak English.

(B)   Winn is mentally incompetent to testify.

(C)   Winn may testify, but only if he was officially adjudicated as competent when he was released from the mental institution.

(D)   Winn may testify through a qualified interpreter.

21.   Prosecution calls Nurse to testify that Pond, a patient at the hospital, told her, "I know I'm about to die. I saw Dent shoot Victim." Pond died a few minutes later.

This testimony is:

(A)   Admissible as a dying declaration.

(B)   Admissible as an admission of a party opponent.

(C)   Inadmissible hearsay.

(D)   Not hearsay.

Questions 22-24 are based on the following fact situation.

Pemberton and three passengers, Bale, Baker and Charley, were injured when their car was struck by a truck owned by Mammoth Corporation and driven by Edwards. Helper, also a Mammoth employee, was riding in the truck. The issues in *Pemberton v. Mammoth* include the negligence of Edwards in driving too fast and in failing to wear glasses, and of Pemberton in failing to yield the right of way.

22.   Pemberton's counsel proffers evidence showing that shortly after the accident, Mammoth put a speed governor on the truck involved in the accident. The judge should rule the proffered evidence:

(A)   Admissible as an admission of a party.

(B)   Admissible as res gestae.

(C)   Inadmissible for public policy reasons.

(D)   Inadmissible, because it would lead to the drawing of an inference on an inference.

23.   Pemberton's counsel seeks to introduce Helper's written statement that Edwards, Mammoth's driver, had left his glasses (required by his operator's license) at the truck stop which they had left five minutes before the accident. The judge should rule the statement admissible only if:

(A)   Pemberton first proves that Helper is an agent of Mammoth and that the statement concerned a matter within the scope of his agency.

(B)   Pemberton produces independent evidence that Edwards was not wearing corrective lenses at the time of the accident.

(C) Helper is shown to be beyond the process of the court and unavailable to testify.

(D) The statement was under oath in affidavit form.

24. Mammoth's counsel seeks to have Sheriff testify that while he was investigating the accident, he was told by Pemberton, "This was probably our fault." The judge should rule the proffered evidence:

(A) Admissible as an admission of a party.

(B) Admissible, because it is a statement made to a police officer in the course of an official investigation.

(C) Inadmissible, because it is a mixed conclusion of law and fact.

(D) Inadmissible, because it is hearsay, not within any exception.

Question 25

Drew is charged with the murder of Pitt. The prosecutor introduced testimony of a police officer that Pitt told a priest, administering the last rites, "I was stabbed by Drew. Since I am dying, tell him I forgive him." Thereafter, Drew's attorney offers the testimony of Wall that the day before, when Pitt believed we would live, he stated that he had been stabbed by Jack, an old enemy. The testimony of Wall is:

(A) Admissible under an exception to the hearsay rule.

(B) Admissible to impeach the dead declarant.

(C) Inadmissible, because it goes to the ultimate issue in the case.

(D) Inadmissible, because irrelevant to any substantive issue in the case.

Questions 26-27 are based on the following fact situation.

Peri sues Denucci for a libelous letter received by investigator. The authenticity and contents of the letter are disputed.

26. Peri's attorney asks Investigator to testify that, a week before receiving the libelous letter, he had written to Denucci inquiring about Peri. The testimony is:

(A) Admissible provided this inquiry was made in the regular course of Investigator's business.

(B) Admissible without production of the inquiry letter or the showing of its unavailability.

(C) Inadmissible unless Peri's attorney has given Denucci notice of Investigator's intended testimony.

(D) Inadmissible unless the inquiry letter itself is shown to be unavailable.

27. Investigator, if permitted, will testify that, "I received a letter that I cannot now find, which read:

Dear Investigator,

You inquired about Peri. We fired him last month when we discovered that he had been stealing from the stockroom.

Denucci"

The testimony should be admitted in evidence **only** if the:

(A) Jury finds that Investigator has quoted the letter precisely.

(B) Jury is satisfied that the original letter is unavailable.

(C) Judge is satisfied that Investigator has quoted the letter precisely.

(D) Judge finds that the original letter is unavailable.

Questions 28-29 are based on the following fact situation.

In a trial between Jones and Smith, an issue arose about Smith's ownership of a horse, which had caused damage to Jones' crops.

28. Jones offered to testify that he looked up Smith's telephone number in the directory, called that number and that a voice answered, "This is Smith speaking." At this Jones asked, "Was that your horse that tramped across my cornfield this afternoon?" The voice replied, "Yes." The judge should rule the testimony:

(A) Admissible, because the answering speaker's identification of himself, together with the usual accuracy of the telephone directory and transmission system, furnishes sufficient authorization.

(B) Admissible, because judicial notice may be taken of the accuracy of telephone directories.

(C) Inadmissible unless Jones can further testify that he was familiar with Smith's voice and that is was in fact Smith to whom he spoke.

(D) Inadmissible unless Smith has first been asked whether or not the conversation took place and has been given the opportunity to admit, deny or explain.

29. Jones seeks to introduce in evidence a photograph of his cornfield in order to depict the nature and extent of the damage done. The judge should rule the photograph:

(A) Admissible if Jones testifies that it fairly and accurately portrays the condition of the cornfield after the damage was done.

(B) Admissible if Jones testifies that the photograph was taken within a week after the alleged occurrence.

(C) Inadmissible if Jones fails to call the photographer to testify concerning the circumstances under which the photograph was taken.

(D) Inadmissible if it is possible to describe the damage to the cornfield through direct oral testimony.

Question 30

Patty sues Mart Department Store for personal injuries, alleging that while shopping, she was knocked to the floor by a merchandise cart being pushed by Handy, a stock clerk, and that as a consequence, her back was injured.

Handy testified that Patty fell near the cart but was not struck by it. Thirty minutes after Patty's fall, Handy, in accordance with regular practice at Mart, had filled out a printed form, "Employee's Report of Accident—Mart Department Store," in which he stated that Patty had been leaning over to spank her young child and in so doing had fallen near his cart. Counsel for Mart offers in evidence the report, which had been given him by Handy's supervisor. The judge should rule the report offered by Mart:

(A) Admissible as res gestae.

(B) Admissible as a business record.

(C) Inadmissible, because it is hearsay, not within any exception.

(D) Inadmissible, because Handy is available as a witness.

Question 31

A leading question is LEAST likely to be permitted over objection when:

(A) Asked on cross-examination of an expert witness.

(B) Asked on direct examination of a young child.

(C) Asked on direct examination of a disinterested eyewitness.

(D) Related to preliminary matters such as the name or occupation of the witness.

Question 32

Price sued Derrick for injuries Price received in an automobile accident. Price claimed Derrick was negligent in (A) exceeding the posted speed limit of thirty-five m.p.h., (B) failing to keep a lookout, and (C) crossing the center line. Bystander, Price's eyewitness, testified on cross-examination, that Derrick was wearing a green sweater at the time of the accident. Derrick's counsel calls Wilson to testify that Derrick's sweater was blue. Wilson's testimony is:

(A) Admissible as substantive evidence of a material fact.

(B) Admissible as bearing on Bystander's truthfulness and veracity.

(C) Inadmissible, because it has no bearing on the capacity of Bystander to observe.

(D) Inadmissible, because it is extrinsic evidence of a collateral matter.

Question 33

Cars driven by Pugh and Davidson collided, and Davidson was charged with driving while intoxicated in connection with the accident. She pleaded guilty and was merely fined, although under the statute, the court could have sentenced her to two years in prison.

Thereafter, Pugh, alleging that Davidson's intoxication had caused the collision, sued Davidson for damages. At trial, Pugh offers the properly authenticated record of Davidson's conviction. The record should be:

(A) Admitted as proof of Davidson's character.

(B) Admitted as proof of Davidson's intoxication.

(C) Excluded, because the conviction was not the result of a trial.

(D) Excluded, because it is hearsay not within any exception.

Question 34

Pitt sued Dow for damages for injuries that Pitt incurred when a badly rotted limb fell from a curbside tree in front of Dow's home and hit Pitt. Dow claimed that the tree was on city property and thus was the responsibility of the city. At trial, Pitt offered testimony that a week after the accident, Dow had cut the tree down with a chainsaw. The offered evidence is

(A) Admissible, because there is a policy to encourage safety precautions.

(B) Inadmissible, because it is irrelevant to the condition of the tree at the time of the accident.

(C) Admissible to show the tree was on Dow's property.

(D) Admissible to show the tree was in a rotted condition.

Question 35

Dean, charged with murder, was present with her attorney at a preliminary examination when White, who was the defendant in a separate prosecution for concealing the body of the murder victim, testified for the prosecution against Dean. When called to testify at Dean's trial, White refused to testify, though ordered to do so.

The prosecution offers evidence of White's testimony at the preliminary examination. The evidence is:

(A) Admissible as former testimony.

(B) Admissible as past recollection recorded.

(C) Inadmissible, because it would violate White's privilege against self-incrimination.

(D) Inadmissible, because it is hearsay not within any exception.

Question 36

Potts, a building contractor, sued Dennis for failure to pay on a small cost-plus construction contract. At trial, Potts, who personally supervised all of the work, seeks to testify to what he remembers about the amount of pipe used, the number of workers used on the job, and the number of hours spent grading.

Dennis objects on the ground that Potts had routinely recorded these facts in notebooks which are in Potts's possession.

Potts's testimony is:

(A) Admissible as a report of regularly conducted business activity.

(B) Admissible as based on first-hand knowledge.

(C) Inadmissible, because it violates the Best Evidence Rule.

(D) Inadmissible, because a summary of writings cannot be made unless the originals are available for examination.

Question 37

Dryden is tried on a charge of driving while intoxicated. When Dryden was booked at the police station, a videotape was made that showed him unsteady, abusive, and speaking in a slurred manner. If the prosecutor lays a foundation properly identifying the tape, should the court admit it in evidence and permit it to be shown to the jury?

(A) Yes, because it is an admission.

(B) Yes, because its value is not substantially outweighed by unfair prejudice.

(C) No, because the privilege against self-incrimination is applicable.

(D) No, because specific instances of conduct cannot be proved by extrinsic evidence.

Question 38

In Polk's negligence action against Dell arising out of a multiple car collision, Witt testified for Polk that Dell went through a red light. On cross-examination, Dell seeks to question Witt about her statement that the light was yellow, made in a deposition that Witt gave in a separate action between Adams and Baker. The transcript of the deposition is self-authenticating.

On proper objection, the court should rule the inquiry:

(A) Admissible for impeachment only.

(B) Admissible as substantive evidence only.

(C) Admissible for impeachment and as substantive evidence.

(D) Inadmissible, because it is hearsay not within any exception.

Question 39

In a civil suit by Pine against Decker, Decker called Wall, a chemist, as an expert witness and asked him a number of questions about his education and experience in chemistry. Over Pine's objection that Wall was not shown to be qualified in chemistry, the trial court permitted Wall to testify as to his opinion in response to a hypothetical question.

On cross-examination, Pine asked Wall if he had failed two chemistry courses while doing his graduate work. The answer should be:

(A) Admitted, because it is relevant to the weight to be given to Wall's testimony.

(B) Admitted, because specific acts bearing on truthfulness may be inquired about on cross-examination.

(C) Excluded, because the court has determined that Wall is qualified to testify as an expert.

(D) Excluded, because Wall's character has not been put in issue.

Question 40

In a tort action, Fisher testified against Dawes. Dawes then called Jones, who testified that Fisher had a bad reputation for veracity. Dawes then also called Weld to testify that Fisher once perpetrated a hoax on the police.

Weld's testimony is:

(A) Admissible, provided that the hoax involves untruthfulness.

(B) Admissible, provided that the hoax resulted in conviction of Fisher.

(C) Inadmissible, because it is merely cumulative impeachment.

(D) Inadmissible, because it is extrinsic evidence of a specific instance of misconduct.

ANSWERS TO THE MULTIPLE-CHOICE QUESTIONS

Answer to Question 1.

(A) is the correct choice.

Experts may give opinions in response to hypothetical questions. (B) is incorrect; the physician is being asked to assume the truth of Phillips' testimony and is not judging his credibility. (C) and (D) are both incorrect statements of the law. Hypothetical questions may be based on prior testimony; experts may base opinions solely on information provided by lay persons.

Answer to Question 2.

(B) is the correct choice.

An expert's opinion may be based on facts even if they would be inadmissible evidence so long as they are the type of facts reasonably relied upon by experts in the field. The status of the lab reports as business records is thus irrelevant and (A) is incorrect. This also eliminates (D). (C) is wrong because the expert need only have to understand the significance of the lab results; she doesn't have to be qualified to conduct the lab tests (or any of the other tests that she might use to forming her opinion).

Answer to Question 3.

(D) is the correct choice.

An exception to the best evidence rule is made when the matter is collateral. Therefore (A) is the wrong answer. The payroll records would qualify under the business records exception, so (B) is incorrect. (C) goes to judicial notice. The question does not ask whether judicial notice might be taken of the date. In any event, the judge's personal knowledge would not establish that judicial notice is proper.

Answer to Question 4.

(D) is the correct choice.

A witness may invoke the privilege against self-incrimination if her answer might constitute a link in a chain of evidence that might lead to her conviction. Answers (A), (B), and (C) all state higher standards than the law requires.

Answer to Question 5.

(B) is the correct choice.

(D) is clearly proper. Because it inquires about a conviction for a crime involving false statement, the judge must allow it. (C) inquires about a specific act that bears on truthfulness. (A) is proper because it seeks to show bias. (B) is the thus the correct answer. The only possible impeachment technique that it could fall under is capacity; but the fact that the witness is known as Louie the Lush and is an alcoholic says little about his capacity to testify accurately.

Answer to Question 6.

(B) is the correct choice.

A defendant is permitted to offer evidence of his good character to prove he acted in conformity with that good character on the occasion in question, i.e., that he is not guilty. This is true regardless of whether the defendant testifies, so (C) is wrong. Since he has not yet testified, his believability as a witness is not yet an issue, so (A) is wrong. (D) is wrong because reputation is always a proper way to prove character.

Answer to Question 7.

(A) is the correct choice.

This is clearly hearsay; the testimony is being offered to place the defendant far from the scene of the crime. This eliminates (B) and (C). (A) is the correct answer and (D) is wrong because a statement of an existing intent to do something in the future is admissible to prove the declarant followed through on his expressed intent. This falls within the state of mind hearsay exception, FRE 803(3).

Answer to Question 8.

(A) is the correct choice.

Bias is always a proper impeachment technique and bias may be inferred from the fact that a witness is related to a party. (B) is incorrect; all witnesses are competent unless otherwise expressly provided and the witness here did not give reputation testimony as is suggested in the answer. Cross-examination as to credibility is always permissible, so (C) is wrong. And the evidence is clearly relevant, so (D) is wrong.

Answer to Question 9.

(A) is the correct choice.

Evidence that a defendant committed another crime using the same distinct modus operandi as the charged crime is admissible to prove identity. Thus, (A) is right and (D) is not. Given the unique nature of the gun, the probative value of this evidence far outweighs the danger of unfair prejudice. The evidence is not admissible to prove willingness to commit the crime, so (B) is wrong. (C) is incorrect because the evidence is not being offered here to prove character.

Answer to Question 10.

(D) is the correct choice.

All of these are permissible ways of proving what Dunn said at the committee hearing. (A) and (C) involve the testimony of persons who have personal knowledge of what Dunn said. (B) involves using the transcript, which can qualify as a business record or past recollection recorded if a proper foundation is laid.

Answer to Question 11.

(D) is the correct choice.

The only possible objection would be the marital communication privilege, but that is not applicable because Wendy's finding a watch in Donat's nightstand does not constitute a communication. Therefore, (D) is correct. (A) is incorrect because the privilege not to testify applies only to current spouses. Wendy would testify as to what she saw; no hearsay is involved, so (B) is wrong. Donat's privilege against self-incrimination is not implicated when someone else testifies against him, so (C) is incorrect.

Answer to Question 12.

(D) is the correct choice.

Communications made to a lawyer by a person who consults the lawyer with a view toward obtaining legal services fall within the attorney-client privilege. Thus, (C) is wrong. (A) and (B) are wrong because the communications are considered confidential despite the presence of Lawyer's secretary or the eavesdropping by the FBI agent.

Answer to Question 13.

(A) is the correct choice.

Any object may be used to refresh recollection as long as the purpose is legitimate. Although the court may be suspicious and demand to view the refreshing item before it is used, this is not a requirement and so (B) is wrong. A refreshing item is not itself evidence and so does not have to meet any evidentiary prerequisites, including authentication; thus, (C) is wrong. (D) is incorrect because no foundation has been laid to offer that this is a past recollection recorded.

Answer to Question 14.

(D) is the correct choice.

(B) is incorrect because if the statement can be read aloud at all, it is used as evidence for substantive purposes. Therefore, no limiting instruction would be proper. (C) is wrong because the presence of a jury is irrelevant. (A) is incorrect because the estimate is hearsay and it has not been qualified as a business record or as past recollection recorded. Since it is hearsay and not admissible under any exception to the hearsay rule, it may not be related to the jury. Thus, (D) is the right answer.

Answer to Question 15.

(B) is the correct choice.

The estimate has been qualified as a business record. All four elements of "KRAP" have been met: it was the regular practice of the business to **keep** such records; made in the **regular** course of business; made **at** or near the time of the event or condition recorded; and made by an employee with **personal** knowledge of event or upon information provided by someone with a duty to provide such information. (A) is wrong because the witness who lays the foundation need not have personal knowledge of the data contained in the record. (C) is incorrect because the estimate is not the statement of a party opponent. (D) is incorrect because it was not a statement against the estimator's interest at the time it was made.

Answer to Question 16.

(B) is the correct choice.

(A) is clearly wrong. The fact that a witness may lie is not a ground for exclusion. The plaintiff is offering it and it is the defendant's statement, so it is an admission by a party opponent. Admissions are admissible regardless of the availability of the declarant, so (C) and (D) are wrong.

Answer to Question 17.

(A) is the correct choice.

The statement is being offered for the effect it had on Doppler, not for its truth. Thus, it is not hearsay and (C) and (D) are wrong. Whether Doppler reasonably believed the statement goes to merits of his defense of coercion and does not effect the hearsay status of the statements. Therefore, (B) is wrong.

Answer to Question 18.

(B) is the correct choice.

The letters are hearsay if offered to prove that the stop sign was not visible and are not covered by any exception; thus, (A) and (C) are wrong. They are not hearsay if offered as proof that the city was put on notice and so are admissible for that purpose. Thus, (B) is right and (D) is wrong.

Answer to Question 19.

(C) is the correct choice.

Although George's statement is an out-of-court statement offered for for its truth, it would survive a hearsay objection because it is an admission by party opponent. Thus (B) is wrong. Nevertheless, FRE 408, which protects offers to settle cases, provides an independent ground for exclusion. Thus, (A) is wrong. (D) is obviously wrong.

Answer to Question 20.

(D) is the correct choice.

FRE 601 provides that every person is competent to be a witness, unless expressly otherwise provided in the rules. Nothing in the rules deems a witness incompetent due to mental illness or inability to speak English. Thus (A), (B), and (C) are wrong.

Answer to Question 21.

(C) is the correct choice.

A trick question. The statement is clearly hearsay, so (D) is wrong. Although it sounds like a dying declaration, the statement does not concern the causes or circumstances surrounding Pond's death. (A), therefore, is wrong. Pond is not a party so (B) is wrong. (C) is correct because it is hearsay not admissible under any exception.

Answer to Question 22.

(C) is the correct choice.

To further the public policy of encouraging people to take safety precautions after an accident has occurred, evidence that a party took a subsequent remedial measure is inadmissible to prove the party's negligence or culpable conduct. Thus, (A), (B), and (D) are wrong. (D) is a silly answer and would not be the correct answer to any question.

Answer to Question 23.

(A) is the correct choice.

Statements by an agent or employee of a party are considered the vicarious admissions of the party if they concern a matter within the scope of the agency or employment. (C) is incorrect because admissions of a party opponent are admissible regardless of the availability of the declarant. (B) and (D) are both clearly incorrect.

Answer to Question 24.

(A) is the correct choice.

Defendant is offering a statement made by plaintiff; it qualifies as an admission by party opponent. (B) is wrong because there is no special hearsay exception for statements made to an officer conducting an investigation. (C) and (D) are both clearly wrong; (C) makes no sense and (D) is wrong because the statement is admissible.

Answer to Question 25.

(B) is the correct choice.

Wall's testimony may be offered to impeach Pitt, whose hearsay statement to the priest was admitted as a dying declaration. The statement related by Wall does not qualify under any hearsay exception, so (A) is wrong. (C) is a red herring answer. The testimony is obviously relevant to the case, so (D) is wrong.

Answer to Question 26.

(B) is the correct choice.

The best evidence rule does not apply here because the content of Investigator's letter is collateral. What is at issue is the allegedly libelous response. (A) is not right for much the same reason. The content of the letter of inquiry is not important, so it doesn't matter if it was made in the regular course of business. (C) and (D) are similarly incorrect.

Answer to Question 27.

(D) is the correct choice.

The best evidence rule does apply here. The contents of the letter lie at the heart of the case. Therefore, the original must be produced unless some exception applies. (A) and (B) are wrong because this is a question for the judge to decide. (C) is wrong because it is ridiculous; how can the judge know if Investigator has correctly quoted from the lost letter?

Answer to Question 28.

(A) is the correct choice.

FRE 901(b) provides that a voice heard over the telephone may be authenticated by testimony that the caller looked up the number in the directory, dialed it, and the answerer identified himself. (B), (C), and (D) all therefore all incorrect.

Answer to Question 29.

(A) is the correct choice.

All that is required to authenticate a photograph is testimony that it is a fair and accurate representation of the scene at the relevant time. The remaining answers are therefore incorrect. (B) is wrong because there is no evidence that the damage necessarily existed when the photograph was taken. (C) is wrong because it is not necessary to have the photographer testify. (D) is wrong because it is still helpful to the trier of fact to view a photograph of the damage; such evidence is just as probative as oral testimony.

Answer to Question 30.

(C) is the correct choice.

(A) and (D) are both obviously wrong. Res gestae is a red herring answer. Business records are admissible regardless of the availability of the maker of the record. Thus, either (B) or (C) is the correct answer. (C) is the preferred answer. Even if an accident report is routinely made, self-serving accident reports made with an eye toward litigation are usually not admitted under the business records exception.

Answer to Question 31.

(C) is the correct choice.

No facts here, just a straight question of law. Leading questions are generally permissible during cross-examination of any witness, expert or not, so (A) is wrong. They may also be used if necessary when examining children and on preliminary matters. This eliminates (B) and (D). (C) is left and is consistent with the general rule that leading questions are ordinarily impermissible on direct examination.

Answer to Question 32.

(D) is the correct choice.

The fact that the eyewitness may have been mistaken about the color of the sweater worn by the defendant the day of the accident is of no consequence, except insofar as it might lead the factfinder to believe that the eyewitness is mistaken about matters important to the case. Thus, it is a collateral matter and extrinsic evidence is not permitted. This also eliminates (A) as an answer. (B) and (C) are wrong because the fact of contradiction might lead to an inference that the eyewitness is lying or lacking in capacity to observe. Extrinsic evidence is nevertheless excluded as to collateral matters because the probative value is insufficient to counterbalance the danger of confusion, waste of time, etc.

Answer to Question 33.

(B) is the correct choice.

Evidence of a conviction of a felony entered after a trial or upon a plea of guilty is admissible to prove any fact that was essential to sustain the conviction. Thus the conviction may be used to prove Davidson was intoxicated. It may not be used as proof of her character, so (A) is wrong. (C) is inconsistent with the facts and (D) is wrong because there is a hearsay exception for this evidence.

Answer to Question 34.

(C) is the correct choice.

Although evidence of a subsequent remedial measure is inadmissible to prove negligence or culpable conduct, it is admissible to prove other things; in this case, ownership or control of the tree. (A) is thus wrong. (B) is wrong because the evidence is not being introduced to prove the condition of the tree and (D) is wrong because the evidence would not be admissible if offered to prove the condition of the tree.

Answer to Question 35.

(A) is the correct choice.

Past recollection recorded requires the witness to testify that he lacks memory of the event and then vouch for the accuracy of a writing he made near the time of the event. (B) is thus wrong. (C) is patently wrong: White is not being compelled to do anything. This leaves (A) and (D). White's former testimony will be admissible if White is unavailable (he is), the testimony was taken under oath (it was), and Dean had the opportunity and motive to cross-examine White at the preliminary examination. Although this is not free from controversy, most courts would say that this requirement is met. Therefore, (A) is the right answer.

Answer to Question 36.

(B) is the correct choice.

The witness is testifying to his personal knowledge. (A) is wrong because the notebooks are not being offered. (C) and (D) are wrong because the witness is not testifying to the contents of these notebooks. He is testifying to facts of which he has personal knowledge which also happen to be recorded.

Answer to Question 37.

(B) is the correct choice.

This question is easiest to answer by eliminating all the wrong answers. (A) is wrong because there is no hearsay problem that requires resort to the admissions "exception." It is the manner in which Dryden acted which is significant, not the content of what he said. (C) is wrong because the tape does not involve any compelled testimonial activity. (D) is wrong because disallowing extrinsic evidence to prove specific instances of conduct applies only to impeachment. This leaves (B). The evidence is probative of Dryden's intoxicated state and it is hard to see how it would be unfairly prejudicial.

Answer to Question 38.

(C) is the correct choice.

Prior inconsistent statements by a witness that were made under oath, subject to the penalty of perjury, at another proceeding or in a deposition are defined as non-hearsay, FRE 801(d)(1)(A), and are admissible both to impeach and as substantive evidence. (A), (B), and (D) are therefore wrong.

Answer to Question 39.

(A) is the correct choice.

(B) is wrong because failing chemistry courses does not bear on truthful character. Similarly, (D) is incorrect; the questions go to his qualifications, not his character. (A) is right and (C) is wrong because a party is permitted to explore just how qualified an expert is even after the court has determined that he meets the threshold standard for qualification as an expert.

Answer to Question 40.

(D) is the correct choice.

Extrinsic evidence is not allowed to prove the specific act of a witness as proof of his untrustworthy character. (A) is thus incorrect. Even if the conduct resulted in a conviction and would thus be admissible under FRE 609, it could be proved only by asking Fisher himself or by proof of the conviction. (B), therefore, is wrong. (C) is wrong because this is not cumulative of reputation evidence.

XVI. PRACTICE ESSAY QUESTIONS

Question No. 1

P and D were each driving automobiles involved in a right angle collision at an intersection. P was driving in a northerly direction on a through street; D was driving in a westerly direction on a street with a stop sign. P sued D, contending that D had failed to stop at the stop sign. D countered that P had passed a truck (which blocked D's view) at high speed at the intersection. Determine the admissibility of the following evidence.

(1) P called K, a pedestrian who saw the accident, and proposed to have him state that ten minutes after the collision occurred when both drivers were standing on the sidewalk discussing the matter, K looked at D and said, "Why in the world did you ever run that stop sign?" K would further testify that D glared at him but said nothing at all in reply.

(2) D called J, who worked with P, and proposed to have him testify that he often rode with P at the intersection where the collision occurred, and that on many occasions, P, passing slower moving vehicles, drove through the intersection at more than sixty miles per hour. J would further testify that he had often mentioned the dangers of these actions to P.

(3) D called E, a highway safety engineer, who described the highway on which P was driving as having a short but fairly steep rise which made a car on that highway difficult for a driver on D's street to see until it was within about 150 feet of the intersection. E was then asked whether, in his opinion, the intersection where the collision took place was dangerous, and whether D could have avoided a collision by exercising ordinary care.

(4) D called W, who testified in support of D's version of the accident. W stated that he had lived on the corner where the collision occurred and had seen at least six similar collisions in the prior year. When asked how he recalled the one on trial, W stated that it was on his birthday, Friday, March 13, 1989. In his closing argument, counsel for P produced a 1989 calendar (not in evidence) and showed that in 1989, March 13 was a Monday.

Question No. 2

P sued D for damages to P's auto. D's car, driven by C, D's chauffeur, sideswiped P's auto as C attempted to pass P. In the pleadings, D denied that C was his agent. Discuss the admissibility of each of the following evidentiary rulings:

(1) P offered the testimony of M, a motorist who saw the collision, that he spoke to C after the accident and asked C where he was going, and C replied, "D told me to pick up his wife at the airport."

(2) D's counsel called H, a hitchhiker whom C picked up prior to the accident, who gave testimony which, if believed, would have completely exonerated C of negligence. P then offered to prove that H had demanded $1,000 from D for the injuries H sustained from the accident, and that D settled with H for $800.

(3) P's counsel, at the close of his case, asked the court permission to have the jury view D's car which W parked near the courthouse on the ground that "this would be the best evidence of the condition of D's car." The court denied the request.

Question No. 3

P sued D for personal injuries. P claimed that D had negligently manufactured a wooden ladder which broke while being used by a man named Carpenter, causing Carpenter to fall upon P. Carpenter died as a result of the injuries received.

(1) A police officer was called as P's witness. He testified without objection that when he arrived at the scene, Carpenter was conscious but had lost consciousness before the ambulance arrived and that when the ambulance arrived, it backed over the ladder and broke it in several pieces. Over D's objection, the police officer was allowed to testify that at the scene of the accident, he asked Carpenter what happened and Carpenter said, "The ladder broke and I fell."

(2) P called Dr. Able. It was stipulated that he was an expert in the field of materials and accident reconstruction. Over D's objection, Dr. Able was permitted to testify that based upon information obtained from the police report, wood fiber analysis reports from an independent laboratory, records of the company from which Carpenter rented the ladder, and his own inspection of the scene, it was his opinion that at least one of the breaks in the ladder pre-existed the ladder's being smashed by the ambulance.

(3) D called Hood as a witness. Hood refused to answer any questions about the falling of the ladder on the ground that his answers might tend to incriminate him. D then called Baker who testified, over P's objection, that Hood told him that he, Hood, had kicked the ladder out from under Carpenter.

(4) On cross-examination, Baker had difficulty remembering anything else that happened the day Hood made the statement to him, but the court sustained D's objection to the question, "How can you remember what Hood said so clearly when you can't remember anything else that happened that day?"

Assume that all appropriate objections were timely made. Were the court's rulings correct? Discuss.

Question No. 4

Seller, a used car dealer, sued Buyer, a truck driver, for breach of contract to purchase a truck. The following occurred at the trial:

(1) Wills, called as a witness for Seller, testified over objection, that on March 3 Seller, while standing beside a 1985 green and white pickup truck, said to Buyer, "You can have it for $299," and Buyer replied, "I'll let you know tomorrow."

(2) The only question asked Wills on cross-examination was, "Isn't it a fact that you hate truck drivers?" An objection to this question was sustained. Counsel for Buyer asked no further questions of Wills.

(3) Tillie, Seller's office manager, was called as a witness for Seller, and testified over objection that on March 4, she answered the telephone and a man's voice said, "This is Mr. Buyer. Tell Mr. Seller I'll take the green and white 1985 pickup for two ninety-nine."

(4) Ralph, an investigator employed by the Better Business Bureau, called as a witness for Buyer, testified over objection that about three weeks after the suit was filed, Wills told him what Buyer had actually replied to Seller's offer was, "I wouldn't give you 99 cents for the piece of junk."

(5) After the defense rested, Able, Seller's attorney, made an offer of proof that he, Able, would testify that prior to filing suit, he interviewed Wills and Wills told him about the conversation between Seller and Buyer in the exact words that Wills testified to in court. Buyer's objection was sustained.

Assume that all appropriate objections were timely made. Were the court's rulings correct? Discuss.

Question No. 5

Dee, a city official, was found guilty by a federal district court jury of the crime of willful evasion of federal income taxes. Dee allegedly failed to report a $20,000 "kickback" received in 1991 from Exx, the successful bidder on a city construction job. Dee has appealed, claiming error with respect to the following rulings on evidence during the trial.

(1) A, a certified public accountant, was allowed to testify that while preparing Dee's 1993 tax return, Dee said, "I didn't report $20,000 I got from Exx in 1991 and I'll need your help if they indict me."

(2) A was also allowed to testify that a short time later he was hired by L (Dee's attorney) to assist L in Dee's defense by helping L to understand Dee's financial personal records (which were in L's

possession, having been delivered to L and Dee) and, in the process, saw an entry in the books indicating a receipt of $20,000 from Exx.

(3) B, a former bookkeeper of the Exx Company, was allowed to testify that the financial records of Exx Company, kept according to accepted accounting principles, showed a disbursement check to Dee of $20,000 in June, 1991.

(4) On cross-examination, B was asked if he had not been fired for embezzlement by falsifying the records of Exx Company. B denied this. Exx was called but the judge sustained a general objection when Exx was asked, "Was not B discharged for embezzlement by falsifying records of Exx Company by showing fictitious disbursements to various city officials?"

Assuming that all appropriate objections were timely made, did the trial court err in any of the above instances? Discuss.

Question No. 6

Parks was the owner of a residence which he had insured for fire and which was destroyed by fire. Parks was criminally prosecuted for arson, the state contending he had set the fire. A criminal trial was had but the jury disagreed and, before a retrial of the criminal case, a civil suit brought by Parks against the insurance company came to trial. The insurer's defense was that Parks had set the fire.

(1) At the trial of the civil case, the defendant offered a certified transcript of testimony of one James, who had testified for the state at the criminal trial, that he saw Parks set the fire. James died before the civil trial. The court, upon objection, refused to admit this transcript. Parks was represented by counsel at the criminal trial but he had not cross-examined James.

(2) The insurer also offered the testimony of Dobbs who, over objection of Parks, was permitted to state that Parks had asked him to testify falsely that at the time of the fire he saw Parks in Chicago which was several hundred miles distant.

(3) The insurer also called Walker as a witness, but before doing so, had Walker refresh his memory by reading certain documents defense counsel then had in court. On cross-examination, Walker admitted that he had forgotten certain facts but had refreshed his memory as above stated just before taking the stand. Parks demanded that he be permitted to examine the refreshing documents but the court denied his request.

(4) Robbins, a defense witness, testified he saw Parks set the fire. On cross-examination, he was asked if he had not stated to one Williams that he knew nothing of the fire. Robbins answered in the negative. On rebuttal, Parks called Williams who testified Robbins told him he knew nothing of the fire. Over objection by Parks, the court then

permitted defendant to call as a witness Smith, who testified that a week after the fire, Robbins had told him he saw Parks set it.

Discuss the propriety of the court's rulings.

Answer to Question No. 1

(1) **Silence of D.** P will contend that D's failure to respond to K's question is a tacit admission and admissible over a hearsay objection. The test for determining whether this is a tacit admission is whether, under the circumstances, D would have responded to K by denying that he ran the stop sign if, in fact, he had not run the stop sign. The burden is on the proponent of the evidence (P) to establish that this is the case. Since this is a question of preliminary admissibility (FRE 104(a)), it is for the judge to decide whether P has met his burden. In this case, the judge would have to decide whether D glared at K merely because he interrupted his conversation or because of the substance of K's remark, or even if D heard K's question. If the judge determines that D heard the question, it is likely that she would find the evidence admissible. A reasonable person in D's situation (i.e., discussing the accident with the other driver soon after it occurred) who had not run the stop sign would likely respond to such a question by denying that he had run the stop sign. P might also argue that K's question to D is not hearsay under the federal rules since it is not in the form of an assertion (it was a question). Therefore, K's question is (according to this argument) not a "statement" as defined in FRE 801 and cannot be hearsay.

(2) **Testimony of J.**

    (a)   **As to P's Prior Conduct.** This is inadmissible character evidence. Its relevance flows solely from the inference that because P drove recklessly on previous occasions, he did so on the occasion in question. D might argue that this is admissible habit evidence. This argument would fail, however, because the testimony fails to establish that P routinely, invariably and habitually drove recklessly through this intersection.

    (b)   **As to J's Mentioning Dangers to P.** This is inadmissible. Nothing in the question indicates that there is an issue as to whether P failed to realize the danger in fast driving. Therefore, if offered to prove that P was put on notice about the dangerousness of that type of behavior, it is irrelevant. If offered to prove that P drove dangerously on previous occasions, it is inadmissible for the same reason J's testimony about P's prior conduct was inadmissible. In addition, J's statement to P is hearsay if offered to prove that driving in that manner is dangerous.

(3) **Testimony of E.**

    (a)   **Description of Scene.** The condition of the intersection ("short but fairly steep rise") at the time of the accident is a relevant consideration for the jury. If E had personal knowledge of the condition, and the road was in the same condition at the time it was examined by E as it was at the time of the accident, E's testimony describing the scene should be admitted. This is not expert testimony. Any witness who had seen the highway and could describe its condition would be permitted to so testify. E's testimony about the difficulty in spotting a car on the highway until it was within 150 feet of the intersection is somewhat more problematic. The effect of a steep rise in the road is probably not one which requires the expertise of a highway safety engineer. Nevertheless, the federal rules permit both lay and expert opinion testimony if it would assist the factfinder in the determination of the case. Thus, irrespective of whether you classify this as lay or expert opinion, it is probably admissible.

(b) **E's Opinion as to Dangerousness.** P will argue that this testimony is inadmissible. Ordinarily, the jury is perfectly capable of deciding whether a described situation is dangerous without the "assistance" of an expert. Not only is there no need for expert testimony on this matter, P will argue that there is a great risk that the jury will overvalue the "expert" opinion and substitute the expert's judgment for its own. D will contend that the liberalized standards governing admission of expert testimony argue for admission. Unlike the common law, which allows expert opinion only when it concerns a matter beyond the ken of the ordinary juror, the modern rules (like FRE 702) allow such testimony when it would be helpful to the trier of fact. This is a judgment call for the court. Whatever it decides, it will be reversed only for an abuse of discretion.

(c) **E's Opinion as to Avoiding the Collision.** At common law, this question would provoke an objection that it goes to an ultimate issue. This objection would not work under the FRE and most modern evidence rules. The fact that testimony goes to an ultimate issue in the case is no longer a ground for objection. Nevertheless, P could object on the ground that the question calls for a response that goes beyond E's field of expertise; he is a highway safety engineer, not an expert on what driving techniques could have been used to avoid a particular accident. In addition, it is not clear that E's idea of what constitutes "ordinary care" coincides with how the law defines "ordinary care." Thus, this question involves a mixed question of law and fact and so presents the danger that the jury could easily be misled. Many (but not all) courts would exclude it.

(4) **Production of Calendar.** This is inappropriate for two reasons. First, counsel must base final argument on the evidence adduced in court or judicially noticed by the trial judge. Here, counsel is trying to present evidence to the jury during closing argument. This is improper. If counsel wanted to establish that March 13 was a Monday, counsel should have introduced the calendar into evidence or asked the court to take judicial notice of such fact. The second reason goes to the use of extrinsic evidence for impeachment purposes. The impeachment technique being used here is contradiction. The general rule is that extrinsic evidence may not be used to contradict a witness as to a collateral matter. Since the point of the impeachment seems to be merely to establish that W was in error as to whether his birthday fell on a Monday or a Friday (a fact of no direct consequence to the case), this would be collateral, and extrinsic evidence should not be permitted.

Answer to Question No. 2

(1) **Testimony of M.** D will object on hearsay grounds to M's testimony about C's out-of-court statement. P will argue that it is admissible as a vicarious admission. At common law, an agent's statement is admissible against the principal only if the agent was authorized to speak (as well as act) for the principal. Under the FRE, however, an agent's statements are admissible as vicarious admissions of the principal so long as they are made while the agency relationship is in existence and concern a matter within the scope of that relationship. The issue here is whether C's statement can itself be used to establish the existence of an agency relationship. Traditionally, courts have held that the fact of agency must be established through evidence independent of the purported agent's statements. The *Bourjaily* case, however, casts considerable doubt on the viability of traditional caselaw. In *Bourjaily*, the Supreme Court held that the hearsay statements of a co-conspirator may be considered in determining whether the requirements of the co-conspirator's exception had been met. The same logic applies here, and leads to the conclusion that C's statement ("D told me to pick up his wife") can be used to establish that C was acting as D's agent. Therefore, a strong argument can be made for admissibility.

(2) **H and D Settlement.** D will object to this evidence, arguing that the law of evidence ordinarily prohibits evidence of compromise offers or actual settlements to prove liability. P may counter this by pointing out that the rule allows such evidence to be used to show the bias of a witness. The demand of H for $1,000 and his acceptance of $800 may be used to impeach H. If, in effect, H was paid for his testimony, the testimony is suspect. P will thus urge the court to admit the evidence under the doctrine of limited admissibility, as proof of H's bias as a witness, not D's liability. D will respond first by arguing that no showing has been made that the $800 payment was anything other than a reasonable payment for injuries suffered by H. If the facts indicate that the H/D settlement was an arms' length settlement, it does not show bias. Moreover, D will argue, even if it does show bias, the jury will be unable to follow the limiting instruction and D will be unfairly prejudiced because it will construe the fact that D settled with H as evidence of D's liability. This latter argument is unlikely to be accepted by the court. The admissibility of this evidence will likely turn, therefore, on whether the court thinks the H/D payment was a pay-off or a reasonable settlement of a valid claim.

(3) **View of D's Car.** The best evidence rule applies to the contents of writings and has no application in this case. Aside from this spurious ground, a judge has the discretionary power to permit such activity if she feels it is important and relevant. Here, the condition of D's car appears to have minimal probative value. A photograph would show the jury everything it needed to decide the case. Although a judge could have granted a jury view of the car, the refusal here seems justified and there was no abuse of discretion.

Answer to Question No. 3

(1) **Carpenter's Statement.** C's response to the police officer's question is a hearsay statement. It is being offered to prove that the ladder broke while C was on it (the matter asserted). P will argue, however, that it is admissible as an excited utterance. Under the common law, P would probably lose because statements made in response to inquiries would not be considered spontaneous. The more modern approach,

however, is to treat the fact that a statement was made in response to an inquiry as just one fact to consider in determining whether it was made under the stress of an exciting event so as to reduce the likelihood of fabrication. In this case, it is not clear exactly how soon after the event C made the statement and what condition he was in — calm, excited, in shock, — at the time he made it. With excited utterances, the condition of the declarant, rather than the time, is the key element. Even if C made the statement upon regaining consciousness after a significant passage of time, the court might still find it to be spontaneous and admissible.

(2) **Dr. Able's Testimony.** One possible objection to Dr. Able's testimony is that it goes to an ultimate fact in issue. Such an objection is clearly a loser. Under the FRE and most modern evidence rules, the fact that testimony goes to an ultimate issue is not ground for objection. A second possible objection is that his opinion is based on hearsay — reports and records from three different sources — as well as his inspection of the scene. This objection is also likely to fail. Experts may base their opinions upon facts and data that are not admitted (or even admissible) in evidence, so long as they are of the type reasonably relied upon by such experts in drawing such conclusions. Thus, if experts in Dr. Able's field reasonably rely upon police reports, wood fiber analysis reports, and company records in drawing conclusions about how such accidents occur, his opinion is admissible.

(3) **Testimony of Baker.** Baker's testimony as to Hood's prior statement is hearsay. It is an out-of-court declaration by Hood that he caused the ladder to fall. The statement is being used to prove its truth and so a hearsay exception is required. The most likely hearsay exception is declaration against interest. First, unavailability of the declarant (Hood) must be shown. Under the federal rules and in many jurisdictions, Hood's invocation of the privilege against self-incrimination will be sufficient to establish unavailability. Second, the statement must qualify as a declaration against interest. It is certainly a statement that would tend to subject Hood to criminal liability. Thus it would be admissible in those jurisdictions that recognize declarations against **penal** interest (e.g., the federal rules and many modern codes). In those jurisdictions that do not recognize declarations against penal interest, D could argue that Hood's statement is against his **pecuniary** interest, as it would tend to subject him to civil liability. A court might or might not buy this argument.

(4) **Cross-Examination of Baker.** It was certainly within the discretion of the trial judge to allow the question to be put to Baker on cross-examination. Baker put his credibility into issue by testifying, and a cross-examiner should be given broad leeway in challenging credibility. While the thrust of the question may seem to be argumentative, it does ask Baker to reconcile his lack of memory as to some details with his comparatively precise memory of other details or events which occurred on the same day. This is a legitimate inquiry into the credibility of the witness and is appropriate cross-examination.

Answer to Question No. 4

(1) **Testimony of Wills.** The testimony of Wills relating the conversation between Seller (S) and Buyer (B) raises hearsay issues. Hearsay is an out-of-court

statement offered to prove the truth of the matter asserted. The testimony here includes out-of-court statements of both B and S. However, the statements are not being offered to prove their truth. Their probative value flows from the fact that they were made, irrespective of the declarant's credibility. Words of offer, acceptance and rejection have independent legal significance and thus are not hearsay.

(2) **Cross-Examination of Wills.** The question asked Wills on cross-examination was proper. Every witness puts his credibility in issue, and a classic form of impeachment is to demonstrate bias on the part of the witness. If Wills really did hate all truck drivers, it would indicate a bias against B and would, therefore, cast doubt upon Wills's credibility. In defense of the court's ruling, one could argue that the likelihood that a witness would lie based upon such a bias is so small that the court acted within its considerable discretion in sustaining the objection.

(3) **Testimony of Tillie.** Two evidentiary problems are raised by Tillie's testimony. The first question is one of hearsay, but as discussed above, statements of offer, acceptance and rejection are not being offered here for their truth, and thus are not hearsay. The serious problem is one of authentication. In order to admit the statement purportedly made by B, S must offer evidence sufficient to warrant the conclusion that the statement is what it purports to be, i.e., a statement of B. Authentication of a voice heard on a telephone may not be accomplished solely by self-identification. Nor did Tillie recognize the voice. It may, however, be authenticated by the reply message doctrine. The statements attributed to B specifically refer to a green and white '85 pickup for the price of $299, the precise elements of the offer shown to have been made to B the day before. It could be interpreted that this telephone call was, in essence, a reply to the offer, and that repetition of these specifics indicates that the speaker must be B. B could argue that S may have told every potential buyer that the green and white '85 pickup was priced at $299, and thus many people could have known the same information. However, if Wills is to be believed, B said he would "let S know" the next day. When, on the following day, a call is received by one representing himself to be B, there is sufficient evidence to support the finding of authenticity. The judge should admit the evidence, leaving it to the jury to weigh the evidence.

(4) **Testimony of Ralph.** Ralph's testimony relates a statement made to him by Wills regarding a statement made by B to S. Breaking down the testimony out-of-court statement by out-of-court statement, we see first that B's statement to S is not hearsay. As pointed out above, it is not offered to prove the truth of the matter asserted. The out-of-court statement of Wills to Ralph (that B said "junk" to S) is also not hearsay. Rather, it is being offered to impeach Wills by showing that he previously made a statement inconsistent with his trial testimony ("B said, 'I'll let you know tomorrow.'"). The problem here is that B is trying to use extrinsic evidence (Ralph's testimony) to prove that Wills made a prior inconsistent statement without having first cross-examined Wills about the prior inconsistent statement. Common law jurisdictions (and a number of post-FRE evidence codes) require that a witness must be asked about his prior inconsistent statements before they may be proved through extrinsic evidence. As part 2 of this question indicates, B did not do this. Therefore, in these jurisdictions, Ralph's testimony would be inadmissible. Under the FRE, however, extrinsic evidence of a witness's prior inconsistent statement may be offered so long as the witness is afforded the opportunity to explain or deny the statement and opposing counsel may ask the

witness about it. If Wills is still in the area and may be recalled as a witness, Ralph's testimony would be admissible under the FRE.

(5) **Able's Offer of Proof.** Able's offer of proof also relates to an out-of-court statement made by Wills. If it is offered for its truth, it is hearsay and a hearsay exception must be found. None is applicable. But Able will argue that it is being offered for a non-hearsay purpose. Wills's credibility was attacked by showing he made a prior inconsistent statement. Able will argue, therefore, that Wills's prior consistent statement is being offered to rehabilitate Wills's credibility. Unfortunately for Able, however, prior consistent statements ordinarily may not be used to rehabilitate a witness whose credibility has been attacked with a prior inconsistent statement. Prior consistent statements may be used only if offered to rebut a charge of recent fabrication or improper motive or influence and only if they were made before the motive to fabricate arose. Although the question does not indicate that a charge of recent fabrication was leveled at Wills, the charge need not be express. Thus, depending on the context and manner surrounding the introduction of Wills's prior inconsistent statement and the use to which it was put by Buyer's counsel, this requirement may be met. Not enough information has been given to determine the circumstances under which Wills made the prior consistent statement to Able, so it is not clear whether it was made before the motive to fabricate arose. Finally, although the rules of ethics may prove a bar to Able testifying, the rules of evidence do not render attorneys incompetent to testify.

Answer to Question No. 5

(1) **Testimony of A Concerning Dee's Declaration.** Two possible grounds for objection may be raised by Dee, but both are weak. Dee can object to the admission of his out-of-court statement on hearsay grounds. Unfortunately for him, it clearly qualifies as an admission by a party opponent, so the hearsay objection will be unavailing. Second, Dee can argue accountant-client privilege. However, this privilege is not recognized by federal courts and since the problem stipulates that Dee is being tried in federal court for a federal offense, federal privilege law governs. If Dee was being tried in state court in one of the few jurisdictions that recognize the accountant-client privilege, he would stand on somewhat firmer ground. Nevertheless, the prosecution could still argue that the statement is not privileged because (a) A was preparing Dee's 1993 tax return and the statement related to 1991 income; and (b) Dee's statement, "I'll need your help if they indict me," could be construed as a solicitation to conceal evidence (hence asking for advice or assistance in the commission of a crime or fraud). Dee could argue, however, that (a) A was hired to handle all of Dee's accounting and tax problems, so the statement did fall within the scope of the accountant-client relationship; and (b) his statement, "I'll need your help," was a request for legitimate assistance in a potential legal battle and was not a solicitation of a crime or fraud.

(2) **Testimony of A Concerning the Entry in Dee's Books.**

(a) **Attorney-Client Privilege.** This presents a tricky issue. Since A was employed by Dee's lawyer to assist in the rendition of legal services to Dee, he qualifies as a representative of the lawyer. Thus, communications made to him by the lawyer or client are privileged under the attorney-client privilege. However, A is not being asked (directly) about a lawyer-client communication. Dee did not prepare the financial records for his lawyer for purposes of obtaining legal assistance; they pre-existed the attorney-client relationship. Therefore, we cannot say that entries in the books are privileged communications. Nevertheless, A was able to examine them only because Dee turned them over to his lawyer for the purpose of receiving legal assistance, and the lawyer showed them to A for the purpose of providing legal assistance to Dee. Dee can argue that this raises an issue analogous to that raised when an individual seeks to quash on self-incrimination grounds a subpoena directing him to turn over documents. The individual may resist the subpoena if the act of turning over the documents involves implicit testimonial assertions that may tend to incriminate him (i.e., "I have the requested records"; "I believe that the records I am turning over are those requested"). By the same token, when Dee gave the financial records to his lawyer, he told the lawyer (explicitly or implicitly), "Here are my financial records." This would be a privileged communication, and Dee can argue that A cannot testify about individual entries in the records without first revealing the privileged communication, "Here are my financial records."

(b) **Best Evidence Rule.** A is attempting to testify as to the contents of a writing — the financial records. His only knowledge of Dee's receipt of the $20,000 comes from having reviewed the writing. Thus, the Best Evidence Rule requires that the books themselves be introduced unless some exception to the rule applies. The prosecution should argue that such an exception applies: the defendant has possession of the books and was clearly on notice that their contents would be a subject of proof at trial. It is unclear from the facts given whether or not the defense was on notice, but if it was, the prosecution should prevail on this argument.

(3) Testimony of B Concerning the Books of Exx.

(a) **Best Evidence Rule.** Again, we have a witness testifying to the contents of a writing. Unless an exception to the Best Evidence Rule can be found, therefore, the financial records of Exx Company must be produced. This time, no exception is apparent.

(b) **Hearsay.** The books of Exx Company, while hearsay, could be admissible under the business records exception and would be admissible to show the disbursement to Dee. However, a proper foundation must first be laid by the proponent of the evidence — the prosecution — that it was the regular practice of the business to keep such records, that they were made in the regular course of business, that they were made at or near the time of the event in question, and that they were made by an employee with personal knowledge or upon information provided by someone with a business duty to report. The facts do not indicate that any such showing has been made.

(4) **Testimony of Exx.** Under FRE 608 and in many jurisdictions, a witness may be asked (in the court's discretion) about specific things the witness has done that bear on the witness's trustworthiness. Thus, the question asked of B on cross-examination would probably have been allowed by the court, even if an objection had been raised. (The prosecution could have argued that B should have been asked whether he had embezzled from Exx Company, not whether he had been fired for embezzlement. Some courts would have sustained such an objection and forced Dee's lawyer to rephrase the question.) When B denied that he had been fired for embezzlement, Dee's lawyer was bound by the answer. Although such questions may be asked of a witness, no extrinsic evidence may be offered to prove that the witness actually engaged in the conduct. Thus, the court properly sustained the objection to Exx's testimony. The fact that the prosecution's objection was not specific is of no consequence, since the objection was sustained. So long as there exists a valid ground for exclusion, the trial court's decision to exclude will be upheld. Dee might, however, make another argument for admissibility. Evidence that B falsified Exx Company records to show fictitious disbursements to various city officials might call into question the validity of the entry showing the disbursement to Dee, who is, after all, a city official. The question does not seem to indicate that this was the reason for calling Exx, and this line of inquiry would seem proper only if the records of Exx Company were offered as proof of a disbursement to Dee. According to the stated facts, this was not done.

Answer to Question No. 6

(1) **Testimony of James.** The transcript of James's testimony at the criminal trial should have been admitted by the court in the subsequent civil trial under the former testimony exception. Under FRE 804(b)(1), former testimony is admissible if (a) the declarant is unavailable and (b) the party against whom it is now being offered had the opportunity and similar motive to develop the testimony in the previous hearing. (Common law jurisdictions require that the issues (and in some jurisdictions, the parties) be identical in both proceedings.) The unavailability requirement clearly is met: the declarant, James, is dead. The former testimony is now being offered against Parks, who had the opportunity and similar motive to develop James's testimony in the previous hearing. James's testimony was highly adverse to Parks and he had every incentive in the criminal trial to show that James was mistaken or lying. Therefore, the trial court should have admitted the former testimony. (In a common law jurisdiction that still requires identity of parties, Parks could argue for exclusion on the ground that the insurance company was not a party to the criminal proceeding.)

(2) **Testimony of Dobbs.** This testimony was properly admitted. The request of Parks constituted an implied admission by conduct, and the jury would be justified in inferring that Parks believed he had a weak case. Note that this really does not present a hearsay problem under the federal rules because Parks did not intend to assert his belief that he had a weak case by engaging in such conduct.

(3) **Testimony of Walker.** It is clear that had Walker used the documents to refresh his recollection while on the witness stand, opposing counsel would have had the right to examine the documents. When a witness refreshes recollection prior to taking the stand, however, no such right exists. Under the FRE, the trial court has

discretion to order that documents used by a witness to refresh his recollection prior to taking the stand be turned over to opposing counsel. The court here refused to do so; in so doing, it acted within its discretion.

(4) **Impeachment of Robbins.** The witness Robbins has been impeached by proof that he made a prior inconsistent statement to Williams. The issue is whether Robbins can be rehabilitated by showing that he made a prior consistent statement to Smith. Ordinarily, the fact that a witness made a prior consistent statement may not be used to rehabilitate him. A prior consistent statement may be used only if offered to rebut a charge of recent fabrication or improper motive or influence, and only if it was made before the motive to fabricate arose. We can't tell from the facts whether the impeachment of Robbins amounted to an express or implied charge of recent fabrication. If it did, we would still need to know whether the motive that supposedly caused Robbins to fabricate arose prior to the time he made the prior consistent statement to Smith. If so, the court should not have allowed Smith to testify.

ANALYSIS OF
ESSAY QUESTIONS

XVII. CASE SQUIBS

RELEVANCY

PEOPLE v. COLLINS

This case exemplifies misuse of statistical evidence. Defendants were tried for robbery and assault. Although the victim was unable to positively identify the defendants, they matched the description she gave of her assailants. One defendant was a black male with a beard and mustache; the other was a white female with blond hair and a ponytail. They drove a partially yellow convertible. The prosecution called a mathematics professor who testified about a law of probability: that the probability of the joint occurrence of a number of mutually independent events is equal to the product of the individual probability of each event (e.g., the odds of a coin landing heads up three times in a row are 1/2 x 1/2 x 1/2 or 1/8). Then, based on an assumed probability for each described characteristic of the assailants (e.g., partly yellow car: 1/10; man with mustache: 1/4; blond woman: 1/3; interracial couple: 1/1000; etc.), the prosecutor used the law of probability to calculate that there was but one chance in 12 million that any couple possessed the characteristics of the defendants. Thus, there was only a one in 12 million chance that the defendants were innocent. The Supreme Court of California reversed, holding that such evidence was too confusing, misleading and prejudicial. Among other things, the court pointed out that the prosecution failed to establish the accuracy of the probability factors upon which the 1/12,000,000 calculation was based. To the contrary, the prosecutor had made them up. In addition, the prosecution failed to prove that the various probability factors were mutually independent, as is required by probability theory in order to make the calculation. Therefore, any probative value the statistical evidence had was far outweighed by its tendency to mislead and confuse the jury.

State v. Poe, 21 Utah 2d 113, 441 P.2d 512 (1968).

This is one of the relatively few cases in which a court has held that the trial judge abused his discretion in admitting gruesome pictures. In this case, the prosecution had already established the identity of the deceased and the cause of his death and introduced black and white photographs showing him, lying on his bed with two bullet holes in his head. Nonetheless, the trial judge allowed the prosecutor to introduce color slides made during the course of victim's autopsy and showing, among other things, the base of victim's skull after the skull cap and brain had been removed by the pathologist. The appellate court stated that such pictures could have been offered only to inflame and arouse the jury.

Michelson v. United States, 335 U.S. 469 (1948).

This famous Supreme Court case lays out the common-law rules regarding the admissibility of character evidence. Michelson was accused of bribery and called character witnesses to testify to his reputation for honesty. The prosecution was then permitted to ask these witnesses "Have you heard [that Michelson committed various acts of dishonesty]." The opinion makes no attempt to justify the rules of the game on any ground other than "this is the way we've done it and it seems to work pretty well." In fact, Justice Jackson commented that the character evidence rules illustrate the dictum that "the system may work best when explained least."

SQUIBS

United States v. Beechum, 582 F.2d 898 (5th Cir. 1978).

This case demonstrates the admissibility of other crimes evidence to prove intent. Orange Jell Beechum, a postal carrier, was charged with possessing a silver dollar stolen from the mails. He admitted possessing the property, but denied that he intended to steal it, claiming that it had fallen out of the mailbox and that he had been unable to find his supervisor in order to turn it in to him. The prosecution offered evidence that Beechum had stolen other items from the mail: he possessed two credit cards that had been mailed ten months earlier to addressees on his postal routes. The Fifth Circuit held that this evidence was admissible to prove that Beechum intended to steal the silver dollar.

Tucker v. State, 82 Nev. 127, 412 P.2d 970 (1966).

This case adopts the plain, clear, and convincing evidence standard for the admission of other crimes evidence. Tucker called the police and told them that he had been asleep in his home, had awakened, and had found an old man, Evans, shot dead on a couch. Tucker was charged with second degree murder. At his trial, the prosecution offered evidence of a similar incident that occurred six years before in which Tucker called the police and told them that he had awakened to find a man, Kaylor, shot to death in his dining room. The prosecution claimed that the evidence was admissible to prove Tucker intended to kill Evans, that the killing of Evans was part of a common plan or scheme, and to negate any defense of accidental death. The Nevada Supreme Court held that it did not have to decide whether the evidence would be admissible for any of these purposes because the prosecution had failed to establish that Tucker had killed Kaylor. The court held that the prosecution must prove by **plain, clear and convincing evidence** that the defendant had committed the other crime.

Huddleston v. United States, 485 U.S. 681 (1988).

In this case, the Supreme Court considered the proper standard for the admissibility of other crimes evidence. Huddleston was charged with the knowing possession and sale of stolen video cassette tapes. There was no dispute that the tapes were stolen; the only question was whether Huddleston knew that they were stolen. To prove that he did, the prosecution introduced evidence of Huddleston's involvement in a series of sales of allegedly stolen televisions and appliances. On appeal, Huddleston argued that the evidence regarding the sales of the television sets should not have been admitted because the prosecution failed to prove that the sets had been stolen. He argued that other crimes evidence should not be admissible unless the court finds by a preponderance of the evidence that the defendant committed the other crime. The Supreme Court rejected this argument. Admissibility of other crimes evidence is a question of conditional relevancy falling under Rule 104(b). All the trial court should do is determine, after considering all the evidence, whether the jury could reasonably find that the defendant had committed the other crime. Given the low price at which Huddleston offered to sell the televisions, the large quantity he offered for sale, his inability to produce a bill of sale, and his involvement in the sale of other stolen appliances, the jury could reasonably have found that the televisions had been stolen. Thus, the evidence was properly admitted. Any danger that this evidence would be unfairly prejudicial to Huddleston should have been raised by an objection under Rule 403 that its probative value was substantially outweighed by the danger of unfair prejudice.

Dowling v. United States, 493 U.S. 342 (1990).

In this case, the Supreme Court held that the Double Jeopardy Clause does not bar the admission of evidence of a defendant's participation in another crime, even if the defendant has already been tried and acquitted for the other crime. Dowling was on trial for robbing a bank in the Virgin Islands. Testimony showed that the robber had worn a ski mask and carried a small gun. To strengthen its identification of Dowling as the bank robber, the prosecution called Henry, who testified that two weeks after the bank robbery, her home had been burglarized by a man wearing a ski mask and carrying a small gun. She identified Dowling as the intruder, stating that she had unmasked him during a struggle. In addition, according to the prosecution, Henry's testimony linked Dowling to another man who was implicated in the bank robbery. This testimony was admitted even though Dowling had already been tried and acquitted for the Henry burglary. Dowling contended that this violated the Double Jeopardy Clause. The Supreme Court rejected his argument. Although the collateral estoppel component of the Double Jeopardy Clause bars the government from relitigating an issue of ultimate fact that has been determined by a final judgment, it does not necessarily bar the evidentiary use of alleged criminal conduct for which a defendant has been acquitted. Since the government only had to present enough evidence so that a jury could reasonably find that Dowling had committed the earlier crime, the prior acquittal (which was determined on the basis of the reasonable doubt standard) did not preclude it from offering evidence of the other crime.

Olden v. Kentucky, 488 U.S. 227 (1988).

Olden, a black man, was charged with raping Matthews, a white woman. Matthews testified that she met Olden at a bar. She left the bar with Olden and his friend Harris to go looking for a friend. She testified that Olden then threatened her with a knife and, with Harris's assistance, raped her. Olden sought to elicit the fact that Matthews was then living with Russell, a black man. Olden's defense was that he and Matthews had consensual sex and that Matthews had concocted the rape story to protect her relationship with Russell, who had seen her emerge from Harris's car and would have otherwise been suspicious of her. The trial court excluded the evidence because it felt that the jury would be prejudiced if it learned that the complainant was involved in an interracial relationship. The Supreme Court reversed. It held that the jury might have received a different impression of Matthews's credibility had Olden been permitted to pursue his proposed line of cross-examination and demonstrate that Matthews had a motive to falsely accuse him of rape.

HEARSAY

Wright v. Tatham, 5 C. & F. 670 (1838).

This famous English case demonstrates the common-law view that all out-of-court statements or conduct whose probative value depends on the declarant's credibility are hearsay. Tatham, the heir at law of the estate of Marsden, challenged Marsden's will, by which he had devised his property to his servant Wright. Tatham claimed that Marsden was mentally incompetent. Among the evidence offered by Wright in defense of the will were several letters that had been written to Marsden. Although the letters contained no direct assertions regarding Marsden's competence, they were said to be relevant because they addressed Marsden as if he were competent, and thus implied that the authors believed Marsden to be competent. Ultimately, the letters were held to be hearsay. Most casebooks reproduce the opinion of Baron Parke, which gives a very broad reading to the definition of hearsay, and contains the famous sea captain hypothetical. Evidence that a sea captain inspected a boat and then took his family sailing would be hearsay if offered to prove the boat's seaworthiness, according to Baron Parke, because the inference that the boat was seaworthy depends on the captain's belief that the boat was seaworthy and the accuracy of the belief. Thus the captain's non-verbal conduct, which was not intended as an assertion, was said to be hearsay.

United States v. Zenni, 492 F.Supp. 464 (E.D.Ky. 1980).

In contrast to *Wright v. Tatham*, above, this case illustrates that under the federal rules, some out-of-court statements whose probative value depends on the declarant's credibility are not hearsay. Defendant was prosecuted for illegal bookmaking activities. During a legal search of her premises, government agents answered the telephone several times and heard unknown callers state directions for placing bets on various sporting events. The government offered these out-of-court statements as proof that the defendant's premises were used in betting operations. In other words, the government offered the callers' statements (such as "Put $2 to win on Paul Revere in the third at Pimlico") as proof that the callers believed the defendant ran a bookmaking operation and that their belief was correct. The court, in explaining the function of Federal Rule 801 and the Advisory Committee's Note to the rule, held that this was not hearsay. The callers' statements were in the form of commands or directives and were not assertions (i.e., these were Category 4 statements). Therefore, under the federal rule, they were not hearsay.

Silver v. New York Cent. R. Co., 329 Mass. 14, 105 N.E.2d 923 (1952).

Silence might easily be viewed as hearsay under the common law approach. As this case illustrates, however, when the silence was sufficiently probative, common-law courts often regarded it as non-hearsay. Plaintiff, who suffered from a circulatory ailment, sued defendant railroad, claiming that it had allowed the temperature in the car in which she was a passenger to become unreasonably cold. The defendant offered the testimony of the porter in plaintiff's car that none of the other eleven passengers complained about the temperature. The court held that the testimony should have been admitted over hearsay objections.

HEARSAY EXCEPTIONS

Mahlandt v. Wild Canid Survival & Research Center, Inc., 588 F.2d 626 (8th Cir. 1978).

This case holds that no personal knowledge requirement exists for vicarious admissions. Poos, the director of education of the defendant Wild Canid Survival Center, was keeping Sophie, a wolf, at his home. One day, a neighbor heard a child's screams and saw little Daniel Mahlandt lying on his back within Poos's fenced yard, with the wolf straddling him. Poos's son quickly ran out and got the wolf off Daniel. Daniel had lacerations and bruises over his body. At trial, the defendants claimed that the lacerations were from the barbs of the fence, and that Sophie had not bitten Daniel. The plaintiffs offered a note written by Poos to the head of Wild Canid which stated that "Sophie bit a child", as well as an oral statement by Poos to the same effect. Wild Canid objected to the statement being admitted as its vicarious admission since Poos lacked personal knowledge of what had occurred. The court held, however, that no such personal knowledge requirement exists for vicarious admissions, and that the statements were, therefore, admissible as the vicarious admissions of Wild Canid.

Bourjaily v. United States, 483 U.S. 171 (1987).

In this case, the Supreme Court decided several issues relating to the admissibility of co-conspirators' admissions. First, the Court held that the elements of the admission by co-conspirator exception must be proved by a preponderance of the evidence. That is, the proponent of the hearsay must convince the judge by a preponderance of the evidence (a) of the existence of the conspiracy; (b) that the defendant and declarant were members of the conspiracy; and (c) that the statements were made during the pendency and in furtherance of the conspiracy. Second, departing from the common law tradition, the Court held that the trial judge could consider the hearsay statements of the alleged co-conspirator in deciding whether the proponent had successfully proved the elements of the co-conspirator exception. The Court based its decision on the plain language of Rule 104(a), which provides that in making preliminary admissibility determinations, the court is not bound by the rules of evidence (except those with respect to privileges).

United States v. Iron Shell, 633 F.2d 77 (8th Cir. 1980).

This case illustrates that in child abuse cases, some courts have been quite lenient in finding that statements made by the child victim qualify under the the excited utterance exception. Defendant was accused of assault with the intent to rape a nine-year-old girl. A police officer interviewed the girl between 45 and 75 minutes after the assault. He testified that although she was neither hysterical nor crying, she appeared nervous and scared. Her hair was messed and had leaves in it. The officer testified that he asked her a single question: "What happened?" Her response, which implicated Defendant, was offered at trial as an excited utterance. The trial court admitted the evidence and the court of appeals affirmed. Although the appellate court said it was a close question, it found that the trial court had not abused its discretion.

Mutual Life Ins. Co. v. Hillmon, 145 U.S. 285 (1892).

In one of the most famous evidence cases, the Supreme Court first held that a statement of an existing intent to do something in the future is admissible under the state of mind exception to prove the declarant actually followed through with his plans. Sallie Hillmon sued several insurance companies to recover on policies on the life of her husband, John Hillmon. The companies claimed that Hillmon had not died. They claimed that the body found at Crooked Creek was not Hillmon's, as Sallie claimed, but was that of one Adolph Walters. To support their theory, they offered letters written by Walters to his family two weeks before the body was found, in which Walters said that he planned to go to Colorado (where Crooked Creek is located) with Hillmon. The Supreme Court held that the letters were admissible under the state of mind exception as evidence that Walters carried out his stated intent to travel to Colorado.

Shepard v. United States, 290 U.S. 96 (1933).

In another famous case, the Supreme Court held that a statement of a present feeling or belief is not admissible under the state of mind exception if offered to prove the truth of the facts that led to the feeling or belief. Shepard was charged with poisoning his wife. He offered evidence that his wife was suicidal. Near the end of the trial, the prosecution called a nurse to testify that the wife said to her, "Dr. Shepard has poisoned me." The evidence was erroneously admitted under the dying declaration as proof that Dr. Shepard had poisoned her. On appeal, the government shifted ground. It argued that the evidence was admissible not as evidence of what was said, but for a non-hearsay purpose: as evidence of a state of mind inconsistent with suicide (i.e., someone who was suicidal wouldn't say something like that). The Court rejected this argument on two grounds. First, the evidence was not offered for so limited a purpose and thus there was no opportunity for the defendant to seek a limiting instruction. Second, even if it had been so offered, a jury could never have followed a limiting instruction. The government then sought to have its admission upheld under the state of mind exception as a statement of the wife's then existing belief (that Dr. Shepard had poisoned her). The Court rejected this argument, holding that the state of mind exception does not reach backward looking statements such as this. Indeed, if it did, the hearsay rule would be eviscerated, because every out-of-court statement could be cast as a statement of the declarant's then existing belief.

United States v. Pheaster, 544 F.2d 353 (9th Cir. 1976).

This case holds that a declarant's statement of his intent to do something may be used to prove someone else's conduct. The defendant was charged in the kidnapping of Larry Adell. The prosecution offered the testimony of two of Larry's friends that he told them he was going to meet Angelo [the defendant] at 9:30 in the parking lot of Sambo's North. This was offered not just to prove where Larry had gone (there was no doubt about that), but also to prove that Angelo was there. The court noted the difficulty posed by the issue. (For example, testimony that, "Larry told me, 'Angelo is going to the parking lot tonight.'", would clearly not have qualified under the state of mind exception.) The court ultimately held that evidence was admissible, noting that Hillmon involved a similar statement ("I am going to Colorado with Hillmon") and that the legislative history of FRE 803(3) was ambiguous about the admissibility of such statements.

United States v. Iron Shell, 633 F.2d 77 (8th Cir. 1980).

This case illustrates that in child abuse cases, statements pertaining even to the identity of the assailant, may be pertinent to diagnosis and treatment, and thus admissible. Defendant was accused of assault with the intent to rape a nine-year-old girl. About two hours after the incident, she was examined by a physician who asked her a series of questions about the incident, including questions such as "When he pushed you down, did he hold you down?" and "What did he say to you?" The court held that these questions were pertinent to diagnosis and treatment; the doctor testified that a discussion of the general cause of the injury was important to provide guidelines for his examination. In this case, however, there was no question as to the identity of the assailant and the court noted that the questions and answers related to what happened rather than who assaulted the girl.

Johnson v. Lutz, 253 N.Y. 124, 170 N.E. 517 (1930).

This famous evidence case illustrates the multiple hearsay problem that arises when the maker of a business record lacks personal knowledge of the event recorded. Following an accident, a police officer spoke to bystanders and filed a report which contained their observations. This report was held inadmissible. Admission of the report involved multiple hearsay: the police officer's report ("The bystanders told me, 'The motorcycle ran a red light.'"); and the bystander's statements ("The motorcycle ran a red light."). Although the logic of the business records exception provides assurance that the police officer accurately recorded what the bystanders said, it does not guarantee that what the bystanders said was accurate. The police officer had a business obligation to report accurately; the bystanders did not. Thus, the business record exception covered only the police officer's statement. Because no hearsay exception covered the bystanders' statements contained in the report, the report was held inadmissible.

Palmer v. Hoffman, 318 U.S. 109 (1943).

A record made with an eye toward litigation may be deemed not to have been made in the regular course of business. In this case, the Supreme Court excluded an accident report containing the statement of a railroad engineer (offered by the railroad) even though it was recorded by the railroad's investigator as part of his regular practice to investigate accidents. As one reason for its decision, the Court stated that this was **not a record kept in the regular course of business:** the business of the company was railroading, not investigating accidents. A second reason hinted at by the Court was the **danger of inaccuracy.** Records that are made with an **eye toward litigation** tend to lack the reliability that other, more traditional business records hold. This second reason is more likely to be cited by courts in excluding such records.

Lewis v. Baker, 526 F.2d 470 (2d Cir. 1975).

This case demonstrates that courts sometimes find that accident reports are trustworthy and admissible. The defendant railroad company offered an accident report made shortly after plaintiff, a freight brakeman, was injured. Distinguishing *Palmer v. Hoffman*, the court found that this report was made in the regular course of business and that it was trustworthy. The court found that the employees who took part in making the report had no motive to lie about what happened. Unlike the engineer whose statement was excluded in *Palmer v. Hoffman*, none of the employees was involved in the accident or the possible target of a lawsuit.

United States v. Oates, 560 F.2d 45 (2d Cir. 1977).

This case demonstrates that law enforcement records are not admissible against defendants in criminal cases under either the public records or business records exceptions. In defendant's trial for heroin possession, the prosecution had to prove that the white powdery substance that it seized from the defendant actually was heroin. Rather than calling the Customs Service chemist who performed the lab test, it offered his report. The Second Circuit held that it was inadmissible hearsay. **Construing "law enforcement personnel" to include all employees of a government agency that has law enforcement responsibility**, the court held that Customs Service chemists are law enforcement personnel. Therefore, the report could not be offered in a criminal case under FRE 803(8)(B). The court also held that the government could not circumvent the limitation on the use of public reports against defendants in criminal cases by offering the record as a business record, as this would clearly subvert the limitation.

Beech Aircraft Corp. v. Rainey, 488 U.S. 153 (1988).

This case interprets the part of the public records exception that admits "factual findings" resulting from an authorized governmental investigation. Following the crash of a Navy airplane, suit was brought against the manufacturer and servicing company of the plane. The key issue was whether the crash was caused by pilot error or equipment malfunction. The defendants offered the report of the Navy investigator, which included "findings of fact," "opinions," and "recommendations." Among the "opinions" was a statement that pilot error probably caused the accident. The Supreme Court held that this report was admissible under FRE 803(8)(C). Noting that many "factual findings" could be characterized as "opinions," the Court rejected the attempt to draw an arbitrary line between the kinds of "facts" and "opinions" that will inevitably be present in investigatory reports. The requirement in FRE 803(8)(C), that reports contain factual findings, bars the admission of statements not based on factual investigation.

United States v. Barrett, 539 F.2d 244 (1st. Cir. 1976).

This case, decided before *Williamson v. United States* (discussed below), illustrates the difficulty of applying the declaration against interest exception. Bucky Barrett was tried for theft. Barrett sought to introduce testimony that Tilley (now deceased) had said that he (Tilley) and "Buzzy" committed the theft and that "Bucky" (the defendant) was not involved. The prosecution argued that Tilley's statement was not admissible as a declaration against interest because the relevant part—that Buzzy, not Bucky the defendant, was involved—was not a statement against Tilley's interest. The only part against his interest was the part in which he admitted his own complicity. The appellate court rejected the prosecution's argument, holding that the Buzzy/Bucky remark was sufficiently integral to the entire statement, which was itself against the declarant's (Tilley's) interest, to come within the declaration against interest exception. The appellate court remanded the case to the district court to decide whether the statement satisfied the corroboration requirement for declarations against penal interest offered to exculpate a defendant.

Williamson v. United States, ___U.S. ___, 114 S.Ct. 2431 (1994).

This case illustrates the cautious approach the Supreme Court has taken to the admissibility of hearsay under the declaration against interest exception. Harris, the declarant, was stopped by the police, and a search of his car revealed 19 kilograms of cocaine in suitcases in the trunk. After being arrested, Harris admitted that he knew he was transporting the cocaine and implicated an unidentified Cuban and Williamson. Several hours later, he changed his story. He stated that he had lied about the unidentified Cuban, but he continued to implicate Williamson, albeit with a story that differed in some respects from the original. Despite being granted immunity, Harris refused to testify at Williamson's trial for various drug offenses. The prosecution then offered Harris's confession against Williamson, invoking the declaration against interest exception. A majority of the Supreme Court held that the statement was inadmissible. The entire confession cannot be viewed as one big "statement." The policy behind the exception—that people do not make disserving statements unless they believe them to be true—simply does not apply to non-self-inculpatory parts of a broader narrative that is generally self-inculpatory. The fact that a statement is collateral to a self-inculpatory statement says nothing about the collateral statement's reliability. Therefore, in applying the declaration against interest exception, courts must look at each individual remark of the declarant. An individual remark will qualify as a declaration against interest only if, when viewed in context, it can be said that the remark was sufficiently disserving so that a reasonable person in the declarant's position would not have made the statement unless he or she believed it to be true. Justice Kennedy, in an opinion joined by two other justices, disputed the majority's analysis. He argued that the declaration against interest exception allows the admission of neutral collateral statements. He did caution, however, against the admission of confessions to authorities by a suspect who has a motive to cast blame on others. Such statements about the others' involvement may well be self-serving and should not be admitted. All nine justices agreed that the case should be remanded to the Court of Appeals. Two justices voted to remand for an inquiry as to whether each of the statements in Harris's confessions was truly self-inculpatory; four concluded that the statements were inadmissible but voted to remand for a harmless error inquiry; and three justices voted to remand for an inquiry consistent with Justice Kennedy's approach.

United States v. Salerno, 505 U.S. 317, 112 S.Ct. 2503 (1992).

In this case, the Supreme Court rejected the defendants' attempt to jettison the "similar motive" requirement of the former testimony exception. Defendants were being tried for a variety of offenses, including 41 acts constituting a pattern of illegal activity in violation of RICO (Racketeer Influenced and Corrupt Organizations Act). Much of the case concerned an attempt to rig bidding on large construction contracts among a "Club" of six concrete companies. The government called DeMatteis and Bruno, two of the owners of one of the concrete companies, before the grand jury, but they denied any involvement. At trial, the prosecution sought to prove the involvement of DeMatteis and Bruno's company through other evidence. The defense then called DeMatteis and Bruno to testify. After both invoked the privilege against self-incrimination, the defense sought to introduce their grand jury testimony under the former testimony exception. The prosecution argued that it did not have "similar motive" to develop the testimony of these two witnesses before the grand jury. The district court agreed and excluded the evidence. On appeal, however, the Court of Appeals held that adversarial fairness demands that the similar motive requirement should not be applied when the government obtains immunized testimony from a grand jury witness and the witness then refuses to testify at trial. The Supreme Court reversed. It held there was no basis for ignoring the text of Rule 804(b)(1), which clearly states that the party against whom the former testimony is now being offered must have had the opportunity and similar motive to develop the testimony in the earlier hearing.

Lloyd v. American Export Lines, Inc., 580 F.2d 1179 (3d Cir. 1978), cert. denied, 439 U.S. 969 (1978).

Lloyd and Alvarez, crewmen on a ship operated by American Export, were involved in a shipboard fight. Lloyd sued American Export. The latter impleaded Alvarez, who counterclaimed against American Export. Lloyd disappeared before trial and so the trial boiled down to a suit between Alvarez and American Export in which Alvarez claimed American Export was liable because it failed to prevent Lloyd from starting the fight. American Export countered by claiming that Alvarez started the fight. To support its claim, American Export sought to introduce testimony given by Lloyd in an earlier proceeding, a Coast Guard proceeding to determine whether to suspend or revoke Lloyd's merchant marine documents. Lloyd had testified that Alvarez was the aggressor. Since Alvarez (the party against whom the testimony was now being introduced) did not have the opportunity to cross-examine Lloyd at the Coast Guard proceeding, the issue became whether a predecessor in interest of Alvarez had had the opportunity and similar motive to develop the testimony. The court of appeals answered that question affirmatively. It held that the Coast Guard was Alvarez's predecessor in interest. The Coast Guard was seeking to establish the same thing that Alvarez was trying to establish in his case against American Export: that Lloyd was the aggressor. Therefore, it had like motive to interrogate Lloyd about the same matters as would Alvarez and thus qualified as his predecessor in interest.

United States v. Owens, 484 U.S. 554 (1988)

Rule 801(d)(1) provides that certain prior statements of a witness who testifies at trial are not hearsay if the witness "is subject to cross-examination concerning the statement." This case demonstrates the minimal nature of this "subject to cross-examination" requirement. Owens, a prison inmate, was tried for beating Foster, a correctional counselor, over the head with a metal pipe. As a result of the beating Foster's memory was severely impaired. Three weeks after the beating, Foster described the attack to an FBI agent, named Owens as his assailant, and identified Owens from a photo array. At trial, Foster testified that he remembered identifying Owens during his interview with the FBI agent, but admitted on cross-examination that he could not remember seeing his assailant, could not remember any of the numerous hospital visitors he received other than the agent, and could not remember whether any of the other visitors had suggested that Owens was the assailant. Foster's out-of-court identification of Owens was admitted under Rule 801(d)(1)(C) as a prior statement of identification. The Supreme Court rejected the defense argument that Foster was not subject to cross-examination about the statement. This requirement is ordinarily met when a witness is placed on the stand, under oath, and responds willingly to questions. The fact that a witness no longer remembers does not mean that he is not subject to cross-examination about the statement. The Court also held that Foster's presence on the stand was sufficient to meet the demands of the Confrontation Clause. The Confrontation Clause guarantees the opportunity for effective cross-examination, not cross-examination that is effective in whatever way the accused might wish.

California v. Green, 399 U.S. 149 (1970).

This case holds that if a hearsay declarant testifies at trial and can be cross-examined about his hearsay statements, there is no Conformation Clause problem. Porter testified at Green's preliminary hearing, naming Green as his drug supplier. At trial, however, Porter testified that he did not know who his supplier was because he had been on drugs at the relevant time. The prosecution then introduced the statements made by Porter at the preliminary hearing. (California has a hearsay exception for all prior inconsistent statements by a witness.) The Supreme Court found no Confrontation Clause violation. **As long as the declarant testifies at the trial and is subject to full and effective cross-examination,** the demands of Confrontation are met.

Ohio v. Roberts, 448 U.S. 56 (1980).

This case discusses the limitations imposed by the Confrontation Clause on the use of hearsay against an accused. Roberts was charged with forging a check and possessing stolen credit cards. At his preliminary hearing, Roberts' lawyer called the victim's daughter and questioned her at length, hoping to elicit from her an admission that she had given the defendant the checks and credit cards without informing him that he did not have permission to use them. She denied this. By the time Roberts came to trial, the daughter had disappeared. At his trial, Roberts testified that the daughter had given him the checkbook and credit cards with the understanding that he could use them. The state subsequently introduced the transcript of the daughter's preliminary hearing testimony. Roberts argued that this violated his right to confrontation. The Supreme Court set forth a two pronged test for assessing the constitutionality of the use of hearsay against an accused. First, the prosecution must either produce the declarant or show that she is unavailable. Second, if the declarant is unavailable, the prosecution must establish that the hearsay is reliable. This may be done either by showing that it falls within a firmly-rooted hearsay exception or by showing that it possesses particularized guarantees of trustworthiness.

United States v. Inadi, 475 U.S. 387 (1986).

In this case, the Supreme Court limited the requirement set forth in *Ohio v. Roberts* (see above), that the prosecution must either produce the hearsay declarant or establish his unavailability. Inadi was tried for conspiring to manufacture and distribute methamphetamine. Among the evidence introduced against him were hearsay statements made by Lazaro, a co-conspirator of the defendant, admitted under the admission by co-conspirator exception. The government neither produced Lazaro nor demonstrated his unavailability. Nevertheless, the Supreme Court held that no violation of Inadi's Confrontation Clause rights had occurred. The Court held that the produce-or-show-unavailability requirement articulated in *Roberts* was not intended to apply to all hearsay; rather, it was limited to the offer of testimony from a prior judicial proceeding. Unlike prior judicial testimony, a co-conspirator's statements derive much of their probative value from the fact that they were made in the course of the conspiracy, a context very different from the trial setting. Thus, admitting them helps further the search for truth. Moreover, forcing the prosecution to demonstrate the unavailability of every hearsay declarant places a significant burden on it, often without any corresponding benefit. In this case, for example, the defendant was free to call Lazaro and cross-examine him, but chose not to do so.

Bourjaily v. United States, 483 U.S. 171 (1987).

Noting that the admission by co-conspirator "exception" was first established in the Supreme Court in 1827, and that the Court has repeatedly reaffirmed the exception as accepted practice, the Court held that this was a "firmly rooted" hearsay exception.

Idaho v. Wright, 493 U.S. 1041 (1990).

This case decides what factors may be considered in determining whether the prosecutor has established that a hearsay statement possesses particularized quantities of reliability. In defendant's trial for lewd conduct with a minor, statements made by the alleged victim (defendant's 2 year old daughter) to a physician were admitted under Idaho's residual hearsay exception (clearly not a firmly rooted exception). The Supreme Court held that the state failed to establish that the statements possessed particularized guarantees of trustworthiness. Therefore, defendant's Confrontation Clause rights were violated. The Court held that the **particularized guarantees of reliability must come from the circumstances surrounding the making of the statement.** Other evidence that would tend to corroborate the accuracy of the statement cannot be considered in establishing its reliability.

White v. Illinois, 502 U.S. 346 (1992).

In this case, the Supreme Court limited the produce-the-declarant-or-demonstrate-unavailability requirement to those cases in which the challenged hearsay statement was made in the course of a prior judicial proceeding. Defendant was on trial for sexually assaulting a four-year-old girl. Statements that the girl made to her babysitter, mother, and a police officer were admitted under the excited utterance exception. Statements that the girl made to an emergency room nurse and a physician were admitted under the exception for statements made for medical diagnosis or treatment. The girl did not testify at trial and no finding was made that she was unavailable to testify. Defendant contended that the use of her hearsay statements thus violated his rights under the Confrontation Clause. The Supreme Court rejected his argument, finding the reasoning employed in *Inadi* to be persuasive. The rationale underlying the two hearsay exceptions involved here is that the context in which such statements are made provides substantial guarantees of their trustworthiness. Thus, little would be gained by forcing the prosecution either to produce the declarant or establish her unavailability. In such instances, if the proffered hearsay has sufficient guarantees of reliability to come within a firmly rooted hearsay exception, the Confrontation Clause is satisfied. The Court concluded that the exceptions here were firmly rooted—the excited utterance exception, because it is very old; the statements made for medical diagnosis or treatment exception, because it is widely accepted among the states.

WITNESSES

Coy v. Iowa, 487 U.S. 1012 (1988).

This case and the following case explore the extent to which the Confrontation Clause limits the ability of the state to have its witnesses testify without having to confront the accused. Defendant was tried for sexually abusing two 13-year-old girls. The trial court allowed the two complaining witnesses to testify from behind a screen so that they would not have to see the defendant as they testified. The court held that this violated the Confrontation Clause. No finding had been made that these girls would have been traumatized by having to testify in a normal fasion.

Maryland v. Craig, 497 U.S. 836 (1990).

Pursuant to a Maryland statute, a child witness in a child abuse case was permitted to testify outside the defendant's presence via closed ciruit television. As required by the statute, the trial court first found, after a hearing, that testifying in the courtroom would cause the child serious emotional distress. The Supreme Court found that this was sufficient to distinguish this case from *Coy v. Iowa*, above. Thus, the Court rejected the defendant's Confrontation Clause claim. Given the state's interest in the physical and psychological well-being of child abuse victims, and the **individualized** finding that this child witness would be traumatized by testifying **in the presence of the defendant**, the use of closed circuit testimony was permissible.

United States v. Abel, 469 U.S. 45 (1984).

This case invloves the use of extrinsic evidence to prove bias. Abel and Ehle were indicted for robbery. Ehle agreed to testify for the state against Abel. After he did, Abel sought to impeach him by calling Mills. Mills testified the Ehle planned to implicate Abel falsely. The prosecutor then cross-examined Mills by asking him if he and Abel were members of a secret prison organization which had a creed requiring members to deny its existence and lie for one another. Mills denied this. The prosecutor subsequently recalled Ehle, who testified that he, Mills, and Abel were indeed members of such a secret prison organization. The Supreme Court held that the trial court did not err in allowing either the questioning of Mills or the rebuttal testimony of Ehle. Abel's and Mills' membership in the organization supported the inference that Mills slanted or fabricated his testimony in Abel's favor. Therefore, the questions and rebuttal testimony were relevant, and the court acted within its discretion in finding that their probative value was not substantially outweighed by the danger of unfair prejudice.

Tome v. United States, ___ U.S. ___, 115 S.Ct. 696 (1995)

This case raises the issue whether a witness's prior consistent statement, offered to rebut a charge of recent fabrication or improper influence or motive, must have been made prior to the time the alleged improper influence or motive to fabricate arose. Tome was charged with sexually abusing his daughter. Tome, who had been awarded primary custody of the daughter, claimed that she concocted the story so that she could stay with her mother rather than with him. At the time of trial, the daughter was six years old. She became increasingly reticent during cross-examination. The prosecution then produced six witnesses who testified to prior statements made by the child to the effect that the defendant had abused her. These were offered under Rule 801(d)(1)(B) as prior consistent statements of a witness offered to rebut a charge of recent fabrication or improper influence or motive. Tome argued that all the statements were made after the daughter's motive to fabricate had arisen; the prosecution contended that the rule did not include a "pre-motive" requirement (i.e., that the rule did not require that the statement antedate the alleged motive to fabricate). In a 5-4 decision, the Court sided with Tome. It held that the language and history of the rule indicate that it was intended to codify the common law rule, which included a pre-motive requirement. The only real change effected by the federal rules was to define such statements as non-hearsay, thereby allowing them to be used for their truth as well as to rehabilitate the witness. The dissent argued that whether the prior statement was made before or after the motive arose was purely a relevancy question that was not addressed by Rule 801(d)(1)(B), which is concerned with a hearsay problem.

Daubert v. Merrell Dow Pharmaceuticals, Inc., 509 U.S. 579, 113 S.Ct. 2786 (1993).

The parents of two minor children born with serious defects brought suit against Merrell Dow, claiming that the mothers' injestion of Bendectin, an anti-nausea drug manufactured by the defendant, was the cause of the children's birth defects. Merrell Dow moved for summary judgment after extensive discovery. In support of its motion, it submitted the affidavit of an epidemiologist who stated there was no scientific evidence that the use of Bendectin during the first trimester was a risk factor for human birth defects. The testimony of plaintiffs' experts was excluded on the ground that it did not meet the *Frye* general acceptance test. The Supreme Court reversed, and rejected the *Frye* test. Nothing in either the text of Federal Rule 702 or its history indicated an intent to retain *Frye*. Moreover, retaining a general acceptance test would be at odds with the Rules' "general approach of relaxing the traditional barriers to 'opinion' testimony." Therefore, the Court concluded that the admissibility of expert scientific evidence must be judged under the standards announced in Rules 702 and 403. In applying these rules, judges still have an important role to play as gatekeepers, charged with the responsibility of ensuring that scientific evidence must be "not only relevant, but reliable." Admissibility of scientific evidence requires a showing that it is based on scientifically valid principles and that it bears "a valid scientific connection to the pertinent inquiry." The Court then listed a number of factors that a trial judge might consider in determining whether "the reasoning or methodology underlying the testimony is scientifically valid and * * * whether that reasoning or methodology properly can be applied to the facts in issue." First, the trial court should consider whether the theory or technique in question has been or can be tested. Second, the court should ask whether the theory or technique has been subjected to peer review and publication, since "submission to the scrutiny of the scientific community is a component of 'good science.'" Third, the court should inquire as to the known or potential rate of error of the particular theory or technique and whether means exist for controlling its operation. Finally, although general acceptance is no longer the sole standard for admissibility, the trial court should take into account the extent to which the theory or technique has been accepted. Then, even if the court determines that the demands of Rule 702 have been satisfied, Rule 403 may still provide grounds for exclusion.

BEST EVIDENCE RULE

Meyers v. United States, 84 U.S.App.D.C. 101, 171 F.2d 800 (1948), cert. denied, 336 U.S. 912.

This case illustrates that a witness's testimony concerning an event about which he has personal knowledge does not violate the Best Evidence Rule simply because the event happened to be recorded or transcribed. Lamarre was indicted for committing perjury before a United States Senate subcommittee. Meyers was indicted for subornation of perjury. At trial, the prosecution sought to establish the content of Lamarre's testimony before the Senate subcommittee through the testimony of Rogers, the subcommittee's chief counsel. Rogers had examined Lamarre before the subcommittee. In a dissent often included in Evidence casebooks, Judge Prettyman argues this violated the BER, because a transcript of the subcommittee hearing was available and this constituted the best evidence. The majority correctly responds that no BER violation took place. The fact that Lamarre's testimony was memorialized in a transcript does not mean that Rogers was testifying to the contents of a writing. Rogers was merely testifying to his own independent knowledge of what took place.

United States v. Duffy, 454 F.2d 809 (5th Cir. 1972).

This case illustrates the problem of determining whether an object is a writing or a chattel under the Best Evidence Rule. Duffy was convicted of transporting a stolen car. At trial, the government offered a great deal of evidence linking Duffy to the stolen car. Among the evidence was testimony that two suitcases were found in the trunk of the car, one of which contained a white shirt imprinted with the laundry mark "D-U-F." On appeal, the defendant argued that the government should have been required to produce the shirt because it was proving the contents of a writing. The court rejected his argument, combining the chattels and collateral matters exceptions. It first stated that the evidence constituted both a chattel and a writing. Therefore, the trial judge had discretion to treat the evidence as either. Since the writing was simple (D-U-F), the danger of error was slight. The court then pointed out that the evidence was not crucial. It was only one piece of evidence linking Duffy with the crime. Furthermore, Duffy was not charged with possession of the shirt.

PRIVILEGES

Upjohn Co. v. United States, 449 U.S. 383 (1981).

In this case, the United States Supreme Court rejects the control group test for determining who is the representative of a corporate client. The Internal Revenue Service sought to obtain documents relating to an internal investigation conducted by Upjohn's lawyers of illegal payments made by Upjohn employees. The investigation included interviews with and questionnaires answered by numerous Upjohn employees. The Supreme Court held that the documents were protected by the attorney-client privilege. **The Court rejected the control group test but declined to set forth a test for courts to follow.** Nevertheless, the factors cited by the Court in siding with Upjohn seemed consistent with the criteria set forth in the *Diversified Industries* case.

Clark v. State, 159 Tex.Crim. 187, 261 S.W.2d 339, cert. denied, 346 U.S. 855 (1953).

This case demonstrates the rule in some jurisdictions that an eavesdropper is permitted to testify as to a lawyer-client communication. A telephone operator overheard a conversation between Clark and his lawyer in which Clark stated, "I killed her." The court allowed the operator to testify, giving as one of its reasons the lack of confidentiality. The privilege should not be extended to prevent third parties who learn of lawyer-client communications from testifying.

Clark v. State, 159 Tex.Crim. 187, 261 S.W.2d 339, cert. denied, 346 U.S. 855 (1953).

This case also demonstrates the proposition that the attorney-client privilege does not attach to communications made by a client seeking a lawyer's advice to enable the client to commit what he knew or should have known was a crime or fraud. A telephone operator overheard a conversation between Clark and his lawyer in which Clark told the lawyer that he had "killed her." The lawyer asked if Clark still had the weapon. When Clark said no, the lawyer told him, "Get rid of the weapon." The court allowed the operator to testify, giving as its second reason (see §65.321 above) the crime or fraud exception. Although communications regarding the past commission of a crime are privileged, here the client received (and apparently followed) the lawyer's advice as to the commission of a second offense: the destruction of material evidence of a crime.

Jaffee v. Redmond, 116 S.Ct. 1923 (1996).

This case recognizes that the psychotherapist-patient privilege applies in federal court. Redmond, a police officer, shot and killed Allen. Allen's estate brought a civil rights action against Redmond, and sought to discover notes made by a licensed clinical social worker during counseling sessions she had with Redmond after the shooting. The Supreme Court held that the notes were privileged. The Court first found that recognition of a psychotherapist-patient privilege would serve the public interest. It would help promote an atmosphere in which patients could confide in their therapists and thus would foster the mental health of the citizenry. In contrast, the Court stated that recognition of the privilege would cost little in the way of lost evidence; without a privilege, the communications would not be made. The Court also drew support for its conclusion from the unanimity with which the states have embraced this privilege. The Court then found that the privilege extended to communications made not only to psychiatrists and psychotherapists, but to licensed social workers in the course of psychotherapy.

Trammel v. United States, 445 U.S. 40 (1980).

This case illustrates the modern trend of vesting the spousal testimonial privilege in the witness spouse. Elizabeth Trammel testified against her husband, Otis, in his drug conspiracy trial. She testified she was doing so voluntarily, in exchange for the government's promise that she would receive lenient treatment for her involvement in the conspiracy. Otis argued that under the common law he held the privilege, and could prevent his wife from testifying against him. The Supreme Court rejected his argument. Noting that the trend in the state courts was to give the privilege to the witness spouse, the Court held that Elizabeth was the holder of the testimonial privilege. As such, she was free to testify or to refuse to testify.

McCray v. Illinois, 386 U.S. 300 (1967).

This case holds that the government may refuse to disclose the identity of an informer. During a hearing on defendant's motion to suppress the fruits of a search, the prosecution called the arresting police officers to establish that they had probable cause to stop and search the defendant. The officers testified that they relied on a tip from an established informer, but refused to identify him. The Supreme Court rejected the defendant's argument that this violated his constitutional rights. In a probable cause hearing, the trial court need not require disclosure if it is satisfied that the officers relied in good faith on credible information supplied by a reliable informant.

United States v. Nixon, 418 U.S. 683 (1974).

This landmark case decided the breadth of the executive privilege. The Watergate Special Prosecutor issued a subpoena to President Nixon demanding that he produce the tape recordings of certain meetings he had with various advisers. The grand jury had already indicted seven individuals for various offenses, including conspiracy, and had named the President as an unindicted co-conspirator. President Nixon resisted the subpoena, claiming executive privilege. The Supreme Court rejected his claim. Although it recognized an executive privilege, it held that the privilege is a qualified one. If there exists a demonstrated, specific need for the information in a criminal trial, the privilege must yield and the information be produced.

Matter of Farber, 78 N.J. 259, 394 A.2d 330 (1978).

This case stands for the proposition that the jounalist's statutorily-based privilege may have to yield to a defendant's right to compulsory process. Farber, a reporter for the *New York Times*, was held in contempt of court for his failure to produce certain materials in the course of a murder trial. The New Jersey Supreme Court, following *Branzburg*, rejected Farber's constitutional claim of privilege. The court also held that Farber could not rely on the state statutory journalist privilege even though he fell within its terms. The defendant's constitutional right to compel the attendance of witnesses and production of documents and other material needed for his defense trumped Farber's statutory right not to disclose.

United States v. Doe, 465 U.S. 605 (1984).

A grand jury served five subpoenas on Doe, the owner of several sole proprietorships, demanding production of various specified documents. The Supreme Court held that the act of producing the documents would involve implied testimonial activity, and thus was covered by the privilege against self-incrimination.

Griffin v. California, 380 U.S. 609 (1965).

This is the case in which the Supreme Court established that it is improper for the prosecutor to comment upon the defendant's failure to take the stand. It also held that the court may not instruct the jury that may draw a negative inference from the defendant's failure to testify. The Court reasoned that allowing such conduct would place too high a price on the exercise of this constitutional right.

JUDICIAL NOTICE

United States v. Gould, 536 F.2d 216 (8th Cir. 1976).

This case illustrates the distinction between judicial notice of adjudicative and legislative facts. Defendants were convicted of violating the Controlled Substances Import and Export Act. Listed among the controlled substances covered by the act are "coca leaves" and "any derivative thereof." The substance smuggled by the defendants was identified as cocaine hydrochloride. The judge instructed the jury that cocaine hydrochloride is a controlled substance. The defendants objected first on the ground that the court could not judicially notice such a fact. The court rejected this contention, holding that this was a readily verifiable fact. Second, citing FRE 201(g), the defendants argued that it was improper to instruct the jury in a criminal case that it must accept a judicially noticed fact. The court rejected this argument also, pointing out that FRE 201 covers only judicial notice of **adjudicative facts.** Whether cocaine hydrochloride is a derivative of coca leaves is a question of scientific fact independent of the facts of the particular case; thus, it is a **legislative fact.**

BURDEN OF PROOF AND PRESUMPTIONS

Sandstrom v. Montana, 442 U.S. 510 (1979).

This case demonstrates the limits on the ability of the state to use a presumption to prove an element of a crime. Defendant was charged with "purposely or knowingly" killing Victim. Although his attorney conceded that Defendant killed Victim, he argued that he did not do so "purposely or knowingly", and put on expert testimony to this effect. The judge charged the jurors that "the law presumes that a person intends the ordinary consequences of his voluntary acts." The Supreme Court held that this was unconstitutional. The jury may have interpreted the instruction as requiring them to find that Defendant intended to kill Victim (acted purposely). **This would have relieved the prosecution of its constitutional obligation to prove the mental element of the crime beyond a reasonable doubt.** Even if the jury merely interpreted the instruction as requiring Defendant to prove that he did not act purposely or knowingly, it would have unconstitutionally shifted the burden of persuasion on this issue to Defendant.

County Court of Ulster County v. Allen, 442 U.S. 140 (1979).

This is the case in which the Supreme Court first draws the distinction between permissive and mandatory inferences in criminal cases. When Defendants were stopped for speeding, the investigating officer noticed two handguns in the car. Defendants were charged with and convicted of illegally possessing the firearms. The judge told the jury that it could infer Defendants possessed the firearms from the fact that they were in the car, but also told the jury that the prosecution had to prove each element of the crime beyond a reasonable doubt. The Supreme Court held that this was a permissive inference in that the jurors were free to reject the inference. Under the facts of the case, the Court held that the inference was a rational one; given the circumstances of the case, the presumed fact (possession) more likely than not flowed from the basic fact (presence in the car with the guns). Thus, the Court upheld the convictions.

XVIII. Table of Cases

CASES

CASES

References are to section numbers